The Development of Controversies: From the Early Modern Period to Online Discussion Forums

Linguistic Insights

Studies in Language and Communication

Edited by Maurizio Gotti,
University of Bergamo

Volume 91

PETER LANG
Bern · Berlin · Bruxelles · Frankfurt am Main · New York · Oxford · Wien

Manouchehr Moshtagh Khorasani

The Development of Controversies: From the Early Modern Period to Online Discussion Forums

PETER LANG
Bern · Berlin · Bruxelles · Frankfurt am Main · New York · Oxford · Wien

Bibliographic information published by Die Deutsche Bibliothek
Die Deutsche Bibliothek lists this publication in the Deutsche Nationalbibliografie; detailed bibliographic data is available on the Internet at ‹http://dnb.ddb.de›.

British Library and Library of Congress Cataloguing-in-Publication Data: A catalogue record for this book is available from *The British Library,* Great Britain.

Library of Congress Cataloging-in-Publication Data

Moshtagh Khorasani, Manouchehr.
The development of controversies : from the early modern period to online discussion forums / Manouchehr Moshtag Khorasani.
p. cm. – (Linguistic insights, ISSN 1424-8689 ; v. 91)
Includes bibliographical references and index.
ISBN 978-3-03911-711-6 (alk. paper)
1. Persuasion (Rhetoric)–History. 2. Electronic discussion groups. 3. Discourse analysis. I. Title.
P301.5.P47M67 2008
808.53–dc22

2008051853

Zugl.: Gießen, Univ., Diss., 2008

Die vorliegende Dissertation ist eine Dissertation des FB 05 der Justus-Liebig Universität Gießen.

This doctoral thesis was submitted to the FB 05 at the Justus-Liebig Universität Gießen.

Printed with financial support by the Hans-Böckler-Stiftung.

ISSN 1424-8689
ISBN 978-3-03911-711-6

Hochfeldstrasse 32, Postfach 746, CH-3000 Bern 9, Switzerland
info@peterlang.com, www.peterlang.com, www.peterlang.net

Dedicated to my parents
for their support and love

Acknowledgements

This book is a slightly modified version of my PhD thesis, which was submitted to the Institut für Anglistik (Fachbereich 05 Sprache, Literatur, Kultur) at the Justus-Liebig Universität Gießen in December 2007.

First, I would like to thank my supervisor and mentor, Professor Dr. Andreas H. Jucker, who has not only been an excellent professor but also a significant source of encouragement through all these years, for his support during this research project. And my special thanks go to Professor Dr. Joybrato Mukherjee for his support and generous feedback. I would also like to thank Professor Dr. Gerd Fritz for his generous input and help and Professor Dr. Thomas Gloning for his encouragement.

This volume is based on a corpus of internet conversations taken from two threads out of two online discussion forums dedicated to the study of arms and armor. I would like to thank all my friends on the forums. I would like to express my special gratitude to John Cooksey, Gordon Frye, Dan Howard, Russ Mitchell, Arun Singh, Doug Mullane, and Greg Thomas Obach for their input.

I would also like to thank my parents for their generous support over the years. Last but not least, I would like to thank my wife Aline for her love, friendship, and support. I would also like to thank my daughter Niloufar for her love and presence.

Manouchehr Moshtagh Khorasani
Frankfurt am Main, August 2008

Contents

1. Introduction

The establishment of online discussion forums has opened up a new range of interaction between different members of the online community on the Internet. As the most recently developed mass medium and communication tool of the 21st century, the Internet has provided new dimensions of communication (Janoschka, 2004:1).

Particularly, online discussion forums have established new forms of communication as large numbers of people can read responses and have access to the information provided there. At the same time, online discussion forums also offer private/interpersonal-like communication as registered members can interact with each other via posting and contact each other via a private message system offered by each respective forum. Online discussion forums are a type of computer-mediated communication (CMC)[1] device and are described as virtual communities. Rheingold (2000:xx) states:

> Virtual communities are social constructs that are the direct result of continued interaction and discussion between a sufficient number of people on the Internet, with the involvement of human feeling to create webs of personal relationships in cyberspace.

Online communities have a defined and articulated purpose; offer flexible and extensive gathering places; establish meaningful membership profiles; allow for a range of roles, such as newcomers, regulars, administrators, and moderators[2]; design a strong leadership program by inviting community leaders to participate; foster appropriate etiquette and rules; support cyclical events; integrate the rituals of community life; and facilitate member-run subgroups (Kim, 2000: xiii–xiv). Online communities are not restricted to online discussion

1 For this expression, see Cherny (1999:2).

2 A moderator of a forum is a member with special rights who regulates and monitors the forum based on a prescribed set of rules and principles.

forums as there are different types of online communities, such as chat rooms, blogs (that offer interaction), and mailing lists.

The communication in online discussion forums is asynchronous (see Crystal, 2006:135), meaning that individual contributions to such forums are saved and kept as they are posted, and these individual posts can be separated by any period of time (Crystal, 2006:140). Today, online discussion forums are ubiquitous on the Internet, dedicated to the discussion of a wide range of topics, and are a part of an online community of users, the purpose of which involves a wide range of topics, such as exchanging information about rare plants, discussing local government, aiding students via distant education (see Preece, 2000:7), talking about games (Crystal, 2006:137), and discussing different aspects of historical arms and armor. The group constituency is also diverse, such as academic, professional, governmental, commercial, and social groups (Crystal, 2006:137). Different people associate different meanings with online communities. Regarding this point, Preece (2000:8–9) states that these associations range from a warm and fuzzy environment, where people chat and help each other, to disturbing images of conspiracy, subversive and criminal behavior, and invasion of privacy. Theoretically, a community of online discussion groups consists of people with common goals and interests, who get together to share resources and satisfy each other's needs, and this is the goal of every online community.

Online discussion forums have a range of strategies at their disposal to encourage repeat visitors to post and to ensure the maintenance of a busy online community, where people can interact and share resources. The interaction takes place when participants post on the forums, revealing their individual behavior or, more specifically, posting behavior. This type of behavior and manner of posting makes up a virtual profile and a virtual character for each person. Hence, an individual's behavior can be attributed to that person in online communities. Online communities share many similar behavioral patterns as their counterparts in social communities in real life. According to Preece (2000:10), an online community consists of a) people who have social interactions with each other to satisfy their own needs or play special roles, b) a shared purpose that provides a reason for the community`s existence, c) policies, such as tacit assumptions, rituals, protocols, rules, and laws, that guide people's interaction, and d) computer systems that assist and mediate social interaction and create a sense of togetherness.

Participants in online discussion forums who make up online communities make friendships and argue with each other and also become involved in long and tedious conflicts and controversies. Kim (2000:xiv) rightly states that every community (including online communities) has its internal conflicts, and these conflicts can be fruitful and vitalize the community if they are handled well by the administrators and moderators and can be disastrous and tear a community apart if the internal conflicts are not handled well. One of the reasons for the existence of conflicts in online discussion forums is that linguistic 'footprints' left by each contributor have a permanent, pragmatic effect. According to Crystal (2006:140), contributions are saved for an indefinite period of time, hence, they can be used out of context at any time. This, of course, provides a potential pretext for conflicts and controversies at any time. To deal with conflicts and controversies, each online discussion forum is managed by one person or a small team of people. Different names are used for people in this function, such as administrator, list owner, editor, host, postmaster, maintainer, moderator, or staff (see Crystal, 2006:138).[3] According to Crystal (2006:138), moderators variously apply their power, such as deciding whether a posted message on a discussion board is relevant or offensive. Further, Crystal differentiates between the filtering and editing powers of moderators and points out that there are moments where moderators have the discretion to decide whether to allow a message appears or not. In other discussion boards, moderators have editing as well as filtering abilities.[4] Moderators with editing powers are able to shorten a lengthy message, to cut the obscene parts out of a

---

3 I will use the term "moderator" as a general term in my research unless otherwise specified.

4 Filtering abilities means that after a member posts in a forum, his/her post does not appear on the open forum. First, the message goes to a waiting line and is checked by moderators. At times, moderators prune/filter the message and then let it appear on the forum.

message or post, to delete spam or unauthorized advertising, and to remove other unwanted material (Crystal, 2006:138–139).

Like chatrooms, online discussion forums are virtual communities in which participants can talk to each other via the posts they make.[5] Similar to online news portals, online discussion forums can be considered a type of media transported via the Internet. Although there are similarities between online discussion forums and chatrooms, there are also some differences that influence the mode of communication behavior. According to Jucker (2003:140), a discussion board (online discussion forum) is a site where anybody can post questions and opinions and can read these contributions and react to them by providing his own opinions. On the other hand, Jucker adds that chatrooms are sites where participants exchange text contributions in real time in a type of immediate interaction. In this respect, Crystal (2006:134–136) distinguishes between synchronous communication, as is the case with chat rooms, and asynchronous communication as takes place in online discussion forums.

Further, Anglemark (2006:295) describes Internet chat forums (chat sites) as communicative environments where electronic interaction between two or more interlocutors happens in real time. Anglemark (2006:295) adds that this type of written dialogue shares certain characteristics with spoken conversation, such as the presence of vocatives, indicating a 'speech-like' quality of the interaction. Janoschka (2004:2) explains that these chatrooms have the tendency to be synchronous or live interactions and consist of real-time mutual exchange of written information.

Anglemark (2006:296) also describes an Internet chat room as a real-time communicative situation where two or more participants can take part in and talk about any topic in a written dialogue over the Internet. Anglemark (2006:296) adds that the utterances or conversational turns in Internet chat rooms are placed sequentially in a window on the computer screen. All participants in a chat room can immediately see each conversational turn after it has been written, and

5 Cherny (1999:1) states that to have a virtual community, an Internet site must provide chatting possibilities, and by providing this, a virtual community is created.

it is not possible to edit the message after it has been posted (Anglemark, 2006:296). Anglemark (2006:296) emphasizes that for these reasons, some researchers describe chatroom language as a type of spoken language in writing (see Davis and Brewer, 1997:2). Janoschka (2004:2) also points out that as the communicative interaction on chat rooms is synchronous, participants have less time to think about and conceptualize their text messages as in the case of synchronous e-mail communication.

Jucker (2003:140) distinguishes between moderated and unmoderated chats and explains that, in moderated chats, a convenor screens each contribution before it is passed on. In contrast, moderation in online discussion forums dedicated to the study of arms and armor transpires in a different way. There is no screening process. Thus, the moderators do not have filtering ability. On the other hand, moderators of the forums dedicated to the study of arms and armor have editing ability. This means that participants can post their contributions, and if there is any violation of the agreed principles of that forum, either the participant is warned or banned, depending on the gravity of the breach of forum rules, and/or the post will be edited or deleted completely.

There are many participants who post in online discussion forums dedicated to the study of arms and armor. Each topic or discussion starts when a participant opens a thread with a corresponding title, such as 'Swords in Medieval Europe'. Depending on the interest each thread raises, more participants post on the thread, answering questions or adding comments. Hence, a type of 'electronic dialogue' is established this way.[6]

However, online discussion forums are different from chatrooms. For instance, the rate of posting is not as speedy as in chatrooms, and the quality of the posts regarding the content is much more complex as they contain technical and subject-oriented information. Not surprisingly, in contrast to synchronous interaction in chatrooms, the communicative interaction in online discussion forums is asynchronous, meaning that participants have time to devise and conceptualize their text messages. Janoschka (2004:2) points out that

6 For the term 'electronic dialogue', see Crystal (2001:29).

interaction in e-mail communication is asynchronous, and this is a feature that e-mail communication shares with communication in online discussion forums. Another difference to chatrooms is that participants in online discussion forums dedicated to the study of arms and armor have the chance to edit their messages up to twenty-four hours after they have posted their messages. In online discussion forums dedicated to the study of arms and armor, participants can also post pictures and discuss artifacts and pieces of arms and armor in detail. In contrast to real social communities, online communities have different sets of characteristics and features. It is easy for participants in online discussion forums to disguise their true identities. Thus, they do not fear possible reprisal. In short, they can escalate a conflict situation much more easily than they could do in their interactions in real social life. Additionally, provided that they can use different IP addresses, participants can employ different identities. A majority of online communities are moderated so that a harassment-free environment for communication can be provided to some extent. In spite of this moderation, controversies and conflicts in online discussion forums occur very often.

1.1 Research question

The objective of this volume is to introduce and analyze controversies in online discussion forums dedicated to the study of arms and armor. As a moderator of the Forum of Swords, I have been acquainted with the procedures of moderating an Internet site dedicated to the study of arms and armor for five years. I have been answering questions, and in the case of controversies, I have tried to mediate and find resolutions. And if all possibilities are gone, the respective controversial thread is locked. I have had a unique chance to be a part of an online community and to experience the sense of belonging to a virtual community first-hand during all these years as a moderator and as a member of the Forum of Swords for three additional years before that.

No one without having personal experience of being a member of an online discussion forum can understand how much one becomes emotionally involved in an online community.

As a linguist, I have found all these years very inspiring. I have gotten to know many people, exchanged private messages (via the special function the site offers) with other members, and also maintained e-mail contact with some of them.[7] I have found the experience of seeing the development of the identification and involvement of a person in an online discussion forum both fascinating and scary. Reimann (2007) reports about Alex Schuman, the most famous blogger from Sweden, who had over 250,000 visitors to his internet site per week. Schuman decided to stop his blogging on his site Att vara Alex Schulman (To be Alex Schuman) on the online version of the Swedish newspaper Aftonbladet as he realized that his readers were keen and eager to read his malicious and spiteful comments. They especially wanted to hear bad things about people with celebrity status, and Schuman had provided them with these malignant contributions. By the time he stopped his blogging, Schuman admitted that he could not even recognize himself and how far he could go in being malicious and asked himself whether he was the person writing all those scathing contributions when he looked at them in retrospect. He calls this a phenomenon that can only happen on the Internet. This is an important point for the analysis of controversies in online discussion forums. Many participants involved in them admit that they would never have said or done the things that they had done in online controversies in real life.

One can only imagine the level of involvement in an online community if one is a member of an online discussion forum. One can feel sadness, happiness, anger, frustration, and a range of other human emotions when participating in online discussion forums. Additionally, one shares these feelings with other members. During all these years, I have also seen many controversies and controversial threads.

---

7 Note that e-mail addresses are not exposed and visible to the general public and forum regulars. On the other hand, the moderators and administrators have access to the hidden profiles of forum members, including their e-mail addresses.

In spite of our continuous efforts as moderators with editing powers, controlling the language in an online discussion forum is a difficult task. Although the forums are moderated environments, the Internet is not, meaning that once certain participants are banned due to the violation of certain rules, they can always avenge themselves by posting controversial threads on other forums or even opening up new online sites to spread their perspectives, no matter how distorted or in error such perspectives could be. This is an aspect that moderators of online discussion forums should always be aware of. As moderators are equipped with certain moderating powers in online communities, the banned participants might use anything the moderators post or have posted against them by quoting them out of context in other online discussion forums, or they might simply open up new sites and rant about moderators. This is also one of the reasons that few academics are ready to join online discussion forums and share their experiences as they fear that their statements might be used against them one day.

Crystal (2006:214) stresses that the language of the Internet is under no control, and, therefore, there are sites that, contrary to conventional standards of politeness and decency, have the aim of giving people the chance to rant about anything they wish. This is exactly the problem with controversies in online discussion forums analyzed in this study. Controversies in online discussion forums cannot be considered as separate entities as they are interconnected with each other, meaning that each one is the result and consequence of the other; moreover, controversial threads are the result of a series of activities on different forums and Internet sites. Therefore, when a forum participant opens a controversial thread against a certain person or a certain book, one can never be sure whether he/she is trying to take revenge against someone or is merely criticizing a certain author or an article. For the purpose of this volume, I have studied two controversial threads from two different discussion forums. One controversial thread on the Forum of Swords and another related controversial thread from the main competitor forum, the Forum of Ethnographic Swords, build up the corpus for my study of controversies in online discussion forums.

One should take into consideration that these two online discussion forums were competing against each other for a period of four months, and as is the case with any type of conflict, the polemical situation between two competitor forums has its acute and dormant stages. There are periods where there are many controversial threads in both forums. This is an acute stage of controversies and conflicts. On the other hand, there are also stages where there are not many conflicts and controversies on the forums. This does not mean that the controversies or conflicts are resolved but could represent that contesters in polemical discourse during this stage are planning their next moves or are simply tired of the mental toll of being engaged in a controversy and refraining from posting for a while. This is the dormant stage of controversies.

The analysis of controversies has been an area of interest for pragmaticists, linguists, and philosophers. Early research has concentrated on the analysis of pamphlets in Early Modern Controversies, such as religious, scientific, and medical controversies; hence, the new medium for carrying out controversies, namely the Internet, has not been the focus of research until now. Although there are good studies regarding the communication patterns in chatrooms on the Internet (see Cherny, 1999), Web advertising, and new forms of communication on the Internet (Janoschka, 2004), there has not been a systematic study of controversies in online discussion forums. The Internet is a very powerful medium of communication. In the 2000 edition of his book *The Virtual Community: Homesteading on the Electronic Frontier*, Howard (2000:323) states that in contrast to the 1980s, when tens of thousands of people had been involved in the Internet, in the year 2000 the number increased to hundreds of millions of people who were involved in communication on the Internet and started to transform civilization's most powerful institutions, such as commerce, politics, science, scholarship, entertainment, education, and health care, by being engaged on the Internet. Howard further stresses that the sudden appearance of the Internet as a new communication medium has changed the world fundamentally. Today, this development is progressing faster and faster, and more and more people interact and communicate via the Internet.

According to Janoschka (2004:83), communication on the Internet is a hybrid form, making use of traditional communication but also constructing its own communicative features that have not been used before. Speed and an increased pace seem to be characteristic features of the communication on the Internet, not only in exchanging information but also in other types of communication, such as polemical discourse. In contrast to the Early Modern Controversies, controversies in online discussion forums are carried out at an unbelievably fast pace, where each participant can increase his/her level of participation by simply increasing the amount of his/her posts. Therefore, online discussion forums offer special advantages for carrying out controversies. One of the main advantages is, of course, speed. An article or a book can easily be attacked on the Internet. The interaction in online discussion forums is very fast, and the participants have a number of possibilities to attack their opponents.

Additionally, participants can also post pictures and, hence, discuss the items in more detail. The presence of pictures increases the level of interest and involvement of participants who can pass judgments on the age and authenticity of a piece of historical arms or armor. Member-posted information can not only be read by other members but also is open to the general public. As a matter of fact, many non-registered members use the information posted in both online discussion forums: the number of non-members who access these sites is by far greater than the number of registered members. Thus, the information posted in online discussion forums can be considered as mass communication since the information is available to masses of people and read by them.

Quoting Große (1998:344), Janoschka (2004:87) states that in spite of the fact that there is no widely accepted and comprehensive theory of mass communication, mass communication is usually described as having one sender who basically transfers one message to a wide and anonymous audience (Rötzer, 1999:53) of dispersed individuals. Further, Janoschka (2004:87) quotes Maletzke (1998:46), who describes mass communication as public, technically transferred by a medium, indirect, and uni-indirectional. There should also be an interconnecting carrier medium, such as newspapers or the Internet, that enable people to transfer messages. Online discussion forums dedicated to the study of arms and armor and the contents posted in them have one dimension of mass communication because they are public and read widely by many readers who are not registered members of the forums and are anonymous to the forum administration and the registered members.

Crystal (2006:214) also points out the mass communicative aspect of the Internet and states that people, by writing in the Internet, are providing content for a potentially worldwide readership. This is an important factor to take into consideration for the focus of my volume. Participants who are involved in an online controversy are not only aware that their contributions are read by registered members of the forums but also know that a worldwide readership is reading the whole thread. Naturally, the amount of pressure is significantly higher for those involved in an online controversy. By way of comparison, pamphlets in the Early Modern Period were read aloud to a number of mostly illiterate people, and participants in Early Modern Controversies also complained about the high emotional toll of getting involved in a controversy. In today's world of the Internet, participants in online controversies are well aware that a significant number of people read their contributions.

Additionally, registered members of online discussion forums dedicated to the study of arms and armor post on the forum and interact with each other. On top of this, each member has the possibility of communicating with his/her friends and cohorts via a PM (private message) system on the online forum, and, they can stay in touch via e-mail and plan their moves and strategies when posting on forums. Thus, online discussion forums provide the possibility of private communication that resembles interpersonal-like communication.[8] Online discussion forums dedicated to the study of arms and armor are a good example of the boundaries between mass communication (referring to many members who read the contents of the forum and also many readers who visit and read the forums without being members) and private communication/interpersonal-like communication (the possibility of contacting the other members via private

8 Janoschka (2004:97) uses this term and states that the Internet offers possibilities of interpersonal-like communication.

message system of the forum) becoming increasingly blurred on the Internet (for this point, see O'Sullivan, 1999). As I mentioned above, members of both forums can contact each other via the private message system of each forum. Additionally, some of them exchange e-mails and some even meet in real life.

This intensive involvement, of course, leads to a high level of involvement and interaction in a controversy by each member. Taking the fact into consideration that the Internet combines both traditional forms of communication with new forms of communication, the purpose of my study is to find out to what extent the new medium of the Internet has changed the nature of carrying out controversies. The research questions of this volume are as follows:

a) What are the similarities and differences between Early Modern Controversies and controversies in online Internet discussion forums?
b) Have the individual tactics and strategies applied changed over time?
c) What are the similarities and differences of applied principles, norms, and rules between Early Modern Controversies and online controversies?
d) Has the online medium been accepted as a tool for carrying out controversies?
e) What are the rules and principles that guide controversies in online discussion forums dedicated to the study of arms and armor?
f) What are the characteristic types of moves and strategies used in these types of controversies?
g) What are the patterns of text production in these types of online controversies?
h) What is the future of the Internet as a medium for carrying out controversies?

Based on the questions above, I will take the following as working hypotheses for my research:

Hypothesis 1: There are some individual moves and strategies that are the same in controversies from the Early Modern Period and controversies in online discussion forums.

Hypothesis 2: There are new moves and strategies that are used in controversies in online discussion forums due to the new communication medium, the Internet.

Hypothesis 3: There are some communication principles from the Early Modern Period that are similar to communication principles of online discussion forums.

Hypothesis 4: There are some new communication principles in online discussion forums due to the effects of the new medium of communication, the Internet.

Hypothesis 5: The communication in online discussion forums is dialogic in nature.

Hypothesis 6: The Internet is used often as a medium to carry out controversies.

1.2 Objectives of the research

Based on controversies in general and focused on Early Modern Controversies[9] in particular, another purpose of this study is to analyze whether the individual tactics, strategies, and principles for carrying out a controversy have changed over time and whether the new medium, namely the Internet, has influenced and changed the tactics, strategies, and norms accordingly. During the course of this volume, the individual tactics and strategies applied in the Early Modern Controversies will be discussed first. These points will be a baseline for an analysis of which similar types of these individual tactics and strategies in controversies take place on the Internet and whether new individual tactics and strategies have been added to the

9 Fritz (2008:164) calls controversies in the 16th to 18th centuries the "Golden Age" of controversies.

repertoire of moves[10] and strategies. In my volume, I hope to uncover some new, individual tactics and strategies that have been developed during the course of time and due to the new principles and rules of online communication, which should have an impact on the nature of controversies.

The corpus of my study consists of two controversial threads that were posted on two different forums dedicated to the study of arms and armor: a) the Forum of Swords and b) the Forum of Ethnographic Swords.[11] The controversial thread posted on the Forum of the Swords is titled *keris*[12] controversy, for the main controversial topic of the thread is the criticism of a print article on the history of the *keris* that had led to an online controversy that lasted for thirty days. The controversy started when Manolo Rodriguez,[13] a member of the Forum of Swords, started a thread criticizing the theories written by Melborn[14] in a published article on the development of the *keris*. Melborn is a moderator[15] of the rival forum, the Forum of Ethnographic Swords, and does not take part in the controversy on the Forum of Swords. However, as I will show later, Melborn is a participant in a related controversial thread, entitled *nationalism* controversy, on the Forum of Ethnographic Swords.[16] Nevertheless,

---

10 A move is a specific rhetorical device and line of argumentation used in a controversy.

11 Note that the names have been changed for privacy reasons and are pseudonyms.

12 A *keris* is a ritual dagger from Indonesia. For more information on this type of dagger, see Hamzuri (1988) and Solyom and Solyom (1978). Note that I changed the original title of the thread due to anonymity reasons and coined the title *keris* controversy for the controversial thread on the Forum of Swords.

13 Note that the personal names have been altered for privacy reasons and are pseudonyms.

14 Note that the personal names have been altered for privacy reasons and are pseudonyms.

15 As I will explain later, a moderator of a forum is a member with special rights who regulates and monitors the forum based on a prescribed set of rules and principles.

16 I coined the title *nationalism* controversy for the controversial thread on the Forum of Swords due to privacy reasons. The original thread's name is different.

some of his supporters participated in the *keris* controversy to defend his position. During the life of the *keris* controversy, there was a constant rhetorical war in the form of a controversy between the supporters and the critics of the article. The whole controversy lasted 30 days before it was closed by a moderator of the Forum of Swords.

A number of controversial threads were opened on both forums during a period of four months as a response to each other. During this period, members of both forums were not only fighting each other on different threads on two different sites, but the number of controversial threads rose during this time from October 2006 to March 2007. To illustrate, the *nationalism* controversy thread is used for comparative purposes for the research of this study. This controversial thread posted on the Forum of Ethnographic Swords deals with the accusation that a moderator of the Forum of the Swords follows nationalistic interests. This thread has also been a main area of controversial communication. This controversy lasted only two days until it was closed by one of the moderators of the Forum of Ethnographic Swords.

It is important to take into consideration that moderators regulate both forums: this means that contributors participate in a moderated environment, and, hence, not all moves are tolerated. This, of course, leads to the establishment of a set of rules that need to be followed and respected by forum members. Some of these rules are explicitly written as the formal rules of the forums that each participant agrees to follow before the registration process for each forum is completed. Additionally, there are other rules and principles that are subject to the subjective and individual assessment of each moderator. Failure to respect the rules and principles may result in a written reprimand, suspension of the posting privileges of the member temporarily, or simply in being banned permanently from the forum in question.

In my research, I will analyze the use of personal style in online controversies and hope to find features peculiar to controversies in the online medium. Regarding the personal style in controversies, Gloning (2005:272) explains that contemporary readers and controversialists of the 16th, 17th, and 18th centuries, at times, point to a 'personal style' of operating in a controversy. Gloning suggests that this kind of impression of a personal style can be analytically explained to some extent by a) identifying the types of moves in conjunction with the respective commitments, b) looking for linguistic expressions used in controversies, and c) revealing the communicative principles that the opponents follow. For the purpose of my study, I will analyze the types of moves used in controversies in online discussion forums, the types of principles that participants follow, and linguistic features and expressions used.

In analyzing my corpus that consists of two threads on two different online discussion forums dedicated to the study of arms and armor, namely the keris controversy, consisting of 18,376 words on the Forum of the Swords, and the nationalism controversy on the Forum of Ethnographic Swords, consisting of 5,211 words, I have combined different elements from different theories in my research methods and added new elements to them. I will analyze online controversies by using the traditional methodologies of analyzing controversies in the Early Modern Period and make a comparison to online controversies. Additionally, I will analyze the controversial texts in online discussion forums by using theories of analyzing the language of the Internet and make a comparative study. Therefore, my research here differs from previous work in the field because of the combination of different research methods as indicated above.

1.3 Contents of the volume

This introduction will be followed by a presentation of the socio-cultural context of the forums in Chapter Two, which deals with social networks and communication in online discussion forums. Next to socio-cultural context of online discussion forums dedicated to the study of arms and armor, this chapter provides information on the participants in online discussion forums, such as active participants, passive participants, distribution of rights, motivation of participants, and the goal of participants. Chapter Two also discusses the owners of the forums, types of interests and business interests, time of the establishment of the forums, and other related formats outside of the Internet, such as magazines, newsletters, and scholarly research dedicated to the study of arms and armor. This section also deals with the self-promotion of members. Additionally, this chapter explains the principles and rules of communication in online discussion forums dedicated to the study of arms and armor.

Chapter Three deals with the topic of conflict and controversies in theory and practice and provides a framework to explain the nature of human conflict and its different forms. Then, I will explain the difference between discussion, dispute, and controversy. The explanation of these different forms of polemical discourse is critical for this research so that the true nature of controversies can be explained. This chapter also deals with the ideal model of carrying out controversies proposed by Leibniz who thought logical discussion would solve controversies but did not take into account the strategic decisions by people to win at all costs. Even in the Early Modern Period, contesters used all means to win over their opponents and to impress their audiences. Further, I will deal with the role of emotions in public controversies in this chapter.

Chapter Four provides background information about the République des Lettres and its members and explains pamphlets as an early medium for carrying out controversies. Chapter Five examines communication principles from Early Modern Controversies to electronic communication. First, it deals with controversies as language games ruled by principles. Then, it explains the classification of communication principles. This chapter ends with the changing nature of communication principles over time. Chapter six concentrates on different individual moves and strategies applied in Early Modern Controversies by different members, and this will offer a benchmark for the comparison of individual moves and strategies used in controversies online.

Chapter Seven deals with individual moves and strategies used in online discussion forums, such as opening moves, attacking moves, defending moves, counterattacks, deflecting moves, accusation moves related to violations of principles of communication, neutral moves, and using rhetorical and direct questions in controversies. Each group of these moves is divided into different individual moves and explained in detail. Chapter Eight gives detailed explanations about some stylistic choices of participants in the online controversies analyzed for this study to show the dialogic nature of controversies in online discussion forums. This chapter deals with audience interaction and forms of addressing other participants. It also offers information on lexical choices and emoticons. Chapter Nine summarizes all the chapters and provides a conclusion with suggestions for further research.

2. Socio-cultural context of the forums

2.1 Introduction

This chapter introduces and explains the socio-cultural context of the forums under analysis in this study. Further, this chapter deals with the participants who take part in online discussion forums, providing details about the type of participants, their motivations, and their goals. Additionally, this chapter discusses the principles and rules of communication of both forums.

2.2 Social networks and communication in online discussion forums

Online discussion forums are types of social networks. Humans construct social networks since they have a fundamental need for contact with each other (Agamanolis, 2006:307). According to Rheingold (2006:47), social networks are created when people interact with one another on a continual basis, and social networks need to be useful; otherwise, they cease to exist. Social networks have supporting functions: making the lives of humans meaningful and enabling them to survive (Agamanolis, 2006:308). In the past, social networks were restricted to people who had face-to-face communication. With the invention of writing, public postal systems, the telegraph, the telephone, and the Internet, new ways of extending social networks were introduced (Rheingold, 2006:48). In today's world, people use different modes of communication to keep their social networks at both local and distant levels. One of these media is the Internet, which has been increasingly and extensively used by different people. In a study on the effect of online communication, specifically e-mail communication, within the highly networked community of Blacksburg, VA, in the USA, and surrounding rural Montgomery County, Kavanaugh *et al.* (2006:217) state that computer networking strengthens and cultivates different types of social ties. There are different forms of online communication, such as e-mail, chat rooms, and online discussion forums. Working professionals, scholars, and researchers use online discussion forums to interact with each other and exchange information (see Fayard and DeSanctis, 2005). Similar to other professional online discussion forums, there are online discussion forums dedicated to the study of historical arms and armor. In the following, I will describe two forums: a) the Forum of Swords and b) the Forum of Ethnographic Swords. Note that both forums allow their members to set up their own profiles.

Today, there are a number of forums dedicated to the study of arms and armor. In the early 1990's, this was not the case. In 1998, the Forum of Swords was established as a forum to discuss modern-made swords. The beginning of this forum goes back to the craze when the movie *Highlander* was released. The resulting, initial discussion was limited to communication about the movie and its related arms and armor. Soon, a number of specialists of arms and armor joined the forum, and the forum site owner and his staff realized that they needed to differentiate the subforums to target each section of the community better. So in contrast to the beginning, where all types of swords from different cultures were discussed together in one forum, a later split of forums led to specializations in the specialized fields of arms and armor, such as the Nihonto Forum (dedicated to traditional Japanese arms and armor), Chinese Swords and Swordsmanship (dedicated to the study of historical arms and armor and swordsmanship from China), Edged Weapons from the Middle East (dedicated to the study of Arms and Armor from the Middle East), and so forth. Hence, the Forum of Swords has been catering more to increasingly smaller audiences within the arms and armor community; members who are interested in Japanese swords, for instance, can go to the Nihonto forum and ignore the other specialized forums. Today, the Forum of Swords is the biggest online discussion forum dedicated to the study of arms and armor that has grown steadily up to the present time. As I mentioned above, the Forum of Swords covers a vast range of topics that are divided into different subforums. At least one or two moderators are assigned to moderate each subforum and make sure that the rules of the forum are followed and ensure the flow of conversation there. Additionally, many moderators are specialists in their related fields and make useful contributions to different threads on the forum.

In 2006, the Forum of Swords underwent another organizational change. As shown below in figure 2.1, in the new format, the whole forum is divided into different communities made up of the a) Antique Arms and Armor Community, b) Modern-era Swords and Collecting Community, c) Bladesmiths, Blacksmiths, Artisans and Professionals, d) Swordsmanship Community, e) International Language Sword Fora, f) SPATHA, and g) Arts, Culture, Recreation & Entertainment. Each community serves a special purpose and is, again, subdivided into further subforums. For example, the Antique Arms and Armor Community is subdivided into the i) Antique & Military Sword Forum, ii) Nihon-to Forum, iii) Ancient Weapons Forum, iv) Middle-East, India and Africa Forum, v) Chinese, South-East Asia Forum, vi) The Antique Kukri Forum, vii) Antique Armor Studies, and vii) Archived Forums. As shown below, after the name of each community, the purpose and goal of the community is written. In the case of the Antique Arms and Armor Community, the purpose is to promote "the art, culture, beauty, and metallurgy of swords of our history". By clicking on each community, members can get into the required area and see all subforums of that community next to each other. By clicking on each subforum, such as Antique Armor Studies, members are redirected to the required area. The following figure shows how the Forum of Swords is organized:

Figure 2.1: Different communities of the Forum of Swords.

Welcome
Thank you for joining us. We invite you to read
Our rules and code of conduct before participating.

Forum	Last Post	Threads	Posts	Moderator
Announcements	August 6 Change By Alan 09-07-2007 05:11 AM	8	8	
Rules and Forum Usage	SwordIdentification Inquiries by Alan 09-13-2007 08:29 PM	6	6	

Communities
Click on any of the community categories below to enter that community, and to see the descriptions of its sub-forums.

Forum	Last Post	Threads	Posts	Moderator

Antique Arms & Armour Community
The Art, Culture, Beauty and Metallurgy of Swords of our History.
Sub-Forums: Antique & Military Sword Forum, Nihon-to Forum, Ancient Weapons Forum, Middle-East, India & Africa, Chinese, South-East Asia , The Antique Kukri Forum, Antique Armour Studies Forum, Archived Forums

Modern-era Swords and Collecting Community
Replica, reproduction, production and custom artistic swords made in our current era.
Sub-Forums: General Discussion Forum, Beginner's Sword Forum, Modern Production Katanas, Makers Making a Difference, Sword Ownership and Use – Legal issues, Knives, Axes, Polearms and Bows, Reference Library

Bladesmiths, Blacksmiths, Artisans and Professionals
The professional forums extend the Forum of Swords support of the sword community by providing a set forums dedicated to industry professionals. Everyone is welcomed to read these forums but posting privileges are limited to industry professionals
Sub-Forums: Metallurgical Studies Question and Answer Forum, Performance Swords Question and Answer Forum, Bladesmith Cafe, Japanese-Style Sword Makers Cafe

Swordsmanship Community
Sub-Forums: Historical European Swordsmanship, Japanese Swordsmanship Arts, Chinese, South-East Asian & Pacific Sword Arts (CSEAPSA), Olympic Sport Fencing, Classical Fencing Forum, Theatrical Fight Forum, Archived Forums

International Languages Sword Fora
Sub-Forums: German Language Sword Forum, Classical Latin Language Forum, Spanish Language Sword Forum, French Language Sword Forum, Italian Language Sword Forum, Scandinavian Language Sword Forum

SPATHA
Society for Promotion of Authenticity in the Teaching of Historical Arms.
Sub-Forums: SPATHA Articles, SPATHA Discussion Forum

Arts, Culture, Recreation & Entertainment Sub-Forums: The Nelson Arms Family Pub, Scottish and Borders History, Culture and Life., Fellowship for Tolkien Mythological Studies, Historical Reenactment & Living History, Fantasy Sword Forum, Sword Movies & Movie Swords, "Home Improvements" Projects, Decorative Sword Collectibles, "Bloodgroove" - SFI's Comic Strip!, The Acanthus Swordworks Team
Services Sub-Forums: Classifieds (Non-business Users), Industry Craftsmen Classifieds, Practice Partner Finder, Sword Reviews & Test Results, Stolen Swords Alert, Test, Technical Support and Off-Topic

When a participant clicks on the heading of each community, such as the 'Antique Arms & Armour Community', he/she is directed to another screen shot where different subforums of each community with assigned moderators are shown in the following figure. On the right, one can see that at least one moderator is assigned to each subforum. Note that due to privacy reasons, I changed all names to moderator and numbered them accordingly. I also changed the names of members that appear on the next screen shot. The 'real name policy' of the Forum of Swords requires member to provide their first and last names.

Figure 2.2: Different subforums of 'Arms & Armour Community'.

	Antique & Military Sword Forum Antique swords of all cultures and historical periods	**French or Belgian?** by Christo Today 11:49 AM	2,972	25,720	Moderator 1, Moderator 2
	Nihon-to Forum The discussion of traditional Japanese made edged weapons and related crafts from the Jokoto to the Shinsakuto period	**Teruhide** by Jeniffer Yesterday 07:47 PM	2,175	18,695	Moderator 2, Moderator 3
	Ancient Weapons Forum Weapons from the Bronze Age up to the Late Migration Era.	**Bronze sword festival 2007** by Fabian Today 12:32 AM	913	11,220	Moderator 4, Moderator 5, Moderator 6
	Middle-East, India & Africa The antique arms and armor of the region of Ottoman Turkey, the Middle East, India and Africa.	**Tulwar help required.** by Ardavan Today 11:25 AM	127	1,480	Moderator7, Moderator 8, Moderator 9
	Chinese, South-East Asia The antique arms and armor covering Chinese, South-East Asia.	**Any Real Antique Jian's for...** by Wong Today 08:29 AM	104	664	Moderator 10, Moderator 11

	The Antique Kukri Forum Focusing on one of the world's most recognizable edged weapons.	**Kothimora** by John Today 07:05 AM	124	1,257	Moderator 12, Moderator 13
	Antique Armour Studies Forum The focus and study of the armour of history	**armor questions** by Alexander 09-13-2007 12:28 PM	733	9,408	Moderator 14
	Archived Forums Past Forums can be found here	**Forum Changes - Feb 1, 2007** by Allan 02-01-2007 08:29 AM	2,097	18,536	

By clicking on one of the communities above, participants can enter each subforum and see different threads titled with different names. Here, they can decide where they want to enter and which individual thread they want to read. The following figure shows what the forum dedicated to the arms and armor from the Middle East, India and Africa looks like:

Figure 2.3: Individual threads of the subforum 'Edged Weapons from the Middle East, Asia, and Africa'.

Threads in Forum : Middle-East, India & Africa (MEIA)		Forum Tools Search this Forum		
Rating Thread / Thread Starter		Last Post	Replies	Views
Sticky Threads				
	Sticky: Book on Iranian Arms and Armor (1 2 3 4 5 ... Last Page) Moderator	Yesterday 01:28AM by Moderator	388	16,359
	Sticky: Welcome! (READ FIRST) Allan01-31-2007 08:30PM by Allan	01-31-2007 08:30PM by Allan	0	715
Forum Threads				
	Tulwar help required. Nash McComby	Today 11:25AM by Emil Nicole	1	13
	all steel spear fom india for comment Stephano Ghangu	Today 09:27AM by Dan Zus	15	259
	Bandeye Shah Velayat Abbas Richard Monroe	Today 07:39AM by Richard Monroe	7	95
	Insciption on Yataghan... Richard Monroe	Yesterday 06:52PM by rand milam	9	111

In contrast to the Forum of Swords, The Forum of Ethnographic Swords was created by a number of collectors of antique arms in 1998. First, the forum had two subforums: a subforum dedicated to the study of European arms and armor and another one dedicated to the study of Ethnographic Edged Weapons (note that the term 'ethnographic weapons' is coined and used by members of this forum to refer to any hand-made historical weapon from Asia, the Middle East, Africa, and South America). After some years, due to the lack of participation, the subforum of European arms and armor was closed. Instead, a new subforum dedicated to the study of the *keris* (from Indonesia and Malaysia) was created next to the forum that was dedicated to the study of ethnographic arms and armor. The reason for this differentiation was that a specialist on the *keris*, named Melborn, was selected and was assigned as the moderator to the new subforum. Melborn had written an article in a print magazine on the development of *keris*. This article was heavily criticized by Manolo on the Forum of Swords. The criticism of the article written by Melborn on the Forum of Swords led to the start of the controversial thread called the *keris* controversy, which is a subject of study in this volume. The Forum of Ethnographic Swords is used by collectors of antique arms to discuss and identify different types of antique arms and armor. As I will show below, the new format of the Forum of Ethnographic Swords consists of a) the Ethnographic Weapons forum, b) the Keris Forum, c) the Swap Forum, and d) the Archived Forums.

Figure 2.4: Different forums of the Forum of Ethnographic Swords.

Forum of Ethnographic Swords   Welcome

User CP | Register | FAQ | Members List | New Posts | Search | Quick Links | Log Out

Forum	Last Post	Threads	Posts
General Discussion			
Ethnographic Swords (34 Viewing) General forum for discussion of all ethnographic edged weapons and related topics.	My latest spear. by Freddo Today 11:50 AM	3,757	42,398
Keris Forum (4 Viewing) A forum for the study and discussion of keris	Question by Ganjji Yesterday 02:29 PM	216	3,763
Classifieds			
Swap Forum (3 Viewing) Forum for posting ethnographic edged weapons and related books which are wanted, for sale or for trade.	For Sale: 9 Keris by Joe 14th September 2007 09:39 PM	652	2,141
Archives			
Forum 2000 - 2004	-	-	-
Board Forum 1998 - 1999	-	-	-

By clicking on any subforum mentioned above, participants can enter each subforum respectively. In the following, Figure 2.5 shows what happens when one enters the Forum of Ethnographic Swords. As shown below, different, respective threads are shown with different titles and headings. Participants can choose where they want to enter and read which topic accordingly.

Figure 2.5: the Forum of Ethnographic Swords and its related threads.

Threads in Forum: Forum of Ethnographic Swords	Forum Tools	Search this Forum	
Thread / Thread Starter	Last Post	Replies	Views
Sticky: Classic Threads Moderator1	12th June 2007 05:43PM by Moderator1	5	1,312
Sticky: Welcome to the Forum Moderator2	16th January 2007 03:04PM by Moderator2	0	592
Sticky: PLEASE READ BEFORE YOU POST: FORUM RULES, GUIDELINES AND FEATURES Moderator1	16th January 2006 02:18AM by Moderator1	5	3,568
My Pata Benny Monrow	Today 10:31 PM by richard	8	267
This might be of interest to some. Micky Benn	Today 09:51PM by spunge	14	352
A slightly unique Piha Kaetta danny	Today 09:50 PM by scoop	7	131

One should take into consideration that next to online discussion forums dedicated to the study of arms and armor, other related formats and tools of collecting information exist in the field of arms and armor. As the participants of the Forum of Swords have different interests and comprise diverse groups, the ways to collect information through other formats are different. The members of the subforums dedicated to the study of antique arms and armor resort to scholarly books published in the field, such as *The Craft of the Japanese Sword* by Kapp and Yoshihara (1996), *Arms and Armor from Iran: The Bronze Age to the End of the Qajar Period* by Moshtagh Khorasani

(2006), *Indian Arms and Armour: Volumes I–III* by Pant (1978, 1980 & 1983), and *Persian Steel: The Tanavoli Collection* by Allan and Gilmour (2000). These books are important for the analysis of online controversies as members of both forums dedicated to the study of arms and armor use these books as a reference and source. Of course, opinions differ regarding the content and theories proposed in each book. This, of course, is a source of controversies, which, at times, leads to online controversies.

In addition, there are a number of martial artists who frequent the subforums of the Forum of Swords that are dedicated to the study of historical swordsmanship. These martial artists consult other members, and some of them have written books on swordsmanship that are based on antique manuals, such as *Medieval Combat: A Fifteenth-Century Illustrated Manual of Swordsfighting and Close-Quarter Combat* by Talhoffer (2000) or *Codex Wallerstein: A Medieval Fighting Book from the Fifteenth Century on the Longsword, Falchion, Dagger, and Wrestling* by Walczak and Zabinski (2002). Additionally, there are related academic magazines indirectly dedicated to the study of arms and armor, such as *Iranica Antiqua* (see Masia 2001) and *Acta Iranica* (see Harper, 1996), that publish arms-and-armor-related articles among other topics dedicated to ancient Iranian studies. There is also an academic martial art journal that publishes arms-and-armor-related materials called *The Journal of Asian Martial Arts* (see Jeremiah, 2007). There are also other martial arts magazines that are tailored to martial artists, such as *Black Belt Magazine.* Similar to books, some articles published in these magazines are used as source materials by some members in online discussion forums dedicated to the study of arms and armor. This, at times, leads to controversies as the opinions on the validity of the theories proposed in the articles differ from each other.

2.3 The participants in online discussion forums (active participants, passive participants, distribution of rights, motivation of participants, and the goals of participants)

Different types of people participate in these discussion groups, namely scholars (historians, archaeologists, art historians, military historians, and other scholars from all other fields), private collectors of historical arms and armor, re-enactors of historical events, film directors, stuntmen, filmmakers, practitioners of historical swordsmanship styles, and enthusiasts. Therefore, there are different interest groups that participate in these forums. Thus, different people with different backgrounds make up a diverse community, contributing to an environment where different attitudes and points of view are presented. This is, of course, an environment with high potential for creating controversies. The General Forum (dedicated to general topics regarding arms and armor) on the Forum of Swords has a larger number of controversial threads in comparison with the specialized subforums, such as the Nihonto Forum. In general, this shows that the more specialized a forum is, the less the tendency is of having controversial threads. This is the case for two reasons. First, in specialized subforums, more specialists with specialized backgrounds communicate with each other, whereas in the General Forum more people with diverse backgrounds and attitudes converse. Second, participation in specialized subforums requires specialized knowledge, and, hence, fewer members actively participate there. On the other hand, more members contribute to threads on the General Forum because little if any specialized knowledge is necessary to engage in communication there.

As mentioned before, communication in online discussion forums occurs in a moderated environment, meaning that to each forum a number of moderators are assigned who act as impartial judges and make sure that the principles and rules of the forum are respected. However, it should be noted that moderators do not remain impartial judges at all times and, indeed, show their preferences for certain members. However, showing preference for certain members is a risky deed. In such cases, other members may accuse moderators of being unfair and partial. Since moderators have editing and banning powers, these accusations are normally edited, and if a member repeats his/her accusations in an aggressive way, he/she might be temporarily or permanently banned. Yet being banned is not restricted to the case that a moderator shows preference for a certain member. Due to the very nature of posting and, at times, differing opinions, controversies and conflicts arise on some threads regularly. In such cases, the forum administrators and the moderators try to intervene and facilitate the discussion. Although the Forum of Swords has a strict set of rules of conduct, some contributors use aggressive words, which lead automatically to them receiving a warning, and if this behavior on their part repeats, it leads to a temporary IP ban of the members in question. At times, the IPs are banned[17] permanently due to an aggravated breach of rules of conduct or when a troll[18] posts. A troll is a contributor who keeps provoking other members, involving them in endless arguments and disrupting the flow of communication. The long-term members also help the staff and moderators to monitor the board and report any violation of rules to the moderator team and administrators. This, again, is a sign of the identification of these groups with a certain online discussion forum.[19]

Making a comparison between moderators of online discussion forums and television moderators, one notes that there are similarities

---

17 Nilsson (2003:11) describes IP banning as the computer-generated ban of an IP address, which leads to the situation where a banned person cannot log onto a certain website, using a computer assigned with the banned IP address.

18 A troll is a contributor or a poster who does not respect the rules, and his sole purpose is to ruin the flow of communication. Nilsson (2003:11) describes a troll as a person who lurks in the background, reads posts, and, at times, joins online communication to make rude and unconstructive comments.

19 Fayard and DeSanctis (2005:3) state that there is research conducted on a range of issues related to online discussion groups, such as "member contribution patterns, substantiality, and motivations to contribute (e.g., Constant, Sproull & Kiesler, 1995; Rheingold, 1993; Wasko Faraj, 2005), empathy expression (Preece, 2000), deception, conflict, and social control (see Smith & Kollock, 1999), and how work-oriented groups differ in their contribution pattern from more entertainment-oriented groups (Finholt & Sproull, 1990)".

and differences between the role of moderators in online discussion forums dedicated to the study of arms and armor and the role of moderators on TV talk shows. As I mentioned before, moderators in online discussion forums are supposed to be impartial and encourage a good flow of communication. Nevertheless, moderators occasionally take an active side in controversies and participate keenly in them by protecting one party. This will, of course, lead to a situation where moderators are involved in spreading the effects of a controversy. Regarding similarities to controversies on TV talk shows, moderators either apply a) 'protection strategy' or b) 'confrontainment' (Hess-Lüttich, 2007:1365). Based on Burger (1991:190–197), Hess-Lüttich (2007:1364) explains that the protection strategy represents an instance when the moderator in a talk show attempts to allow guests to appear in a good light. To do so, a TV talk show moderator either presents the guest in a positive way or by granting the guest the opportunity indirectly to portray himself positively. On the other hand, based on Mühlen (1985:209), Hess-Lüttich (2007:1364) explains that in confrontainment, a moderator on a talk show applies the moderator strategies of provocation and disqualification. These strategies lead, of course, to a less comfortable talk show atmosphere. Similar to talk shows, moderators of discussion forums dedicated to the study of arms and armor, at times, use protection strategies towards one member, be it a smith or a dealer that is favored by the site administration, placing him in a favorable position, such as being a reputable seller of antiques or a respected modern reproducer of old weapons. At other times, some online moderators provoke and disqualify some members. In this case, one can see some similarities in the roles of moderators of online discussion forums and TV moderators.

Further, regarding controversies on TV shows, Hess-Lüttich (2007:1365) also identifies 'infotainment' and explains that its primary function is to combine information and entertainment or suspense. As an example, Hess-Lüttich explains that Lea Rosh, hostess of the monthly talk show *Freitagnacht*, based in Berlin, did not narrow her program to harmonious entertainment and mere amusement. Moreover, she applied the journalistic concept of 'clarity through controversy', which meant that through controversial debates, she tried to offer her audience entertainment and, at the same time, information. Hess-Lüttich adds that her program differed from other programs as it presented a debate on a pre-announced topic in both an informative and entertaining way, providing one of the first forms of infotainment. Although this strategy is not actively implemented by moderators of online discussion forums, some of them apply the concept of clarity through controversy. In this case, moderators start a controversial thread where different members take part in the thread and state their differing opinions. Although this strategy is not used very often, examples of this strategy can be seen on both the Forum of Swords and the Forum of Ethnographic Swords. In other words, both TV and online moderators are trying to shape the context of the information to suit their purposes or their advertisers' purposes (for monetary, political reasons or other reasons).

Further, there is also a business aspect to the Forum of Swords. One should note that many modern swordsmiths who make swords for movies and private customers also participate there; therefore, they can position their products in targeted segments of the forum toward specific audiences. The majority of these swordsmiths have their websites, which are interlinked to the Forum of Swords. Some antiquity dealers also participate there and are interlinked to that forum. Therefore, besides a scholarly character, where a lot of information is exchanged between scholars and private collectors, the Forum of Swords also offers a venue for swordsmiths and antique dealers to present their products. As previously mentioned, one should note that besides interlinking in the signature lines of forumites,[20] there are no direct advertisements on the site. One should not think that the type of discourse on these forums is completely academic in nature. There is also casual discourse that takes place in the Off-topic Forum (a subforum dedicated to off-topic discussions). The Forum of Ethnographic Swords also has a business character as some antique dealers who post there benefit from their exposure on the forum.

The Forum of Swords enjoys a high number of registered members of which there are over 60,000 and over 150,000 monthly readers. The members of the forum have different contribution

20 In online discussion forums dedicated to the study of arms and armor, forum contributors are described as forumites.

patterns (some of them post daily, some weekly, some monthly, and so forth).[21] In both forums in this study, the number of posts each member makes appears below his/her name so that, after a while, it becomes a matter of prestige for each member to increase the number of posts he/she has made. Many members are simultaneously members of other smaller Internet forums dedicated to the study of arms and armor. Some of them are very loyal and do not post elsewhere. It means that some members proudly only post on one subforum of the Forum of Swords. This, of course, is due to the fact that they are interested in one field of study and develop a sense of loyalty over a period of time toward that forum, its members, and its moderators. Further, among registered members, one can distinguish between frequent users, who post regularly, and rare users, who make sporadic postings on the forum. There are different motivations to contribute. Some private collectors post their swords, asking the experts or fellow collectors for proper identification and an estimated age; some show museum pieces and exchange information about the provenance of the artifacts; some describe their forging techniques and ask for advice; and some ask about the related techniques in martial arts.

Over the course of time, new and different forums related to arms and armor were also created, which have been competing heavily with the Forum of Swords. As a result, each one of these forums is specialized in one particular area of arms and armor and tries to compete with the Forum of Swords in that focused area. Similar to online discussion forums of information systems professionals in India that were analyzed by Fayard and DeSanctis (2005), online forums dedicated to the study of arms and armor promote an alternative to educational courses and seminars without any fees involved. However, unlike online discussion forums of information systems, the arms and armor forums also indirectly offer tangible products, such as antique arms and armor or newly made pieces, through interlinking to smiths' websites and antique dealers.

21 The level of activity also differs in e-mail communication. Regarding the level of activity of e-mail communication, Kavanaugh *et al.* (2006:217) distinguish between heavy users versus light users and experienced users versus novices.

Each forum decides to support and promote certain smiths and companies who are allowed to introduce their products on the forum, whereas others are discouraged or not allowed to do so. In such a competitive environment, attracting forumites (contributors) and maintaining their numbers are essential for the existence and survival of a forum. One should note that during the course of time, some smaller forums dedicated to the study of arms and armor vanished due to the lack of participation. Therefore, attracting forumites and sustaining them in online discussion forums dedicated to the study of arms and armor are an ongoing challenge not only by the forum staff and moderators but also by key members who feel responsible for these tasks.

Herring (2004:345) explains that the success of a forum depends on 'continuous and self-sustaining' participation of its contributors. This is also the case with the Forum of Swords and its competitors. One of the major competitors to the Forum of Swords is the Forum of Ethnographic Swords. Although, as stated above, this forum can only compete in a small range of specialties that the Forum of Swords offers, members of that forum and staff are, nevertheless, determined to compete for their existence and the maintenance of the number of their contributors. Over the period of the last four years, the competition has become very intense with members of both forums participating in controversies on both forums. As each online forum is a moderated atmosphere and a close-knit community, there are rules that are determined by the staff and are enforced by the moderators of each forum. These rules ensure a free flow of information and discussion and punish any form of unconstructive communicative behavior, such as trolling. Additionally, each forum has set rules that are followed by each community. These rules can be described as accepted norms and rules of each forum.

Before participating in the Forum of Swords, each member needs to register. In the beginning, members could use an Internet hanger (Internet name), but after two years, the forum administrators changed this policy and required each member to register with his/her real name. At that time, this policy was called the 'real-name policy'. Although a majority of participants register with their real names, one needs to take into consideration that there is no definite way to determine whether all participants use their real names. There were cases where some members who were banned from the forum still participated by using false names. On the moderator forum of the Forum of Swords, a discussion was initiated about whether the administrators should introduce a new rule requiring a minimum age requirement. The motivation for this suggestion was that some members who were very young did not respect the rules and ended up trolling the forums for a while and endangering the social fabric of the forum. However, this idea was dropped as the moderators and site administrators of the Forum of Swords came to the conclusion that there was no effective way to find out the real age of a person. To be more effective in handling trolling and to deal with controversial threads, different moderators who were experts in their respective fields were assigned to each forum. The tasks and duties of moderators are to monitor their respective forums, and if they see any violation of the rules, they can take proper action.

2.4 The principles and rules of communication in online discussion forums dedicated to the study of arms and armor

There are a number of tools that moderators can use to control their forums. One of these tools is using a set of rules that serve as principles of communication that the moderators can use as a reference to suspend the posting privileges of members who break these rules or principles. Upon registering, each member receives a warning that emphasizes that by pushing the button that states 'I AGREE', the member needs to agree to and follow all the rules. These rules are explicitly called 'Rules and Online Code of Conduct'. The moderators enforce these rules on the forum. One should note that moderators can be divided into two categories: a) moderators who are responsible for enforcing the rules of the forum, also called administrative duties of moderators, and b) moderators who are specialists in their respective field of arms and armor and who make specific contributions to their subforums. Nevertheless, both types of moderators can enforce the rules and are equipped with administrative functions, such as banning a member due to the aggravated violation of a certain rule.

As will be shown later in this chapter, these rules regulate and determine the individual posting behavior of each member on the Forum of Swords. Further, the Rules and Online Code of Conduct explicitly stress that any violation of the rules will result in the suspension of posting privileges or banning of members who have violated the rules. In the welcome note of the Forum of Swords, it is also written that posting in the Forum of Swords is a privilege, not a right. This, of course, gives the moderators a tremendous amount of power to control the communication processes in the Forum of Swords. If a member complains about his/her banning and asks for his/her posting privileges to be reinserted again, the moderators can always refer to this rule and stress that posting on the Forum of Swords is not a right but a privilege. This rule is not officially stated in the charter of the official rules of the Forum of Swords. The number one official rule is 'Real full name for user IDs'. This rule stresses that nicknames will not be tolerated. Additionally, this rule explains that all registration is approved by site administrators within 24–96 hours, and if they discover any new registration using the same IP, they will immediately delete the account. The second rule stresses that the environment of the Forum of Swords is a moderated environment. That means that not all individual moves are accepted in a moderated environment. The third rule requires that the participants provide their real e-mail addresses, meaning that after each member registers, a confirmation e-mail will be sent to him or her. Then, the new member needs to answer to that e-mail so that his or her account will be activated. The administrators of the site review the e-mail within 1–3 days and will delete all nickname accounts.

In addition to these three rules, there are also two principles of a 'Code of Conduct'. The first principle is the principle of being 'warm and friendly'. This principle stresses that disrespect, rudeness, impatience, anger, snide remarks, sideswiping attacks, trolling, cynicism, and poor attitudes will not be tolerated on the Forum of Swords.

Further, this principle identifies the website as a family-friendly website and stresses that no pornographic links or images, spam, discussion of firearms, discussion of politics, and attacks against someone's religious or spiritual beliefs will be tolerated. The next principle of the 'Code of Conduct' is the principle of 'No politics'.[22] This principle explicitly stresses that the politics of another website remain on that website and that the participants of the Forum of Swords are required to keep the politics off the forum. One needs to take into consideration that in spite of these rules, a lot of controversies occur as people bring politics into the forum from other websites, which will be shown later.

Next to these rules and codes of conduct, the Forum of Swords also has an advertising policy. This policy requires participants not to post ads or promotional links indiscriminately to a business website or forum. However, the forum makes an exception for individual artists, swordmakers, and craftsmen who are not involved in retail and in manufacturing, provided that their total number of workers is less than five people. In this case, these people may use a signature link to a business and the forum to network discretely. On the other hand, the advertising policy of the Forum of Swords requires that wholesalers, retailers, businesses, and martial arts schools that want to present themselves openly on the forum support the Forum of Swords through advertising. The advertising policy explicitly states that any violation of these rules and the usage of the Forum of Swords as a free promotional tool will result in account termination.

Next to these rules, there are also other principles that participants in the Forum of Swords follow. One should note that these rules are not explicitly stated in the charter of rules of the Forum of Swords. Nevertheless, similar to the members of an e-mail environment studied by Graham (2007:745), these principles are followed and respected by the majority of the members of the Forum of Swords. These principles are the principles of politeness that are expected from participants in online communication and are similar to

22 Among moderators of the Forum of Swords, this principle is also known as "What happens in Vegas stays in Vegas", meaning that politics and problems of other forums should not be discussed or affect the Forum of Swords.

the politeness principles in an e-mail environment identified by Graham (2007:745). Such principles or 'netiquette rules' include the following: a) threads should be accurately marked with their titles, which should correspond to the content, b) one should not waste bandwidth by using image hijacking,[23] and c) one should not 'blat', meaning that one should not reveal the contents of a private message that one has received on the forum or the contents of a private email on the public forum. These rules are the rules that I call implicit rules of the Forum of Swords in contrast to the explicit rules that are clearly stated and described in the charter of rules in the Forum of Swords.

Similar to other online discussion forums, the rules and principles of the Forum of Swords are constantly being updated due to the needs that occur during the course of time. Some of the rules are updated and revised, and some new ones are added. One of the rules that was updated and resulted in the creation of a new rule, called 'trolling and abuse of forums', was the rule of being 'warm and friendly'. Although the principle of being 'warm and friendly' already prohibits trolling, the owners of the Forum of Swords, nevertheless, saw the necessity to introduce a separate and new rule in September 2007 that specifically bans trolling. This new forum rule is titled 'trolling and abuse of forums' and stresses that there is no 'three strikes' rule on the Forum of Swords. It means that if a person trolls, he/she will be banned immediately, and the moderators and the staff will not give him/her any other chance to rejoin the forum. The introduction of this new, separate rule was due to an increase of trolling activities on the Forum of Swords and also due to the interpretative nature of the principle of being 'warm and friendly'. When moderators reprimanded some members of the Forum of Swords for having violated the principle of being 'warm and friendly' due to trolling activity, some accused members started to counter and say that they were not being unfriendly and denied having violated the rule of 'being warm and friendly'. To avoid these circumstances and

23 Image hijacking involves posting pictures by directing image tags to a third party's server. This rule is looked down upon as it consumes the third party's bandwidth on another site. As I will show later, this rule is explicitly explained in the charter of rules of the Forum of Ethnographic Swords.

the interpretative nature of the rule of being 'warm and friendly', the new rule concerning "trolling and abuse of forums" was introduced.

Some other rules are new and were introduced over time. One of the new rules introduced in September 2007 is named 'sword identification inquiries'. This rule specifically stresses that the Forum of Swords moderators and staff do not answer sword identification questions via private message and email and requires the members to post their inquiries in the respective forums. The introduction of this new rule was due to the fact that an increasing number of members started to ask the moderators and the staff of the Forum of Swords to identify certain types of swords via private messages and email. The introduction of the rule concerning 'sword identification inquiries' led to a decrease in the participation in the forum that was not in the interest of the site owner. Another rule that was added in September 2007 was 'no firearms/guns pictures and posts'. Although the Forum of Swords always discouraged conversations about firearms and deleted such posts, the Forum of Swords saw the necessity to introduce this new rule due to an increase of attempts of some members to discuss firearms on the forum. Finally, a new rule, named 'user account deletion policy', was introduced in October 2007. This rule specifically states that user requests to delete their accounts will not be accepted. The reason for taking this decision was that some members who were banned requested the Forum of Swords staff and moderators to delete their posts and account. As deleting accounts is a very time-consuming process and since the ownership of all posts made by a user would default to 'guest' if the user ID were deleted, the Forum of Swords prefers to maintain the user account and post/thread associations to the user for legal purposes. The Forum of Swords also keeps this information to maintain an institutional memory of these people and to track them if the need ever arises.

Table 2.1: The communication principles and rules of the Forum of Swords.

The communication principles and rules of the Forum of Swords	
Explicit rules / principles	
Rule 1	Posting is a privilege, not a right
Rule 2	Real full name for user IDs
Rule 3	Moderated environment; not all individual moves and posts are accepted
Rule 4	Real e-mail addresses have to be provided
Rule 5	Be warm and friendly
Rule 6	No politics; politics of other sites remain on those sites
Rule 7	Trolling and abuse of forums is not tolerated
Rule 8	Sword identification inquires should be done in the forums and not via private messages
Rule 9	No firearm / gun pictures and posts
Rule 10	User account deletion policy
Implicit rules / principles (netiquette)	
Rule 11	Threads should be accurately marked in their titles
Rule 12	One should not waste bandwidth by using image hijacking
Rule 13	One should not blat

The Forum of Ethnographic Swords has a sticky thread (a thread that is permanently at the top of a discussion forum's page and does not change position on the page as other threads do when new material appears on them) to explain the rules and guidelines of that forum. This forum does not have a real-name policy: participants can take part in the forum by using Internet hangers. However, in the charter of rules of the Forum of Ethnographic Swords, before detailing the explicit rules, it is stated that the forum reserves the right to reveal the true identity of any participant should any complaint or legal case arise from any message posted by the participant. Thus, in contrast to the Forum of Swords, the Forum of Ethnographic Swords does not have an active real-name policy expressed clearly in the charter rules. A part of the reason for not having a real-name policy is that this forum caters to the needs of private collectors of antique arms and armor, and many collectors prefer to remain anonymous. Further, the forum states that the messages expressed are the views of the author of the message, not the views of the forum. Thus, the Forum of Ethnographic Swords' unstated policy is biased toward the benefit of private collectors and discrete individuals, not public disclosure of its members.

The first rule of the Forum of Ethnographic Swords is related to active auctions. This rule prohibits the discussion and interlinking to any online auction or auction that is active.[24] An exception to this rule is that a discussion about a pending auction is permitted if the participant knows that the nature of the auction is fraudulent. This rule is not explicitly stated in the charter of rules of the Forum of Swords due to the fact that in some subforums, such as the Edged Weapons from the Middle East Forum, discussing ongoing auctions is not allowed, whereas in other subforums, such as the subforum dedicated to the study of European Military Swords, the discussion of ongoing auctions is tolerated. In contrast to the Forum of Swords, the Forum of Ethnographic Swords defines the penalties for violation of each rule immediately after each rule is written. In case of the violation of the first rule, mentioning or referring to an open auction, the participant will be banned for the first violation for ten days, for thirty days for the second violation, and permanently for the third violation.

The second rule is about spamming, which states that spamming or intentional business advertisement is strictly forbidden in the general discussion forums. Items for sale by the members should be posted in the Swap Forum. Note that the Forum of Swords also has a subforum called 'Classified Swords', where private members can sell their items. This is taken for granted and not explicitly written in the charter of rules in the Forum of Swords. The third rule is about 'flames, insults, bigotry, and threats'. This rule strictly forbids flames (insulting statements) or insults and asks participants that in case of being flamed they should notify one of the members of the moderator team. This rule also states that if a participant does not get along with a member, he should incorporate the function 'add to ignore list'. By putting someone on the ignore list, a participant does not see the posts of another member who has been

24 Note that this rule specifically refers to any online auction, such as eBay auctions, as well as other items offered for sale by auction houses.

put on the ignore list.[25] Due to the international nature of the forum, this rule also states that intolerant posts against any culture, race, religion, and nationality will not be tolerated. This rule also forbids any type of threatening messages.

The fourth rule of the Forum of Ethnographic Swords is about copyright violations and pornographic material. This rule does not allow the members of the forum to upload pictures or other attachments copyrighted by a person other than the poster himself unless the owner of the picture grants explicit permission. This rule also does not allow 'image hijacking' that involves posting pictures by directing image tags to a third party's server. The rule explains that this practice is forbidden as it consumes the third party's bandwidth that someone else is paying for. However, one should note that an important reason behind this rule is that online discussion forums prefer their members to post pictures directly on their forums by using the attachment function. This way, they can keep pictures on their forums and files. This rule also strictly forbids members from placing pornographic materials on the server or links to pornographic sites, whether in textual or in any other form. The fifth rule is about controversial topics and trolling. This rule states that controversial topics, such as religion and politics, will not be tolerated on the forum, and the topics should be concentrated on arms and armor. Nevertheless, the reality of applying this rule is very different on this forum as members post many controversial posts that are not necessarily related to the study of arms and armor. This rule also forbids trolling or any activity intended to create discord or problems on the Forum of Ethnographic Swords.

The sixth rule involves 'special forum policies'. This rule states that the member who intends to sell an item on the Swap Forum must own and be able to transfer clear title. Additionally, this rule states that participants who sell or trade on the Swap Forum do so at their own risk. The seventh rule involves 'legal discussions'. This rule allows the discussion of laws, regulations, and legal issues, such as the

25 One should note that the Forum of Sword also provides this function. My experience as a moderator of the Forum of Swords shows that few members use this function. Normally, they prefer to get involved in polemical discourse with their opponents.

ownership of edged weapons and their transportation or exportation, but the same rule strictly forbids participants from making suggestions for circumventing mentioned laws or regulations, such as shipping and labelling strategies. This rule also allows the discussions of one's own experiences with customs and local possession laws, but the same rule does not allow discussions about circumventing or avoiding the mentioned laws. The eighth rule is about 'appraisals'. This rule prohibits the members from making public appraisals on the forum. The ninth rule is about the 'Forum of Ethnographic Swords staff', which states that the team includes site/forum administrators, forum moderators, and technical advisors and stresses that decisions made by the staff are not subject to public debate. The tenth rule is a 'summary' recapping of the general rules and guidelines expected from the members as every participant is solely responsible for what he writes, every member must obey the law, each member should refrain from advertising on the forum unless he or she does so on the Swap Forum, and members should keep the communication civil and respectful. The last rule, namely the eleventh 'enjoy' rule, is not a rule per se but asks the members to enjoy the communication on the forum and, hence, theoretically serves the purpose of creating an enjoyable and friendly atmosphere. The following table shows all the moves described above together with the rules of netiquette that are also valid for the Forum of Ethnographic Swords.

Table 2.2: The communication principles and rules of the Forum of Ethnographic Swords.

The communication principles and rules of the Forum of Ethnographic Swords	
Explicit rules / principles	
Rule 1	Discussion and interlinking to any (online) auction is forbidden
Rule 2	Spamming or intentional business advertisement is strictly forbidden
Rule 3	Flames, insults, bigotry, and threats are strictly forbidden
Rule 4	Uploading copyrighted pictures without permission and posting pornographic materials are strictly forbidden; no image hijacking
Rule 5	Posting controversial topics, such as religion and politics, and trolling are forbidden
Rule 6	Special forum policies: to sell an item on the Swap Forum, one must own and be able to transfer clear title

Rule 7	Legal discussions: discussions about circumventing laws or regulations regarding ownership of edged weapons and their transportation or exportation are not allowed
Rule 8	Making public appraisals on the forum are forbidden
Rule 9	Decisions made by site / forum administrators and forum moderators are not subject to public debate
Rule 10	Summary: every member is solely responsible for what he writes, every member must obey the law, each member should refrain from advertising on the forum unless he/she posts ads on the Swap Forum, and members should keep the communication civil and respectful
Rule 11	Enjoy the forum
Implicit rules / principles (netiquette)	
Rule 12	Threads should be accurately marked with their titles
Rule 13	One should not waste bandwidth by using image hijacking
Rule 14	One should not blat

2.5 The background of the keris controversy and the nationalism controversy

To analyze the nature of controversies in online discussion forums, I will analyze two controversies, namely the *keris* controversy in the Forum of Swords and the *nationalism* controversy in the Forum of Ethnographic Swords. In October 2006, a deliberate controversy started in the Forum of Swords. A member of Forum of Swords named Manolo opened a thread that criticized an article entitled 'The Origins of *Keris*' by Alan Melborn, published in an arms magazine in 1998. The same print article was later published online on the Forum of Ethnographic Swords. To understand the level of escalation of this controversy and the rivalry between the Forum of Swords and Forum of Ethnographic Swords, one needs to understand that Melborn is a moderator of the Forum of Ethnographic Swords. Therefore, any open criticism of his work on the rival forum, namely the Forum of Swords, leads to an interforum controversy. Note that *keris* is the traditional, ritual dagger from Indonesia, carried by men and tucked in the sash in front of the body. The blade shape of a keris is asymmetrical where the blade is wider on one side in comparison to the other side. There are two different forms of the blade: wavy and straight blades. The blade length usually ranges from 30 cm to 38 cm. The blade is double edged, and it is sharp on both sides. The surface of the blade usually has a pattern that is the result of the forging process. This pattern is revealed via an etching process. The pattern on the *keris* blade is known as *pamor*. The earlier form of the *keris* is known as the *keris buda*, attributed to the Central Javanese Hindu Buddhist era (circa 700 C.E.–900 C.E.). The central thesis of Melborn's theory is that the earlier form of the *keris budda* was heavier and, hence, used in an overarm stabbing motion. Later on, when the *keris budda* developed into the lighter *keris*, the overarm stabbing technique was abandoned and changed to the rapier grip, which was used to handle the lighter *keris*.

The *keris* controversy started as the member Manolo first raised his criticism of the article in question on the Forum of the Ethnographic Swords. The main criticism of Manolo was that any knife combat system teaches both overarm stabbing and the forward rapier grip and one cannot claim that the *keris budda* was only used in overarm stabbing and the *keris* only with a rapier grip. However, his criticism was not perceived well by the owners and moderators of the site, and this led to Manolo being banned from the Forum of Ethnographic Swords. Hence, one can see that there could be more motivation for Manolo to continue this controversy on another forum.

The controversy on the above-mentioned article started when, after being banned from the Forum of Ethnographic Swords, Manolo began a direct, confrontational thread on the Forum of Swords regarding the same issue. One interesting feature is that the period between Manolo being banned from the Forum of Ethnographic Swords and his criticism of the article by Melborn in the Forum of Swords lasted over one and a half years, proving that online controversies have their acute and dormant stages. Anything that is written in online discussion forums can be used against anyone at any time as long as the thread remains open. Given the nearly infinite duration of online controversies, one should recognize that each online controversy has its own limited life, meaning that in contrast to other informative threads, a controversial thread will be closed sooner or later by the moderators of the respective forum. The question of how long a thread remains open depends on the level and degree of a controversy, whether the heated discussion gets out of control, and how long the moderators who support a certain group allow the members of a team, with whom they sympathize, to state their opinions and, hence, win the favor of the readers. The *keris* controversy had a life of 30 days, meaning that the controversy started when Manolo started his critical post on October 11, 2006. One should note that on October 24, 2006, Alan (the site administrator of the Forum of Swords) closed the thread for administrative review for one day. Alan closed the thread by providing a link to the rules of courtesy on the forum and explicitly explained why the thread was closed. The site administrator pointed out that another controversial thread was running parallel to this one, and he decided to close both:

(1) Alan: Due to administrative review of a related thread – which is locked – this one too will be locked only momentary as a courtesy so that ALL parties will have a chance to share their perspectives.

On October 25, the site administrator reopened the thread. In spite of the short close-down that served as a warning, the heated and intense discussion ensued. Finally, a moderator closed the thread on November 10, 2006. Nine people participated in the controversy. There were also two administrators and one moderator who gave warnings and closed the thread with a total number of five posts. As mentioned before, one administrator locked the thread temporarily for one day. Even after the thread reopened, the participants did not try to maintain a 'warm and friendly' atmosphere. Thus, there were different breaches of the 'Be warm and friendly' rule of the Forum of Swords. The following table shows the number of posts by each participant as well as the average number of words per post, the average number of words in the longest post, the average number of words in the shortest post, and the total number of words posted by each participant in the controversy.

Table 2.3: The Total Number of Words Posted in the *keris* Controversy.

Name of participants	Number of posts	Total number of words posted by the member in the controversy	Average number of words per post	Average number of words in the longest post	Average number of words in the shortest post
Manolo Rodriguez	25	4,686	187	759	29
Charley	5	6,470	1,294	2,481	110
Jonathan	3	817	272	357	160
David	7	2,758	394	1,372	28
Paulo	10	1,754	175	348	12
Ward	2	394	197	342	52
Marco	11	664	60	217	8
Stefano	1	120	120	120	120
Joe	2	707	353	579	128
Alan (site administrator)	2	49	25	38	11
Daniel (site administrator)	1	33	33	33	33
Moderator	3	104	34	91	13
Total number of words used in the controversy			18,376 words		
Life span of the online controversy			30 days		
Total number of posts			72 posts		
Number of participants in the controversy			9 participants		
Number of administrators / moderators involved			3 administrators and moderators		

The above table shows exactly the level of involvement and activity of each member in the *keris* controversy in the Forum of Swords. The following figure shows how many posts each member posted per day and the periods of intense activity (acute stage) and as well periods of inactivity (dormant stage).

Figure 2.6: Level of activity and number of posts of the contributors over the life of the *keris* controversy.

▲ Start of the controversy ■ Number of posts per day ♦ End of controversy

	Manolo R.	Charley	Jonathan	David	Paulo	Ward	Marco	Stefano	Joe	Alan (S.A.)	Daniel (S.A.)	Moderator
11	▲		1	1	1							
12	3				1							
13												
14	1											
15												
16												
17												
18												
19	1	1	2									
20	3						11					
21	2				3							
22				1	1			1				
23				2	1	1						
24		1										
25										1		
26						1				1		
27	3											1
28												
29												
30												
31	3	1							1		1	
01	2			1								
02												
03												
04												
05												
06												
07												
08	3	1		1	2							
09	2			1								1
10	1	1			1							♦

Table 2.3 and figure 2.6 show the degree of involvement of each member and specially the time intervals when he/she posted comments. This information is important as it shows the modus operandi of each individual member involved in an online controversy. For example, Manolo is a frequent poster, and Charley is not. In table 2.3, this is not evident in the first site as Charley has more words, 6,470 words, written, and Manolo has 4,686 words. Yet the number of posts by Manolo (25 posts) and Chaley (5 posts) shows the different modus operandi in posting messages. In one point in the *keris* controvery, Charley accuses Manolo for posting too many posts without thinking carefully about writing down his ideas.

On January 5, 2007, a short-lived but aggressive controversy started on the Forum of Ethnographic Swords. This controversial thread was one of the responses of members of the Forum of Ethnographic Swords to the controversial *keris* thread on the rival forum, the Forum of Swords. A member named Eidel opened a thread entitled 'nationalism'. This thread was started as a subtle attack against certain members and a moderator of the Forum of Swords who had stated in previous threads that in order to study the swords of a related culture, one needs to travel to the respective countries and network with the local academics. This was perceived as a challenge by some members of the Forum of Ethnographic Swords, and, hence, the related thread was started under the title 'nationalism', claiming that one does not need to belong to a certain culture or travel to a certain country to be able to study the respective arms and armor. Although this controversy does not look as active as the *keris* controversy on the Forum of Swords, it is important to note that the thread initiator, Eidel, and his main supporter, Ehud, were both temporarily banned for the period of one month by the Forum of Ethnographic Swords' site owner due to their postings on this thread, which were deemed as offensive and violated that forum's rules. This is an indication that Eidel and Ehud's posts were considered extremely aggressive by the Forum of Ethnographic Swords' site administration.

One of the unique characteristics of this controversy is that, besides the participation of Stefano, all other members of the Forum of Swords refrained from taking part in this controversy on the Forum of Ethnographic Swords. They were either banned from participating or did not participate in this controversy as a number of controversies were escalating on both forums at the same time. This, of course, takes its toll on the participants of both sides as the participation in a controversy is very time consuming and unnerving. A number of posts were also created in this thread that could be considered neutral since these neutral participants were not interested in getting involved or taking sides in the controversy. They simply wanted to express their opinions. Although two administrators, Dick and Donald, intervened in the course of the *nationalism* controversy with a total number of three posts, contrary to the role of two site administrators and one moderator involved in the *keris* controversy, the moderators of the Forum of Ethnographic Swords played an inactive role during the life of this controversy. Donald made two posts and contributed to the thread by stating his own opinion. Only at the end of thread did Dick, the other site administrator, lock the thread on January 7, 2007. The inactivity could be partially due to the short life (two days) of this controversy. In contrast to the *keris* controversy on the Forum of Swords, where many participants with opposing opinions were involved, this controversy seemed to be, more or less, a discussion between people of the same opinion.

Table 2.4: Statistical analysis of the number of words posted on the *nationalism* controversy thread.

Name of participants	Number of posts	Total number of words posted by the member in the controversy	Average number of words per post	Average number of words in the longest post	Average number of words in the shortest post
Eidel	1	677	677	677	677
Val	1	262	262	262	262
Ehud	3	421	140	344	26
Tony	7	1,349	193	617	1
Shahin	2	285	570	396	174
Tom	2	51	25	39	12
Stefano	1	19	19	19	19
Manuel	6	1,427	237	558	38
Donald (site administrator)	2	704	704	704	704
Dick (site ad-ministrator)	1	16	16	16	16

Total number of words used in the controversy	5,211
Life span of the online controversy	2 days
Total number of posts	26
Number of participants in the controversy	8 participants
Number of administrators / moderators involved	2 administrators

Figure 2.7: Level of activity and number of posts of the contributors over the life of the *nationalism* controversy thread.

▲ Start of the controversy

▒ Number of posts per day

♦ End of controversy

	Eidel	Val	Ehud	Tony	Shahin	Tom	Stefano	Manuel	Donald	Dick
5	▲									
6		1								
7			3	7	2	2	1	6	2	♦

2.6 Summary

This chapter has shown that online discussion forums are social networks where members communicate with each other and exchange information. A number of different forums dedicated to the study of arms and armor exist today. Some of them are more general in nature, and some are dedicated to the study of arms and armor from a specific culture.

Different participants take part in online discussion forums, ranging from scholars to re-enactors and from martial artists to enthusiasts. For the purpose of this study, I introduced two different forums, namely the Forum of Swords and the Forum of Ethnographic Swords. These two forums are the locations where two controversial threads of the *keris* controversy and *nationalism* controversy took place. Both forums are moderated environments, supervised by different moderators. The moderators and administrators ensure that forum rules are followed and respected. Each forum has a set of rules that are explicitly written in the charter of rules in each forum. Additionally, there are also rules of netiquette that each member is expected to respect and follow.

I explained the background of two different controversial threads that are the subjects of this study, namely the *keris* controversy that took place in the Forum of Swords and the *nationalism* controversy that took place in the Forum of Ethnographic Swords. The *keris* controversy started, as a member of the Forum of Swords named Manolo criticized the reasons given for the development of the *keris* by Melborn, who is a member of the Forum of Ethnographic Swords. The *nationalism* controversy started when a member of the Forum of Ethnographic Swords named Ehud accused a moderator of the Forum of Swords of having nationalistic ideas. In Chapter 3, I will investigate the nature of conflicts and controversies in theory and practice in order to have a solid basis for the analysis of controversies in online discussion forums.

3. Conflicts and controversies in theory and practice

3.1 Introduction

This chapter focuses on the nature of human conflict and controversies to provide background knowledge about different types of polemic discourse in general before embarking on the analysis of controversies in online discussion forums. This information is important in order to have a firm understanding of the type of polemical discourse that develops in online discussion forums. First, I will describe both the nature of human conflict and some previous models of conflict and conflict resolution. I will show that conflicts are present in the everyday activities of human beings, taking different shapes in different cultural settings. Accordingly, the best way of dealing with conflicts differs from culture to culture. I will show that, in spite of the fact that human conflict is considered a challenge and even a threat, it can also help human beings to achieve better results in their interpersonal relationships and approach problems from different perspectives. This, of course, requires better ways of and approaches to dealing with conflict situations. Conflict situations differ according to both the type of polemical discourse and the intentions of the interlocutors involved in polemical discourse.

Based on this description, the next part of this chapter explains the differences between distinctive types of polemical discourse, namely discussion, dispute, and controversy, and the corresponding intentions and goals of participants involved in each type of polemical discourse. I will explain the variation between each and show that there is no clear-cut difference in the types of polemical discourse used in online discussion forums. Rather, a hybrid form is used. Based on the work of Leibniz and his conception of the role of controversies, I will explain Leibniz's ideal model of how controversies should be carried out in a situation in which all participants are interested in furthering knowledge and learning from each other.

A major part of this chapter deals with the characteristics of controversies as it has been practiced; the evidence indicates that Leibniz's ideal model was not effective in the Early Modern Period. Participants in controversies, whether operating in the Early Modern Period or engaging in recent controversies in online discussion forums as analyzed in this study, largely have been much more interested in influencing the audience and making a good impression rather than furthering knowledge. Thus, individual moves and strategies used in these controversies are greatly influenced by the intentions of participants to gain power and influence. As will be shown, the goal of participants in controversies is to win over and to impress the audience, not to gain higher levels of knowledge.

3.2 Human conflict and polemical discourse

Controversies are a type of conflict and polemical discourse. Before going into a detailed analysis of controversies in online discussion forums, I would like to expand on the role of conflicts in human discourse and interaction. Human conflict, human differences, and the subsequent polemical discourses that ensue from them have always accompanied all aspects and spheres of human existence. Different ideas, opinions, interests, and ways of thinking lead to an array of conflicts that are part of the way how people interact and live together. Human beings are constantly confronted with various types of conflicts, ending in polemical discourse. Dascal (2000) points out that polemical discourse ranges from daily domestic quarrels to everyday disputes in the business world, from political debates to labor conflicts, and from book reviews to courtroom discussions. One could enlarge this list, but above all, one is constantly engaged in a self-debate with oneself as well whenever one wants to make a decision. This can also be considered a state of conflict with oneself: one needs to decide between alternatives. Thus, conflicts and polemical discourses are ubiquitous, and one cannot avoid them but has to find ways to deal with them. There are, of course, different ways of dealing with conflicts. In other cultural settings, different types of conflicts and polemical discourse occur. Although there are cultural differences in dealing with polemical discourse, all cultures see the necessity of dealing with conflict situations in different areas of human communication and interaction. Nevertheless, one should note that the way of dealing with conflict differs from one culture to another. Regarding this point, Dascal (2000) quotes Kerbrat-Orecchioni (1994), who differentiates between societies driven by a confrontational ethos (as an example, she mentions Israeli society) and societies with a consensual regulative ethos, such as modern Japanese society.[26]

Therefore, different cultural norms and rules regulate the way polemical discourse is carried out and handled. However, having a consensual regulative ethos does not mean that arguments or problems are solved in harmony, meaning that in spite of having a consensual regulative ethos and the subsequent, elaborate politeness devices implemented to prevent explicit polemical confrontations, polemical discourse is carried out in a covert way and not an overt way, so even in these societies, the importance of polemical discourse is not overlooked (Dascal, 2000). Nevertheless, in spite of the occurrence and importance of polemical discourse, human difference and human conflict have been considered a challenge for centuries. This challenge is not only perceived in private human relationships but also in the business world, where continuing conflicts are seen as detrimental to the productivity of a company. Analyzing conflicts in the corporate world, Gordon (1979:149) claims that conflicts are annoying and

26 Dealing with conflicts in the field of business, Böning (2000:236-237) claims that there are different types of dealing with conflicts based on the culture and states that Germans, Americans, South Koreans, and Norwegians tend to be more task-oriented and stick to facts, whereas Belgians and Spaniards tend to be more emotional. However, in my opinion, one needs to be careful about these categorizations as they may strengthen existing national stereotyping. Surely, as being social animals and going through the process of socialization, human beings are influenced by social norms and values. Nevertheless, one should never forget that human beings are different from each other due to different individual features and characteristics.

dangerous for the relationship between individuals and unproductive and not profitable for groups and companies. However, Gordon admits that conflicts are inevitable for human relationships; therefore, he suggests that one needs to face two tasks to deal effectively with the challenge of conflicts: a) one needs to keep the number of conflicts as small as possible,[27] and b) one needs to find a solution for conflicts that are inevitable.

Bernhard (1999:158–159) also stresses that conflicts are inevitable and explains that, generally, the defense reactions to conflicts are a) to fight back his/her opponent by using direct attacks (such as insulting, blackmailing, and spreading false information), b) to escape by avoiding a conflict, or c) to resign to the fact that a conflict exists (reactions such as suppressing and compensating).[28] Conflicts happen in all areas of human interaction, frequently in the workplace. Desivilya and Yagil (2005:56) explain that most studies on interpersonal conflict management patterns have used a Dual Concern Model as a theoretical framework (Blake & Mouton, 1964; Pruitt & Rubin, 1986; Rahim, 1983). Desivilya and Yagil (2005:56) add that the basic principle of this model assumes that the conflict-management mode used by an individual derives from two underlying motives: concern for self and concern for the other party.

Dependence on the strength of each of these two motivational orientations may change as a function of the particular conflict situation, with different emphases resulting in five major conflict-management patterns: a) dominating (high concern for self and low

---

27 One needs to take into consideration that in the Early Modern period, Leibniz advocated an atmosphere where carrying out controversies that were governed by a set of rules and principles would be beneficial for furthering the knowledge and understanding gained. This, of course, cannot be applied in the corporate world, where conflicts are seen as impediments for the productivity of a company. Nevertheless, even in the corporate world, one sees the necessity of having a culture of conflict, where problems are discussed and not avoided.

28 Bernhard (1999:161) explains that one of the major problems in dealing with conflicts is the win-lose mentality, where conflicts are considered as a null-sum game. Instead of having this approach, Bernhard (1999:166) suggests a win-win mentality in dealing with conflicts. However, in reality, applying such a mentality is an extremely difficult task.

concern for the other), b) obliging (low concern for self and high concern for the other), c) avoiding (low concern for self and low concern for the other), d) integrating (high concern for self and high concern for the other), and e) compromising (moderate concern for self and moderate concern for the other). Analyzing the language found in the workplace, Holmes and Marra (2004:439) distinguish between four distinct strategies that leaders use to cope with potential conflicts: conflict avoidance, diversion, resolution through negotiation, and resolution by authority. In spite of all these different tactics to deal with conflicts that have been suggested by different scholars in different fields, the general reactions of human beings to conflicts show that conflicts are still a major challenge to human beings and that dealing with conflicts is not an easy task.

Human differences in attitudes, in resolving problems, and in dealing with different tasks are one of the major challenges and, at the same time, the source for potential conflicts and polemical discourse. Conflicts and polemical discourse can happen in any type of environment where human interaction takes place. Face-to-face communication is regulated by social norms, whereas interaction on the Internet is not bound by these norms. Hence, conflicts and polemical discourse in an online environment tend to be very vicious. In spite of the challenge to deal with conflicts, Dascal (1999) considers human difference as something of value, something that has to be preserved and cultivated so as to attain a better life and greater achievements for humanity as a whole. Human differences make sure that, through critical thought and discussion, a topic or theory is analyzed and considered from many different angles and that, eventually, better mutual understanding can be reached. Hence, in an ideal environment, through critical feedback and analysis, humans are constantly able to improve their work and achievements. A very simple suggestion for the improvement of mutual understanding would be to travel and experience different cultures and countries. As a matter of fact, in today's world, through travel and its consequent exposure of different cultures and opinions, human beings are continuing to understand many different cultures and cultural perceptions better, as well as different ways of dealing with conflicts.

In spite of this exposure, Dascal (1999) points out a very exceptional phenomenon, namely that in spite of having an 'open world' with high physical and electronic mobility and direct contact between different groups, immigration results in varying degrees of competition and a strengthening of negative stereotypes. Therefore, Dascal opines that exposure to human diversity alone would not be enough to overcome these preconceptions. One need only to take a cursory look at the countries with high immigration rates to find out that the idea of a melting pot does not operate perfectly and that the invisible lines of segregation and discrimination can be felt in many areas of these societies. In international settings when conflicts occur, people can easily fall into the trap of stereotyping their opponents. For this reason, in dealing with conflicts in intercultural and global settings, Dascal (1999) states that one needs a 'positive attitude towards human difference' along with exposure to other cultures. Dascal (1999) suggests that high valuation of human difference should be placed in the list of moral and other values.

To accept human difference, one needs to create a culture of tolerance, to include tolerance towards other ideas, religions, cultures, and ways of life. However, Dascal (1999) warns that in its traditional sense, toleration would not be sufficient as, in this case, toleration does not assign any positive value to difference, which means that one simply tolerates other ideas, but it does not mean that one accepts these ideas or assigns any value to them. Elaborating on this issue, Dascal explains that following the tradition of liberalism, tolerance towards different beliefs and ways of life is considered an important principle; however, tolerance alone would not be enough as the majority of people allows minority groups to practice their beliefs and customs without attributing any positive value to these practices. Moreover, the majority group often considers the beliefs and customs of the minority group to be peculiar. This, of course, leads to the majority's sense of moral superiority over minority groups (Dascal, 1999). This could lead to the problem that minority groups are simply tolerated but not really accepted.

Dascal (1999) rejects this type of toleration as it does not support a 'give-and-take' interaction with different ideas, and, further, it does not show any admiration and respect for human difference.

Therefore, Dascal (1999) pleads for a 'less restricted conception of tolerance' that attributes some type of intrinsic value to each particular manifestation of difference and to this collective contribution to humankind as a whole. This conception requires that one should get rid of simplistic ranking assumptions and that all individuals and groups should create a self-awareness of their imperfections and limitations. Thus, through this self-critical approach, individuals are aware of their own limitations and more open to the conflicting attitudes of another person or group (Dascal, 1999). However, Dascal (1999) warns that the ideal outcome of interaction with different and conflicting views should not be in one direction only, meaning that one should not necessarily give up one's convictions and accept the other's opinion through 'conversion'. This would result in giving up one's ideas without even presenting them properly to the opposite party. The objective is that different minds work together to reach better objectives through cooperation.

Moreover, Dascal emphasizes that one needs to develop a sense of understanding and make an effort to 'put himself in the other's place'. This approach gives one the possibility to understand the other's views and beliefs without giving up one's own beliefs. Additionally, one should take into consideration that understanding differences is perspective-dependent, meaning that there is no absolute criteria to determine what is correct to think and to do (Dascal, 1999). Therefore, in dealing effectively with human difference, Dascal (1999) proposes the following interrelated points: a) one should make a difference between 'acceptance' and 'understanding' of radically different beliefs and ways of life, b) one should make full and fair use of the 'human critical capacity' and not give it up, and c) one should be aware of the 'contingent and fallible' nature of all human judgments and their underlying criteria.

As is well known, human communication is based on cooperation. The major issue that arises here is to find out how the principle of cooperation works in a conflict setting. Dascal (1999) explains that communication is a cooperative undertaking. To communicate, speaker and addressee play different roles; however, they have a mutual interest to ensure that the 'message' exchanged between the two is properly understood. Therefore, Dascal asserts that whoever is involved in communication "is by default, *presumed* to be cooperative". However, not all human interaction is based on cooperative communication. Through humankind's history, there have been extensive accounts of violent confrontation and conflict. Dascal (2005b) explains that violent conflicts are extreme manifestations of confrontation, where latent antagonisms and animosities become explicit, overt, and irresolvable, except by the use of force. Unfortunately, conflicts cannot be resolved once and for all, and Dascal (2005b) points out that, historically, conflicts tend to be lasting phenomena that are quite difficult to resolve permanently. Dascal describes acute periods of violence as salient episodes in an ongoing dialectical process where conflicts are disguised as political, economic, cultural, or other forms of competition. As will be shown later, this feature can also be seen in controversies in online discussion forums as well. Controversies between members are not always truly resolved. The controversial threads in online discussion forums are normally locked by moderators so that no one can post on the threads anymore. However, the participants open up other threads and continue their controversies. Even when there are silent periods of weeks or months between certain members within controversies, the possibility that the same members will become involved in another controversial thread is very high.

Further, Dascal (2005b) adds that periods of intense verbal activity precede and/or follow a violent phase of a conflict. This intense verbal activity has different forms, such as mutual criticism, accusations and threats, negotiations of cease-fires or other arrangements to decrease the level of belligerent activities, and treaties of cooperation and reconciliation that lead to partial peace agreements (Dascal, 2005). To resolve conflicts, the two involved parties with opposing views could try to consult another neutral group or individual to mediate and arbitrate the whole process. If the two parties with opposing views do not consult an impartial third party but seek to resolve their conflict themselves, this process is called a negotiation. Negotiation can further be divided into the traditional model of hard bargaining, wherein the interests of a group outweigh the working relationships, and the principled negotiation model, which considers both the interests and the working relationships. However, one should note that controversies are a type of conflict in which seeking a resolution is not the goal of opposing parties. Moreover, the opposing parties try to influence and impress an audience that watches the whole controversy.

The research emphasis of this study is a detailed analysis of controversies that happen in the new environment of the Internet. In spite of their similarities to physical communities, online communities have their special features and characteristics. Needless to say, these virtual communities are also exposed to many conflicts and controversies. There are different modes of communication on the Internet by which participants can get involved in quasi-dialog, such as blogs, discussion boards, and mailing lists, and the potential of having a controversy is present in each mode. In the present work, I will solely concentrate on a study of controversies in online discussion boards.

3.3 Different types of polemical discourse: discussion, dispute, and controversy

To understand the nature of controversies in online discussion forums, I need to expand on the meanings of the terms 'discussion', 'dispute', and 'controversy'. As will be shown in this chapter, each type of polemical discourse has its own characteristics, distinguishing one from another. Although making a clear-cut distinction between these three types of polemical exchanges is not an easy task, the difference between each type of polemical exchanges is essential for further analysis. Before starting with the examination of controversies in online discussion forums, one needs to understand what types of polemical exchanges have taken place in each case study presented here. Analyzing the uses of argumentative reasons in religious controversies, Dascal (2001:3) differentiates between three types of polemical exchanges in religious polemics, namely discussion, dispute, and controversy.

To begin with, Dascal (2001:3) highlights the role that rational argumentation plays in each type of polemical exchange. Dascal explains that rational argumentation performs a strictly codified role in discussions, a rather marginal role in disputes, and an important but broadly conceived role in controversies, which means that participants in a discussion use rational argumentation to reach a common consensus on a disputed issue. In such an interaction, every participant strictly follows the rules of rational argumentation, and provided the arguments are correct, he is convinced by the arguments his opponent brings forward. This is not necessarily the case in polemical exchanges that take place in online discussion forums: when a polemical exchange happens in an online discussion forum, it either ends up in a dispute or, in a majority of cases, in a controversy.[29] Dascal (2001:3) continues to say that the participants in a dispute do not pursue rational argumentation to convince each other because rational argumentation plays a marginal role in this type of polemical discourse. On the other hand, rational argumentation plays an important but broadly conceived role in controversies.

The majority of polemical exchanges that take place in online discussion forums resemble a controversy type as the participants try to impress and convince an audience or readers of the forums. Normally, participants in online discussion forums try to avoid an overt dispute as it might lead to the suspension of their posting privileges by the moderators of the respective forums. It is, of course, not an easy task to demarcate between dispute and controversy regarding the polemical discourses that take place in online discussion forums, for each type of polemical exchange is associated with the preferential selection of specific types of argumentative moves and the exclusion of others (see Dascal, 2001:4).

There are also other differences between these three types of polemical exchanges. In religious polemics, Dascal (2001:4) explains that a discussion is a polemical exchange with a well-defined topic or

29 However, I would like to stress that making a clear-cut distinction between controversies and disputes on controversial threads in online discussion forums dedicated to the study of arms and armor is not an easy task, for polemical discourse in online discussion forums shares features of both sides.

problem. He adds that within the course of the discussion, the contenders realize that the root of the problem is a mistake related to some important concept or procedure within a field with distinct features (in spite of the fact that the contenders disagree regarding the nature of the mistake in question and about who makes it). Dascal states that discussions offer the possibility to find solutions that consist of correcting the mistakes based on the application of decision procedures accepted in the field, such as proof, computation, and repetition. Although, in rare cases, this type of polemical exchange happens in online discussion forums dedicated to the study of arms and armor, discussions are not commonplace because either they end up in controversies or in disputes. As I mentioned before, the latter is a dangerous move as it might lead to the suspension of the posting privileges of the participants. Analysis of the polemical exchanges found in online discussion forums supports the idea that the participants are not interested in finding a solution. Moreover, they continuously try to prove their opponents are wrong.

Disputes have a more emotional character, and differences are based more on personal feelings and attitudes. In religious polemics, Dascal (2001:4) explains that a dispute is a polemical exchange with a well-defined divergence. One should take into consideration that the contenders in this case do not consider the definition of the polemical discourse as being based on some mistake. Rather, they see it based on differences of attitudes, feelings, or preferences. Thus, a dispute does not have a solution; in the best-case scenario, it can dissolve or be dissolved, such as in a tribunal, where an instituted authority decides in favor of one of the parties (Dascal, 2001:5). Dascal adds that as dissolution is a form of closure that is external both to the topic under dispute and to the participant's beliefs and attitudes, the underlying divergences reappear either in disputes over other versions of the same topic or in disputes over other topics. In the case of online discussion forums, the instituted authority and power is the group of moderators and administrators who close a thread that ends in a heated dispute. Further, as instituted authorities, they can punish the members who started the heated debates and violated the rules of the forums by suspending their posting privileges.

The third type of a polemical exchange is a controversy. Dascal (2001:5) considers controversies in religious polemics as a polemical exchange that has an intermediate position between a discussion and a dispute. It can start with a specific problem, but it has a tendency to spread quickly to other problems, showing deep divergences. Dascal explains that these divergences contain opposed attitudes and preferences as well as disagreements about the extant methods of problem solving. Therefore, the differences of opinions in controversies are not simply a question of mistakes to be corrected, nor are there accepted procedures for deciding them (Dascal, 2001:5). This, of course, results in the continuation of controversies and, at times, their recurrence. This feature is also present in the controversies in online discussion forums, for they tend to spread quickly to other topics; other threads are opened on the same forum where participants continue their controversies or open up new controversies on other topics. So as two participants may not resolve a disagreement on a topic in one forum, they may take that disagreement to another forum, which may have no relationship to the original controversy but will serve to continue it.

Controversies do not reduce to mere unsolvable conflicts of preferences as Dascal (2001:5) stresses, but in a controversy, the contenders collect arguments to increase the weight of their positions against their adversaries' objections, and in doing so, they try to tilt the 'balance of reason' in their favor. Additionally, in religious polemics, Dascal (2001:5) states that controversies are neither solved nor dissolved; moreover, in best-case scenarios, they are resolved. The resolution of controversies may be the acknowledgement, either by the contenders or by their community of reference, that enough weight has been collected in favor of one of the conflicting positions; resolution may be the emergence of modified positions acceptable to the contenders; or it may be the mutual clarification of the nature of the differences at stake (Dascal, 2001:5). In this respect, the controversies in online discussion forums have a major difference in respect to the religious controversies described by Dascal. Although it is true that the participants in online discussion forums dedicated to the study of arms and armor also collect evidence and arguments to add weight to their positions, a controversial thread is never resolved.

Moreover, in all cases, an instituted authority, namely a moderator or an administrator, locks the thread and, hence, dissolves the polemical discourse. When a moderator locks a thread, no one can post on it anymore. Additionally, moderators have the possibility to trash a thread. 'Trashing' means that the thread is moved to a trash forum that is only visible and accessible by moderators. Normally, very controversial threads are moved to the trash forum. Before moving a thread to the trash forum, the moderators may 'prune' the thread, meaning that they clean it of insulting remarks. Only in polemical threads where the whole topic is very controversial would the moderators decide to trash the whole thread.[30] Thus, controversies in online discussion forums studied here share the characteristics of both controversies and debates as described by Dascal (2001:5).

Dascal (2001:5) makes further distinctions between these three types of religious polemical exchanges and adds that discussions are about establishing the truth, disputes are about winning, and controversies are about persuading the opponent and/or a competent audience to accept one's position. Dascal (2001:5–6) explains that the opposition in discussions is considered as purely logical, in disputes as mainly ideological (attitudinal and evaluative), and in controversies as involving a wide range of divergences concerning the interpretation and relevance of facts, evaluations, attitudes, goals, and methods. Dascal (2001:6) expands on this by stating that each one of these polemical exchanges has a preferential move that is in line with its aims and goals, meaning that the preferential move of the discussions is the proof, of the disputes is the stratagem, and of the controversies is the argument (Dascal, 2001:6).

Gloning (2005:264) stresses that taking the global nature of controversies into consideration, controversies contribute to research and decision-making, and this contribution results in a positive evaluation of this form of communication. However, one should note that involvement in a controversy can be annoying and embarrassing

30 It is also possible for moderators to be corrupt and take advantage of their biases and interests by deleting/modifying threads for reasons wholly their own. It means that even those who are supposed to be responsible are susceptible to the same strategies as anyone else in controversies.

for the parties involved as well. Therefore, there are personal 'costs', such as losing face, for people who are involved in controversies. Additionally, negative feelings generated from controversies, such as anger, hate, or grievance, are not only unnerving but also detrimental to finding a solution for a problem (Gloning, 2005:264). Sharon-Zisser (2005:371) also states that controversies wrench, tear the participants involved in them apart, and traumatize. Nevertheless, she stresses that controversies can be intellectually productive.

In an earlier publication, Dascal (1998:19) differentiates between two macro-levels of controversies, namely strategical and tactical. At the strategical level, Dascal distinguishes between three ideal types of polemical exchanges: 'discussion', 'dispute', and 'controversy'. Further, Dascal (1998:21) uses the following criteria for clarifying this typology: a) the scope of the agreement, b) the kind of content involved, c) the presumed means for solving this disagreement, and d) the ends pursued by the contenders. At the tactical level, Dascal differentiates between three types of moves used in polemical exchanges: 'proof', 'stratagem', and 'argument'. According to Dascal, 'discussion' has an inherent affinity with 'proof', 'dispute' with 'stratagem', and 'controversy' with 'argument'.[31]

Dascal (2001:6) explains that a proof is a move that tries to establish the truth of a proposition beyond reasonable doubt, relying on rules of inference and evidence accepted by the opponent to make him (provided that he behaves rationally) to accept the conclusion. As will be shown later, in polemical discourses in online discussion forums dedicated to the study of arms and armor, the contenders are not interested in the proof that is given to them by their opponents. Even when proof is provided, these online opponents overwhelmingly ignore it and keep arguing for their own theories, showing that the type of polemical discourse under investigation is not a discussion but

31 Senderowicz (2005:283) explains that the above typology proposed by Dascal raises some difficulties. Senderowicz sees the main difficulty in Dascal's distinction between arguments and proofs. Senderowicz quotes Dascal, who opines that, in proofs, the proposition is "established beyond reasonable doubt". Arguments are meant to make one believe or accept a proposition. However, Senderowicz (2005:283) suggests that there is differentiation between "reasons to believe" and "reasons that establish the truth".

a controversy. Additionally, participants in online discussion forums also get involved in disputes by using stratagems in order to try to persuade and even deceive the audience into believing that their propositions are true.

Dascal describes a stratagem as a move that intends to make a relevant audience behave in a special way by persuading the audience that the proposition is true. It is important to take into consideration that when a stratagem makes use of inference, it does not mean that the inference pattern is necessarily valid or that the evidence is true; moreover, as stratagems involve deception, they are only meant to be effective towards the intended addressee and audience. In controversies in online discussion forums dedicated to the study of arms and armor, the stratagem move is often used to influence an audience to behave in a certain way. Thus, this move is not solely restricted to debates. Dascal (2001:6) explains that the particular type of force behind the stratagem is not based on making the addressee accept the intended belief or to perform the desired action, but this move intends to render the addressee speechless so that he cannot retort with a satisfactory counter-move.

The third move, namely argument, is used in controversies. According to Dascal (2001:6) an argument as a move intends to persuade the addressee to believe that a proposition is true. Similar to stratagems and unlike proofs, arguments do not intend to seek the truth but are concerned with belief. This is a preferred move used by contenders in online discussion forums. Participants in online discussion forums are not interested in discovering truth; moreover, they try their best to defend their own ideas and beliefs and to make sure that the audience also believes in these ideas. However, there is a difference between an argument and a stratagem. Unlike stratagems, arguments try to appear effective by providing recognizable reasons for the belief in question. On the other hand, Dascal adds that, unlike proofs, these reasons are not required to be based on valid inference patterns and truthful evidence; in addition, they depend on the propositions the addressee actually accepts as evidence and on the inference patterns that are likely to persuade him or her. In spite of the fact that arguments do not compel the addressee to accept the conclusions but put him or her under some type of obligation to do so, this obligation derives from social norms, such as communicative cooperation (Dascal, 2001:6). However, one should note that in controversies in online discussion forums, both moves, stratagems and arguments, are used. Thus, making a definite distinction between the two and assigning the usage of one move solely to one type of polemical discourse is a difficult task. It seems that controversies in online discussion forums dedicated to the study of arms and armor share some characteristics of debates. At times, participants in controversies try to force their opinions on other members by using different tactics and strategies.

Analyzing religious polemics, Dascal (2001:7) also offers a different model of discourse for each type of polemical discourse. Dascal explains that discussions follow a 'problem-solving' model, disputes a 'contest' model, and controversies a 'deliberative' model. Based on this overall model, Dascal reasons that a discussant tries to use decision procedures that win over the adversary by proving the truth of his/her position or the falseness of his/her adversary's position; a disputant tries to be recognized as the winner, regardless of whether his/her position is true or not; and a controversialist tries to give reasons for believing in the superiority of his/her position, in spite of the fact that such reasons do not conclusively prove it. Dascal adds that in case the opponent provides a compelling argument against the discussant's position, a discussant is ready to admit defeat, and a controversialist is ready to acknowledge the weight of the opponent's reasons. On the other hand, a disputant starts and ends the dispute being convinced he/she is right.

Dascal (2001:7) explains that actual polemical exchanges are seldom 'pure' examples of one of these three types because the contenders' ways of perceiving and conducting a given exchange need not be similar. For example, analyzing a scientific controversy between Lord Monboddo and Richard Price (1780–1781) on Newton's physics and its metaphysical framework, Mishori (2002:143) states that one of the differences between the two is their attitude towards polemic exchanges. Mishori stresses that Monboddo considers polemics as an opportunity for epistemological gains (mutual instruction, clarification of ideas, testing the force of one's arguments), whereas Price seems to consider debating as a pointless activity unless there is a way of convincing the other side.

As mentioned above, in polemical exchanges in online discussion forums dedicated to the study of arms and armor, there is seldom one pure type of polemical discourse. One can easily see a combination between a 'contest' model and a 'deliberative' model. In these types of controversies, there is almost no 'problem-solving' model as the contenders are more interested in proving themselves correct to an audience and do not accept the position of their opponents, no matter what type of arguments they provide. The following table shows different types of polemical discourse identified by Dascal (2001:3–7):

Table 3.1: Different types of polemical discourse.

Type of polemical discourse	Discussion	Controversy	Dispute
The role of rational argumentation	A strictly codified role	An important but broadly conceived role	A marginal role
The root of the problem	Mistake	Starts with a problem and spreads to other issues quickly	Differences of attitudes, feelings, or preferences
Appropriate outcome / answer	Solution	In a best-case scenario, there will be a resolution; otherwise, an ongoing process	Dissolution (differences can dissolve or be dissolved)
Goal	Establishing the truth	Persuading the opponent and/or a competent audience to accept one's position	Winning
The type of opposition	Purely logical	Includes a wide range of divergences	Purely ideological
Preferential move	Proof	Argument	Stratagem
Model	Problem-solving model	Deliberative model	Contest model

The above model can be further divided based on formal and functional criteria as the following table shows:

Table 3.2: Division of different types of polemical discourse based on formal and functional criteria.

Formal criteria	Model
	Type of opposition
	Appropriate outcome / answer
	The root of the problem
Functional criteria	Preferential move
	Goal
	The role of rational argumentation

3.4 The ideal controversy: a model by Leibniz

To understand the role of controversies in the Early Modern Period, I will introduce the model of an ideal controversy proposed by Leibniz in the Early Modern Period in this section. Thus, I will analyze whether the role of controversies in the Early Modern Period followed the principles of the model suggested by Leibniz and whether Leibniz's model is followed and applied in controversies in online discussion forums today. According to Gloning (2005:264), different opinions about the function of Early Modern Controversies exist. These range from the belief that controversies make a contribution to testing personal beliefs and enhancing one's personal mastery of a subject matter to the assumption that controversies contribute to reaching supra-personal 'truth'. Gloning (2005:265) also points out that there are many early theories on controversies, stating that controversies somehow contribute to the progress of knowledge and science.

Gloning states that argumentative mastery of a subject matter is another aspect related to truth and knowledge, and he adds that this aspect is closely associated with the duties of a scientist to provide 'an account of the subject matter'. A scientist who wants to accomplish this task successfully needs to be aware of the counterevidence for competing positions to defend his own position in an efficient way (Gloning, 2005:265). Regarding the argumentative mastery of a subject, Gloning (2005:265) explains that controversies have two basic functions: a) controversies provide the person with counter-evidence not yet known to him, and b) controversies offer a testing ground for argumentative strategies.

Further, Gloning (2005:265) adds that in some Early Modern theories of controversies, the model of science as a collaborative enterprise gains an anthropological motivation. In this respect, controversies and criticism are considered necessary as human nature is too weak for the immense tasks in the field of knowledge and no one is free from making mistakes. In other words, no one is able to build up a proposition free of mistakes without interacting with other people and asking them for their opinions so that the proposition can be double-checked and revised. Hence, mutual criticism contributes to overcoming these shortcomings and limitations (Gloning, 2005:266–267). One of the key figures who believed that controversies would help to reach absolute truth was Leibniz. Thus, in the Early Modern Period, Leibniz developed an idea on how controversies should be carried out in an ideal setting. Although Leibniz dealt with the art of controversies throughout his life, he never wrote a systematic account that could be called the 'Theory of Controversy' (Dascal, 2006:xx). Dascal explains that this is not unusual in Leibniz's *modus operandi* as it is the task of the readers and interpreters to find the relevant pieces and reconstruct Leibniz's mosaic of thought regarding the theory of controversies. In his recent publication, *G.W. Leibniz: The Art of Controversies*, Dascal (2006) offers a wide selection of Leibniz's writings regarding different aspects of conducting controversies and debates with the sole purpose of offering readers the chance to discover a wide range of principles, strategies, argumentative practices, and ideas about how to carry out controversies.

Fritz (2008:165) explains that Dascal's goal in the above-mentioned book is to show that Leibniz's emphasis on a 'softer mode of proceeding (*blandior tractandi ratio*)' in construction of knowledge includes not only a rationality based on calculative-demonstrative rationality alone but also on the use of dialogue. This method is described by Leibniz himself as the 'balance of reason' (Fritz, 2008). Leibniz believed that the growth of knowledge depends on the cooperation of many minds. He advocated a critical spirit in such a cooperation that supports the confrontation of opposed positions, not for the purpose of winning but for its potential contribution to advancing knowledge (Fritz, 2008:165). However, Leibniz's idea of an ideal controversy is not widely practiced in the real world, for his model ignores the human pursuit of power and status in controversies and the public domain. Pursuing power and status, the contenders in a public controversy are more interested in appearing as legitimate authorities and presenting the impression of leadership and reliability in front of the public rather than in pursuing the truth. Nevertheless, one cannot underestimate Leibniz's efforts to find ways for the resolution of conflicts and the effects of his work in dealing with controversies so that they do not end in endless debates or negative outcomes.

Leibniz had a distinct method for carrying out a controversy. His idea provides an ideal model for how controversies need to be carried out so that one reaches the required results and outcome by having different opinions cooperating with each other. This provides a framework to check whether such a model was implemented and used in Early Modern Controversies and whether some ideas of Leibniz's model are still used in controversies in online discussion forums. Leibniz was an Early Modern thinker who maintained a large and highly varied network of correspondents. He exchanged several letters (written every day) with his correspondents, covering a wide range of disciplines. According to Dascal (2006:xx), in spite of the fact that Leibniz condemned the 'spirit of contradiction' that motivates some polemicists, he was not afraid of getting involved in prolonged debates in philosophy, law, theology, politics, or science as long as he considered such debates useful and necessary.

Leibniz implemented the dialogical form as a sharp tool in his major works, and he criticized the theories of his contemporaries and defended his own views against his contenders in contemporary journals (Dascal, 2006:xx). He also asked for the criticism of others as he considered it an invaluable source of learning. Dascal explains that

Leibniz naively believed that others would welcome and enjoy his own serious and well-intentioned criticism.[32] Leibniz was a true believer in constructing the principles that should govern such a time-consuming practice as mutual criticism. These principles should ensure that such an activity would not be a waste of time but a tool in the pursuit of knowledge. Leibniz was of the opinion that the growth of knowledge required the cooperation of many minds. To reach this goal, Leibniz worked for the creation of appropriate institutional frameworks, such as academies, societies, and journals (Dascal, 2006:xxi). Such cooperation, he believed, should be based on a critical spirit that esteems the confrontation of opposed positions, not for the purposes of winning but for its potential contribution to advancing human knowledge. In other words, one should not seek harmony in interaction as knowledge should be constructed and derived from the variety of diverging views.

In such an environment, objections should be appreciated and taken seriously as key contributions to conceptual clarification (Dascal, 2006:xxi). Leibniz believed that one should learn about opposing points of view and their respective contributions to truth, and one should also discover their points of divergence and look for reconciliation between them. The reader should note that Leibniz was born two years after the Peace of Westphalia, signed in 1648. The peace treaty ended the Thirty Years War in Europe. Two years before Leibniz died in 1714, the Peace of Utrecht was signed, ending the 14-year-long Spanish Succession War (Dascal, 2006:xxii). Dascal explains that both were 'world wars' in regard to generalized European wars. Between these two events, European intellectuals and politicians were trying to find ways to foster peace and avoid the devastating effects of these wars. The community of European intellectuals known as the 'République des Lettres'[33] played a key role in this respect.

32 This is never the case in online discussion forums. Contenders in a controversy are more interested in appearing as figures of authority and do not welcome any criticism.

33 I will explain more about the République des Lettres in the next chapter.

Many journals, such as *Nouvelles de la République des Lettres* (founded by Pierre Bayle in 1648), *Philosophical Transactions* (published by the Royal Society of London since 1661), *Journal of Sçavans* (a private publication since 1665), *Acta Eruditorium* of Leipzig (1682), the *Miscellaneous Curiosa*, and the *Ephemerides of Nürenberg*, as well as a number of *Giornale dei Litterati* published in different Italian cities since 1685 and the *Journal de Trévaux* (a Jesuit publication published since 1701), provided a supra-national forum for intellectual communication and exchange of ideas via review of recently published books on theology, politics, philosophy, science, history, and other subjects (Dascal, 2006:xxiii–xxiv).

These journals, alongside an intense private and semi-private correspondence, established a vast network of contacts among intellectuals all over Europe (Dascal, 2006:xxiv). Dascal states that this network included the newly established academies with their international membership. The République des Lettres established an autonomous realm of reason that was independent of issues of faith. Dascal (2006:xxiv) emphasizes that the importance of the République des Lettres is that it allowed for debate based on a living model of coexistence, and even cooperation, in spite of and through dis-agreement. According to Dascal, Leibniz became a key figure in this forum of debate and communication and symbolized the connection between knowledge and politics more than any other intellectual in his time.

Dascal (2006:xxv) points out that the 16th and early 17th century, negotiations were influenced by two quite different ap-proaches: a) a tolerance-based approach and b) a conciliation-based approach. Both approaches blossomed in the second half of the 17th century. The tolerance-based approach had its roots in late-Renaissance skepticism and held that differences were irreducible and irresolvable, and to avoid violent conflict, one needed to 'tolerate' the 'wrong' position, rather than to attempt to suppress it by force (Dascal, 2006:xxv). On the other hand, the conciliation-based approach held that the differences were not so radical and could be overcome via a process of rational negotiation, targeted at finding out a common core shared by both parties.

Dascal (2006:xxv) explains that the model of tolerance as developed, for instance, by Locke turned out to be the most influential model at the time. However, Dascal (2006:xxvi) explains that the Lockean model of tolerance goes beyond the extremely limited notion of tolerance supported and partially implemented earlier. As an example, Dascal (2006:xxvi) states that the Edit de Nantes (1598), the first of the ordinances ensuring religious tolerance, only permitted the Calvinists to preach in the areas where they were already established, but it did not allow them to expand their areas of influence or construct new churches, even within their own areas. Locke understood tolerance on the basis of a distinction between the public and the private sphere. According to Locke, a person has a right to hold any religious opinion privately, and, thus, the state has no right to meddle in this private domain. Based on Locke's model, religious opinions are fully tolerated as long as they are expressed in the private sphere; however, if the public manifestation of these religious opinions changes the public order, they cannot be tolerated either because they are intolerant opinions, such as those of Catholics, or because they question the established social order.

At the same time, Locke believed that opinions that do not conform to the true religion are wrong (Dascal, 2006:xxvi). Dascal (2006:xxvii) stresses that Locke's notion of tolerance is, in fact, a condescending attitude of 'toleration' towards ideas that are considered as false. These false ideas are tolerated on exclusively political grounds, insofar as they are not considered dangerous. Dascal explains that in spite of the fact that Locke's model, without a doubt, shows progress in regard to tolerance in a reflection that goes beyond realpolitik, it remains a minimalist model because it attempts to preserve a peaceful coexistence with a given social fabric and does not make any suggestion regarding the possibility of a reconciliation of the divergent opinions and the encouragement of a rational debate between them.

Dascal (2006:xxvii) explains that in such a model, error and truth are *a priori* assigned to one or another idea, and, therefore, such a model makes a debate between diverging ideas irrelevant and possibly even dangerous. As Leibniz considered debate between people who held diverging ideas important, he was clearly not content with Locke's notion of tolerance. Leibniz considered tolerance to be a starting point that is able to foster the rational debate targeted at overcoming differences (Dascal, 2006:xxvvii). Thus, Leibniz considered tolerance a prerequisite for a passionless debate. Tolerance prepared people for a debate in which they could bring forward and exchange ideas and reasons.

Dascal (xxviii) explains that, in his synopsis, Leibniz differentiates between two strategies for dealing with the solution of controversies: a) *controversiae conciliato per tolerantiam* and b) *controversiae conciliatio per consensum*. The first one is not simply the application of Locke's 'toleration'; instead, it is a strategy, in Leibniz's point of view, where the mere removal of mutual condemnation and passionate discourse leads to a solution as people find out that there is no real opposition, and, therefore, the debate is put to rest. The second strategy is necessary when moderation on its own does not remove the opposition. In this case, moderation is necessary to make preparations for a dispassionate consideration of the arguments and allow the contenders to search for (and possibly reach) an agreed-upon solution (Dascal, 2006:xxviii). According to Dascal (2006:xxviii), Leibniz's 'art of controversy' is made up of an array of attempts to build up the conceptual framework and necessary tools for the implementation of the second strategy, *controversiae conciliatio per consensum*.

Leibniz was involved and concerned with controversies throughout his life. As a child, he read medieval disputations (although his teacher prohibited him from reading them), and two months before his death, Leibniz was still concerned with the topic of controversies. Leibniz knew that his work on controversies did not reach its full mature formulation, and he was aware of the incompleteness of his work (Dascal, 2006:xxix). However, Leibniz trusted future generations to complete his work.

Dascal (2006:xxxvii) stresses that Leibniz distinguishes controversies from war. In Leibniz's opinion, a controversy is "a question debated in a trial (*judicium*)", explaining that 'trial' is "the state of those who contest by means of reasons in the hope of success". On the other hand, war is "the state of those who contest by means of force" (Dascal, 2006:xxxvii). Based on this distinction,

Leibniz concludes that not all forms of polemical exchanges can be considered 'controversies'. As an example, Leibniz does not consider 'the way of rigor' (*la voie de la rigueur*), such as the force or repression shown by the forced conversion of the Jews in Spain, to be a controversy. In similar fashion, a dispute strategically ruled by total submission to the 'way of authority', which is another form of using force in a dispute, cannot be considered a controversy (Dascal, 2006:xxxviii).

Leibniz also excludes the 'way of dispute or discussion' from the realm of 'controversies'. The 'way of dispute or discussion' includes a disorderly way of using arguments, invectives, evasion, and all types of stratagems at will (Dascal, 2006:xxxix). Dascal (2006:xxxix) explains that in such an atmosphere, there is no possibility of reaching a solution based on reason, and it turns out to be a war of all against all, where there is no winner based on rational reasons. Therefore, from a young age, Leibniz was concerned with developing methods to avoid 'vices' that change controversies into disputes. Leibniz also did not consider the 'way of accommodation' (*la voie de l'accommodement*) a controversy. Leibniz stated that the goal of this 'way' is to construct an *ad hoc* means of neutralizing the opposition between the contenders. In this way, the deep reason for the conflict is not addressed, and the solutions are short-lived and remain at a superficial level. Dascal (2006:xxxix) explains that in warfare, the 'way of accommodation' can be compared to the establishment of occasional pacts that are not based on the real, long-term strategic interests of the partners.

In Leibniz's opinion, the desire for compromise may end in 'the way of condescending' (*la voie de la condescendence*). Thus, a contender makes concessions to the demands of the opponents without taking into consideration that there are points where making concessions is not possible. Leibniz also did not consider the 'Huet historical method', which was another method of conducting a debate, or a controversy. Huet's historical method attempts to put an end to the theological-philosophical controversies by establishing the most remote antiquity of truth and the consensus of all ancient people (Dascal, 2006:xl). This method is based on the assumption of the historical priority of Moses over the founders of other ancient religions, which derive from a common, basic source.

According to Dascal (2006:xI), Leibniz sympathizes with Huet to some extent as Leibniz also believes that history can be used to show the truth of religion and proposes the need for a universal history, both sacred and profane. Therefore, Leibniz agrees with Huet's method in regard to the use of antiquity as contributing to the establishment of truth. However, Leibniz does not consider it an absolute proof and stresses that it should be checked by the *ars critica* (art of criticism) so that the imagined and the fabulous can be differentiated from the true and the historical. Based on what Leibniz did not consider a controversy, Dascal (2006:xIii) describes Leibnizian understanding ('identi-kit') of controversies as the following:

> A controversy is an orderly (rather than random) debate where reasons should address the deep and general (rather than superficial and ad hoc) issues; they should consider seriously (rather than condescendingly) the opponent's view; and they should be based on strict methodological control (rather than on ideologically-prone free interpretation).

However, Dascal (2006:xIii) explains that despite the stress on the role of reasons in controversies, there is an initial parallel with war. This is because contenders get involved in a controversy that they hope to win. Further, according to Dascal, the 'serious aim' of a contest of this type, as in similar war-like games, is to end the contest. Nevertheless, based on Dascal, there is a difference between controversies and other war-like games. The prize of a controversy is to persuade the thoughts of "either of the adversary himself or else of some other listener", and "a full victory is the one that subjugates declared enemies also in their mind" by using reason alone (Dascal, 2006:xIii). Based on Leibniz, such reasons are contextually based, plural, and motivated. Therefore, to understand the true nature of controversies, one needs to take into consideration the contestants, the contest's prize, the hope of success based on the laws of competition, and the reasons used in the contest (Dascal, 2006:xIii).

The notion of moderation is very important for Leibniz as he considered moderation a precondition before a rational debate could take place. The central piece for the moderation is the active participation of the *rapporteur* (expounder), who keeps the order of the debate and reformulates and summarizes the contenders' positions and arguments. Thus, a *rapporteur* is not similar to the *judex controversiarium* of Leibniz's earlier writings. In this respect, a *rapporteur* does not have the function of a judge nor that of a conciliator (Dascal, 2006:xlv). Further, Dascal (2006:xlvii) explains that the arsenal of Leibniz's art of controversies includes both the *ars indicandi* and the *ars inveniendi*. The *ars indicandi* shows demonstrative proof (which, when applicable, is meant to decide a dispute conclusively), and the doctrine of mathematical probabilities (which, when applicable, allows for the formalization of non-conclusive proof). According to Dascal, the doctrine of mathematical probabilities contains the traditional tools of rhetoric and dialectics as well as other tools that are either adapted from other domains (for example, the already mentioned *ars deciphratoria* and *ars arguitarium*) or established by Leibniz himself, such as a variety of semiotic means.

As mentioned before, Leibniz's major works do not have the shape of theoretical treatises, for Leibniz liked to show his ideas in the form of dialogical exchanges with his contemporaries (Dascal, 2006:li). Based on Dascal (2006:lvi), in all his intellectual encounters with his contemporaries, Leibniz had three goals: a) to gain a full understanding of the most important metaphysical alternatives to his own ideas as far as possible, b) to find out the shared elements and the remaining divergences, and c) to improve his own system in the light of his competitors' objections.

During his life, Locke was not willing to engage in a controversy with Leibniz. After Locke's death, Leibniz became engaged in a debate with Locke's text, whose result, the *Nouveux essays sur l'entendement humain*, was only posthumously published. Although Leibniz was the sole author of this dialogue, he presented Locke's positions in the most faithful and favorable way possible (Dascal, 2006:lix). Leibniz's goal was to integrate Locke's insights with his own in order to reach a broader comprehensive system. Dascal (2006:lix) explains that by doing so, Leibniz followed his own rules for the conduct of a rational controversy, namely moderation, reformulation, expansion of the basic notions and principles, and conciliation at a deeper level.[34] In the next chapter, I will show that controversies were never carried out in the way Leibniz wished them to take place, even during the Early Modern Period. Thus, the ideal form of controversies as proposed by Leibniz never took place. Nevertheless, one cannot underestimate the suggestions and work of Leibniz. In spite of the pursuit of power and using unfair moves, the audience can still benefit from controversies as they contribute to the demonstration of different points of view and where the audience makes its own decision.

3.5 The characteristics of controversies in practice

As mentioned before, the polemical discourse that generally takes place in online discussion forums dedicated to the study of arms and armor is of the controversy type. Additionally, controversies in online discussion forums have some features of disputes as well. At this stage, describing the nature of controversies in more detail is important in order to understand the similarities and differences between controversies and other types of polemical discourse better. Dascal (2003:280) describes controversies as a written, protracted quasi-dialogue. This type of protracted quasi-dialogue is created by elaborate pieces of discourse. Further, Dascal describes controversies as a specific kind of conflict and adds that, in all controversies, there are one or more inconsistencies between the statements of the two opponents (the defendant and the opponent), meaning that, in a controversy, the defendant and the opponent have differences of opinions.

However, one should note that the last statement is only a simplified description of the nature of controversies because controversies are far more complex than simple differences of opinions between two different interlocutors in a conversation. Controversies have the tendency to reappear: they are not resolved once and for all but have a recurring tendency. Moreover, controversies are prolonged

34 For more details and also original texts by Leibniz, see Dascal (2006).

conflicts with the feature of having the 'principle of charity' between parties blocked, meaning that participants in a controversy are not necessarily interested in a cooperative behavior to achieve better results. Furthermore, participants in a controversy are not necessarily interested in resolving their conflict, nor are they always willing to accept the other's interpretation or the intervention of an impartial judge (Dascal. 2003:281–282). The contenders in online discussion forums do not necessarily accept the intervention of a moderator, an impartial judge. When a controversy in an online discussion forum reaches the climax, the intervention of site moderators and administrators will not stop the contenders from attempting to pursue their goals by subtly attacking their opponents. This invariably leads to the closing of the thread in question by a moderator.

Another interesting point is that controversies are not necessarily conflicts between two fully opposing and different ideas. Mishori (2002:145) points out an interesting phenomenon in the controversy between Mondoddo and Price: when Price finds out that Monboddo's ideas are very different from his own, he loses interest in the debate. Mishori concludes that this feature undermines the characterization of controversy as a "clash between two radically opposing worldviews" since this feature indicates that, in some cases, the realization of the existence of a theoretical gap between participants in a controversy might suppress the will to participate in a controversy.

Regarding the nature of controversies, Dascal stresses that the question at issue (the 'controversy's demand') cannot be addressed and resolved at a content (semantic) level as controversies involve an existential dimension and a public dimension. The existential dimension involves the opponents' reputations (their careers and their intellectual and personal prestige), which are at stake in the dispute, requiring an obligation to be critical and polemic towards the other's viewpoint and person in order not to lose face. The 'public dimension' means that the actual addressee of the opponents' argumentation is not the counterpart himself but the public or the audience that 'assists' the controversy (Dascal, 2003:289). Therefore, the social legitimation of controversialists does not depend on their opponents but on the impression that they make on an external audience (Dascal, 2003:289–290).

Thus, Dascal (2001:6–7) explains that participants in polemical exchanges may not be interested in convincing their opponents; moreover, they try to target an audience that does not participate in the debate, such as 'staged polemics' on live TV debates[35] or in written forms, such as the philosophical genre 'dialogue' or in the heresiological literature. In such an environment, every contributor to a controversy tries to have a convincing argument and to win in front of the audience.[36] In such an environment, if the participant in a polemical exchange makes his opponent look excessively weak or compliant, the audience will not be impressed by the opponent's views (Dascal, 2001:7). This type of controversy is often seen in political debates on TV shows where a moderator asks questions from two different people or parties engaged in a public controversy.

Hess-Lüttich (2007:1361) defines all conversations that are staged for show and address an audience as 'show controversies'.[37] According to Hess-Lüttich, show conversations include shows on television, dialogue on the theatrical stage, poetically designed fictitious conversations, panels, telephone conferences, radio phone-in experts appearing before public audiences, political discussions on

---

35 Hess-Lüttich (2007:1360) describes TV talk shows and (political) debates as "as-if" debates, pseudo cooperation, and pseudo-controversy. Further, Hess-Lüttich states that "verbal violence" in both TV talk shows and (political) debates sabotage a fair and reflected exchange of arguments. By calling political debates on TV a pseudo-controversy, Hess-Lüttich indirectly indicates that there should be a type of controversy where a fair exchange of arguments is possible. However, one should note that political debates on TV are controversies where the goal of participants is not to have a fair exchange of arguments but, moreover, to impress their audience.

36 Luginbühl (2007:1371) describes allegations of incompetence and allegations of insincerity as the main forms of conversational violence in political TV debates. According to Luginbühl, "violence" as the exertion of physical force and language cannot be treated as two completely different categories.

37 Based on Löffler (1984), Hess-Lüttich (2007:1362) states that the show conversation is a form of shadow boxing with rhetorical "winners" and "losers", and quoting Weydt (1980), Hess-Lüttich (2007:1362) states that a debate has been a "cooperation between enemies", a type of contra-operation by co-operation. Further, according to Settlekorn (1989), Hess-Lüttich (2007:1363) says that a show conversation is "pseudo-conversation and a pseudo-dispute of the adversaries with each other, of the adversaries with the journalists, and of all the participants with the implied public".

television, and liturgical rituals. Hess-Lüttich (2007:1362) explains that there are complaints that parliamentary debates, as they are considered show debates or show controversies, are meant to target the audience. These complaints criticize parliamentary debate with its noble ideal of rational discourse and intelligent argument as a show. The critics presuppose that an ideal form of debate should exist that allows a rational discourse and, hence, modern political debates do not follow the rational debate but are merely meant for show to impress the audience. However, in reality, this complaint does not recognize that public debate is not a phenomenon of the triviality of modern times as the show character[38] has been the nature of the ritual of (political) debates since their beginning.

The controversies in online discussion forums about arms and armor have also a show character. On the one hand, some of the participants who are researchers and antique dealers have an existential dimension, for the researcher can lose face and reputation in the community while the antique dealers could lose their reputations in the proper identification of the artifacts they sell if they are proven wrong in some aspects. In the latter case, it will surely hurt the dealer's business as well. Moreover, the controversies in online discussion forums also have a public dimension as each participant knows that a large number of collectors, researchers, and students follow whole online controversies.

In some types of controversies, the mere choice of the language of the written texts reveals the public dimensions of controversies or how the participants try to present to and target their audiences. For example, referring to a controversy about astrology between Kepler, Röslin, Feselius, and Schaerer around 1600, Gloning (2002:41) explains that besides the contribution by Kepler, 'De stella nova in pede Serpentarii', all contributions were written in German. That means that the controversy could not be taken as a pure discussion or debate among specialists because the language of scientific debate at

38 This means that parliamentary debates act as show debates. Although parliamentary debates convey the impression that members of parliament are debating to convince each other by using logical argumentation, in reality the members of parliament try to convince their audience to accept their ideas. Hence, they have a show character.

that time was Latin. Therefore, it is clear that the contributors in the controversy were well aware of the fact that an audience was reading and observing the whole procedure. Thus, Gloning explains that these contributions were written to target the non-expert readers. Interestingly, this was one of the goals of the participants in the controversy as Gloning adds that the dedications show that the controversy over the astrology also had a political dimension. The contributors were not only trying to influence the public but also the political establishment. Additionally, defending astrology also had an economic aspect for authors in the field of astrology, such as Schaerer, as writing and selling of fortune-telling was a lucrative business (Gloning, 2002:41). This shows that the participants in a controversy were bound and constrained by their audience. Thus, in such an environment, the controversy has an existential and a public dimension.

This is also the case with the polemical discourse that takes place in online discussion forums dedicated to the study of arms and armor. The majority of them, if not all, are of the controversy type. The contenders in the controversies in online discussion forums are well aware of the fact that their activities are followed and observed by an audience. Therefore, much of the content provided among participants in controversies is phrased in ways best suited to attract and convince non-participants. In contrast to older controversies, the very nature of the Internet allows a larger and more flexible audience to watch the whole procedure of controversies than the audience of early religious controversies. Thus, controversies in online discussion forums have an even higher level of public dimension than did religious controversies that were carried out via pamphlets since larger numbers of people read online controversies.

On the other hand, the contenders in controversies are not allowed to use all moves that could impress and influence the audience. Regarding this point, Dascal (2003:290) emphasizes that the 'audience-driven constraint' does not mean that every manipulative move is allowed and accepted in such an environment because the audience or public in controversies 'praises reason as well'. Therefore, Dascal (2003:290) describes controversies as 'quasi-dialogues' because, in spite of the fact that they must have a conversational appearance to be effective, their deep, persuasive character is tailored to the audience. This is also the case with controversies in online discussion forums. Since online discussion forums occur in a moderated environment, the participants in controversies are well aware of the fact that very overt, aggressive moves will be punished by the moderators by imposing bans on the members. Therefore, they try to use their aggressive moves against their opponents in subtle ways.

Dascal (2005a:280) states that the major part of academic controversies consists of written texts where each critical move and each reply in a controversy is a normally elaborate piece of discourse. This means that before writing a piece and contributing to any controversy, the contenders carefully plan and think about the consequences of their actions. Dascal adds that the elaborate pieces of discourse in communication in controversies distinguish them from the spontaneous exchanges typical of face-to-face communication. Nevertheless, Dascal (2005a:280) adds that there are typical features of controversies that make them protracted dialogues. In this case, the pragmatic concepts that are developed for the analysis of conversation can be applied to the study of controversies. However, one should be very careful and not conclude that conversations and controversies are the same thing. Regarding this point, Dascal (2005a:280) stresses that there are still major differences between controversies and conversation as controversies are quasi-dialogues. Being quasi-dialogues, the principles of pragmatics should be applied to the analysis of controversies.

Therefore, Dascal (2005a:280) explains that a purely semantic method for analyzing controversies would not be sufficient since semantic analysis usually characterizes a controversy concerning the presence of certain logical relations, such as inconsistency amongst the statements of the disputants. Dascal explains that this approach presumes that a required condition for the resolution of a controversy is that one of the contenders changes his/her mind. However, as Dascal (2005a:281) points out, an actual controversy is not about a single difference of opinion on any single issue but is about different issues at the same time. Therefore, in a controversy, a contender does not simply change his/her mind and accept the ideas of his/her opponent. The contender will insist on his/her ideas. Dascal

(2005a:281) further explains that the disagreement in a controversy includes a range of topics that "cluster around some presumed central divergence". Additionally, contenders in a controversy do not change their positions to resolve a controversy as this would mean that the opponent would win the dispute. Therefore, the positions in controversies tend toward polarization and result in a sustained debate, spreading to new issues and topics. Although controversies are difficult to formalize, Dascal (2005a:281) explains that parameters, such as centrality, entrenchment, degree of polarization, breadth, and depth, might be added to the formal framework.

Taking the public dimension of controversies into consideration, different types of people participate in such polemical discourse. They can generally be divided into active contenders who argue over an issue and passive readers or observers. Gloning (2002:42) explains that the constellation of people involved in the astrology controversy mentioned above is the same as in the theological controversies of the Early Modern Period: a) two or more active opponents, b) readers, or if applicable, listeners, and c) in the circle of readers/listeners, a territorial lord to whom the text is dedicated and who will be consulted as the judge in case of an escalating debate. Gloning further explains that there are different ways of getting involved in a controversy: a) a person is directly and personally attacked by opponent X, b) a contributor defends the person who is personally attacked by opponent X, c) an opponent has attacked a position that is advocated by someone, and d) opponent X has advocated a position that is incompatible with someone else's position. Similarly, there are also two or more active contenders who are involved in online controversies dedicated to the study of arms and armor. In addition to these active contenders, there are participants who support a particular person or group and, hence, get involved in the controversy as well. In case of escalating problems, the participants consult the moderators or the site administrators to intervene in the online controversy.

In spite of asking for the interference of a territorial lord in case of astrological controversies, a religious authority in case of religious controversies, or a moderator or site administrator in case of online controversies, one should note that the advice or interference of these impartial observers is not always or necessarily followed or accepted by the contenders in a controversy. Thus, examples of controversies from the Early Modern Period through modern time show that nothing has changed in this respect. Providing a reason for this behavior in Early Modern Controversies, Dascal (2005a:281) states that controversies are hardly restricted to the object level as they spread easily to meta issues (as explained above). Thus, spreading to the meta level in communication could be one of the reasons for such behavior. Thus, participants in a controversy not only do not accept each others' views but also ignore the interpretations and judgments of a 'neutral' judge unless that judge believes in or is biased toward their own views. Dascal explains that this is the reason why the charges of misrepresentation, misinterpretation, and irrelevance are common in controversies. Therefore, Dascal (2005a:382) argues that disagreement at these levels forms the essence of controversies and is not a logical inconsistency. Therefore, pragmatics is very useful in analyzing the language of controversies. This is because pragmatics, in its broadest sense, is a theory of the uses of language and can adequately analyze the uses of language in a controversy.[39]

Dascal adds that, in typical social use of language, such as in a conversation, interlocutors use linguistic expressions with conventional meanings, such as semantic or literal, so that they can react to each others' utterances with no particular difficulty. Dascal describes this process as 'understanding'. It is important to take into consideration that interlocutors make use not only of the utterances themselves but also their co-text and context. That means that comprehension is not only restricted to semantics itself but also involves the understanding of the related context of use to find out whether utterances have some other intended meaning or can be taken at face value. The application of pragmatic analysis to the study of controversies in online forums dedicated to the study of arms and armor is extremely important as many of the statements and speech

39 However, one needs to make a distinction between socio-pragmatics and not the private and mental uses of the language. By "pragmatics", Dascal (2005:282) means the socio-pragmatics, meaning the study of the social uses of language and not the private and mental uses of the language that could be used.

acts of the contenders involved in the controversy cannot be taken at their face value, meaning their semantic level, as they also have other associated meanings at a pragmatic level. Members of online discussion forums who know the polemical background of controversies in online discussion forums understand clearly what the polemical statements mean. To a casual onlooker, some of these statements might look harmless and absurd. But, knowing the polemical background of the controversies, one develops a clear picture of the pragmatic function of these polemical statements.

Therefore, it is important to analyze controversies from a pragmatic point of view. First, one should look at the communication background of conversations in general and of controversies in particular. Dascal (2005a:282) quotes Grice, who describes conversation as a cooperation game, meaning that all participants should make sure a proper understanding is established. The speaker should make sure that his contribution is understandable to the addressee, and the addressee should make sure that he understands the conveyed message properly, based on the speaker's intentions. Otherwise, an understanding between participants will not be possible. Dascal (2005a:282–283) stresses that although misunderstanding happens, it is not guaranteed to happen as conversation is based on the presumption that the cooperation principle is respected. One should note that the sequential structure of conversations does not only depend on semantic meaning, logical meaning, or 'argumentative' meaning but also depends on pragmatic meaning.

Utterances are linked at the level of their pragmatic interpretation, meaning in terms of the pragmatic notions of relevance and conversational demand. Dascal (2005a:283) explains that in spite of the fact that an utterance is not semantically, logically, or argumentatively 'appropriate', it may have the appropriate structure and fulfill the conversational requirements. Dascal also states that conversations may have 'pragmatic grammar'. In this respect, he adds that a controversy's structure is essentially pragmatic, meaning that a controversy is not a sequence of utterances used by controversialists following turns; rather, a controversy is a sequence of more or less lengthy texts that may have answers addressed to several parts of the opponent's previous text(s). Therefore, in a controversy, there is not a single 'controversy's demand', but a different number of demands could surface at every stage.

However, one should note that there are similarities between controversies and conversation in this respect. Dascal (2005a:283) explains that a controversy may have certain global conversational demands (such as the general topic under discussion, the format under discussion) next to local demands (such as the question-answer sequence). Further, Dascal (2005a:283–284) adds that a controversy reveals a crisscross pattern of 'demands' that the participants try to identify and to react with the corresponding moves. This, in turn, results in the establishment of new demands. Dascal stresses that the strict sequentiality is not a characteristic feature for the analogy with conversations, but the very fact that the participant's evaluations of every move is primarily connected to their pragmatic interpretation is characteristic, both as demand-establishing and as demand-meeting contributions.

According to Dascal (2005a:284), in ordinary conversations, the identification of conversational demands and the process for the pragmatic interpretation are mostly smooth and tacit, whereas in controversies both are problematic and raised to the level of explicit issues in disputes, such as claiming that the opponent did not respond to a specific statement. One can also observe this phenomenon in controversies in online discussion forums very often where participants constantly claim that the opponent did not provide an answer to a statement.

Dascal (1997) distinguishes between the following characteristics of controversies:

a) Spreading: According to Dascal, the first important feature of controversies is that they do not stay restricted to the initial questions that originate them. Moreover, controversies tend to spread quickly in both extent and level of depth. This is also the case with controversies in online discussion forums. Contenders start with a certain topic and, then, move on to controversies on other issues. In this case, they open another thread on the forum with the title of the new controversy and continue their original controversy there. Due to the fast and flexible nature of the Internet, it is very common that the participants get involved in different controversies distributed on different threads on the forums. From a pragmatic point of view, all of these controversies are interrelated. Manolo Rodriguez opened a thread named 'Armed Fashion Theory: A New Theory for Weapons'[40] on the Forum of Swords on August 8, 2006; this lasted until September 7, 2006. His theory was immediately taken as a challenge by his contenders from the Forum of Ethnographic Swords, who also post on the Forum of Swords. The end result was that one of his main contenders, named Marco, opened a new thread named 'Armed Fashion Theory: A Case Study – Pre-1826 Burma' on August 29, 2006, in response to the invitation or provocation of Manolo Rodriguez (note that this highly controversial thread closed on October 22, 2006 by the site administrator):

(2) Marco:

Quote *Manolo Rodriguez: Let's follow Jon's suggestion, and close out by turning Armed Fashion theory (and yes it is a theory because it is predictive and anyway is based directly off Dr. Star's general fashion theory) toward a specific case – like Indochina, home of Marco's beloved dha – on a new thread.*

I guess Manolo wants me to start this thread, even though its his theory we are discussing. So let me lay out some information, and you tell me what Armed Fashion Theory would predict.

The whole idea of Marco opening this thread is to challenge Manolo Rodriguez's Armed Fashion Theory and try to prove to the audience that Manolo's theory does not work when applied to cases analyzing arms and armor. This means that for a period of ten days, two related controversies were running at the same time.

b) Questioning adversary's presuppositions: In controversies, contenders question their adversaries' basic factual, methodological, and conceptual presuppositions to undermine their positions and viewpoints (Dascal, 1997). This is also the case with controversies in online discussion forums. Contenders also question their opponents' basic factual, methodological, and conceptual presuppositions in order to weaken their positions. In the following example taken from the *keris* controversy, Charley, a person who claims not to be involved

40 Note that the original title is changed due to privacy reasons.

with the controversy but specifically supports Melborn's article, questions the basic methodological presupposition of his opponent, Manolo Rodriguez:

(3) Charley: It must be noted that the part of the Melborn article that Mr. Rodriguez has fixed on for his analysis is not central to the conclusions drawn in this article, rather, Melborn has clearly stated:- "– the reasons for this development are pure hypothesis". A hypothesis is a supposition or explanation made on the basis of limited evidence as a starting point for further investigation.

Here, Charley questions Manolo's methodological and conceptual manner of criticism towards Melborn's article. He claims that Manolo's criticism of Melborn's article fails to concentrate on the key issues Melborn wanted to present and, hence, fails to see Melborn's conclusions.

c) Hermeneutical aspect: Dascal (1997) further explains that the third important feature of controversies is their hermeneutical (interpretative, explanatory) aspect. Contenders in controversies accuse each other of misinterpreting their data, theories, and of not responding to objections previously raised. This feature of controversies happens very often in online controversies as well. For example, in the *keris* controversy, Charley accuses his opponents of not having read and having misinterpreted the article written by Melborn:

(4) Some of the contributions to this thread indicate that the contributors may not have read and understood what Melborn wrote in his article

The example above shows that Charley thinks that his opponents have misinterpreted Melborn's article. Therefore, Charley accuses his opponents of misinterpreting the theory suggested by Melborn in his article with the purpose of undermining their analyses.

d) Openness: Dascal (1997) states that the fourth and the most important characteristic of controversies is openness. This feature is the direct result of the ideas discussed above. Openness of controversies means that none of the contenders in a controversy know where the inherent dynamics of it will end up. Furthermore, openness means that controversies are seldom restricted to a single discipline and, even within a discipline, to a well-defined topic. Additionally, controversies show the existence of deep differences regarding the meaning of concepts, methods, and facts so far accepted against dispute. Further, one cannot predict all the possible objections of the opponent. Last but not least, controversies pave the way for the emergence of radical innovation, such as 'non-conventional' ideas, methods, techniques, and interpretations (Dascal, 1997). Controversies in online discussion forums dedicated to the study of arms and armor also share the feature of openness as well. Normally, when a controversy starts on a forum, a number of other threads are also opened that are indirectly related to the first controversy. No participant involved in an online controversy can be sure that his involvement will be restricted in one thread only. Usually, other threads are also opened at the same time, where opponents attack each other on different topics in different threads. The openness makes controversies in online discussion forums very time-consuming activities.

e) Closure: Dascal (1997) describes the fifth characteristic of controversies as closure. Leaving aside 'natural death' and 'abandonment', Dascal differentiates between the 'solution' (of a discussion) and dispute. Further, Dascal explains that 'resolution' and 'sound argument closure' are examples of the solution, whereas 'closure' and 'procedural closure' belong to disputes. Most controversies in online discussion forums eventually are closed by moderators or site administrators. No single controversy ends up as an open thread that participants keep posting on, or it dies a natural death,[41] meaning that online controversies are not resolved on their own. They always require the mediation of a third party – in this case, a moderator to step in and close the thread. Otherwise, the opponents keep attacking each other, and the tone of communication can become and usually becomes increasingly aggressive. In this scenario, participants in an online controversy tend to break many communication principles and forum rules to attack each other.

---

41 In the language of online discussion forums, all threads die a "natural death", meaning that participants lose interest in the thread and do not post on it anymore. Thus, the thread in question becomes inactive and is not of interest due to other active threads.

f) Not anarchical nature: Another feature of controversies is that they are not anarchical (Dascal, 1997). Dascal stresses that in contrast to conversations, controversies are not governed by implicitly or explicitly codified rules; however, this does not mean that controversies allow the extremity of 'anything goes'. There are still communication principles that need to be followed by participants in controversies. This is also the case with online controversies as participants need to follow forum rules and other communication principles, such as maintaining focus on the desired topic.

Table 3.3: Characteristics of controversies.

Characteristics of controversies	
Type of conflict	Prolonged conflict
Goal of participants	To impress an audience
Controversy demand	a) Existential dimension: the opponent's reputation b) Public dimension: the audience
Social legitimation of controversialists	Creating an impression made on an external audience
Type of dialogue	Quasi-dialogue
Limitation of audience-driven constraint	Not all manipulative moves are allowed
Type of disagreement	A range of topics
Level of communication	Spreading easily to meta issues
Topics	Spreading fast in both extension and depth levels
Dealing with contenders	Questioning the opponents' basic factual, methodological, and conceptual presuppositions
Hermeneutical nature	Having a hermeneutical (interpretative, explanatory) aspect
Openness	The end result unknown
Closure	End with closure
Not anarchical	Ruled by communication principles and no toleration for extreme moves

3.6 The role of emotions in public controversies

Public controversies are highly emotional activities that take an emotional toll on their participants. Many participants complain about the high emotional toll of the involvement in controversies in online discussion forums. Group dynamics and their effects play a major role in the course of controversies as well. Blöchliger (1999:115) explains that a human being is never complete on his own; it is only through interaction with other human beings that he reaches a state of completeness. This is, of course, not surprising as human beings are social animals who need affiliation with other individuals and groups (Blöchinger, 1999:115). Therefore, each person is intertwined in different social networks.

When a controversy occurs, all aspects of group dynamics and pressure play an important role. A controversy in online discussion forums starts with a polemical interaction between two members and rapidly transforms into a group activity in which people form groups, defending one side and attacking the opposite side. As a controversy is a highly emotional activity, emotions play an important role in such moves. Moderators of online discussion forums are constantly contacted via private message systems by members of the respective forum who are involved in the controversies who complain about their opponents breaking some forum rules and ignoring communication principles. Very often, moderators are asked to close the respective controversial threads. These threads are also discussed on the moderator forum, a private forum that the general public does not have access to, which is used to discuss the policy of the forum and, above all, how to handle the controversial threads and the participants in them.

In analyzing public controversies, Gross (2005:335) also points to the important role of emotions. He stresses that social emotion plays an important role in public controversies. Borrowing the concept of social drama from the social anthropologist Victor Turner, Gross (2005:335) describes social drama as a type of collective social action that goes from threat to resolution in four stages. The first stage is the breach that reveals an underlying social conflict. If this social conflict is not resolved or closed quickly, it will move to the second stage, namely crisis. In the third stage, the community tries to settle the crisis by judicial procedure, meaning that the community tries to settle rival claims by means ranging from informal mediation to formal justice before a supreme judicial body (Gross, 2005:337). Gross explains that the last stage of a social drama is reintegration, a stage in which a society tries to return to the status quo ante.[42]

Further, Gross stresses that, from a sociological point of view, this pattern of events is interesting as it is repeated across societies and in the same societies over time. This is the same procedure that public controversies in online discussion forums go through, supporting Gross' statement that this pattern of events repeats over time. As an example, I will illustrate this by using the *keris* controversy: the breach in the community is later revealed when Manolo criticizes the article by Melborn on the development of the *keris*. Melborn enjoys a prominent reputation among the collectors of the *keris* and is also a moderator of the Forum of Ethnographic Swords. Therefore, criticizing him openly on the Forum of Swords is considered a breach of etiquette by many of Melborn's supporters. The social conflict – in this case, the controversy – is not resolved at the first stage; therefore, it moves to the second stage of crisis. During the life of this controversy, four different crises happened, with intervals between them, until the thread was closed by the site administrator on October 10, 2006. The crisis on the online discussion forum crystallizes itself in the form of higher activity levels of controversial posts, namely, for the purposes of this study, during October 11–14, 2006 (seven posts), October 19–27, 2006 (nineteen posts), October 31 to November 1, 2006 (six posts), and November 8–10, 2006 (eleven posts). This shows that participants tend to post more often during the periods of

42 After analyzing three controversies, Gross (2005:349) concludes that in some controversies (as public knowledge is at stake), public debate regarding a controversial topic is completely suppressed by a private interest even in so-called free societies. Therefore, Gross differentiates between knowledge available to the public, as in libraries, and public knowledge, where claims can be endorsed and debated in public arenas, such as school books, historical museums, or motion pictures.

crisis and stop posting for a while afterward. There are different reasons for this type of behavior. Mainly, either they use these intervals to plan their next moves, or they get tired of the highly emotional involvement a controversy requires and need to distance themselves from the whole polemical discourse.

During the second stage, namely crisis, emotions play a significant role. In his paper, Gross (2005:341) analyzes the role of emotions in different types of public controversies, such as the political controversy over the Enola Gay, and states that during the crisis stage in the controversy, there was no argument; rather, there was an emotional outburst in the form of an argument.[43] Additionally, the mediation was not in the form of mediation on events but a drive to represent oneself as a loyal member of a particular group by showing moral outrage at a specific target (Gross, 2005:341). This means that each member of the controversy expressed not only his own outrage but also that of the group he belonged to. Another characteristic of social dramas is that the circles of dispute widen and the targets of contention increase as well. This is also the case with the controversy on the *keris*, where many contenders could not hide their emotions and stick to the facts presented in the thread. As a moderator of the Forum of Swords, I received many private messages from different members of the Forum of Swords and the Forum of Ethnographic Swords members (who are also participants on the Forum of Swords) who complained about the improper behavior and false line of argumentation of their opponents. These messages are all highly emotional, revealing the fact that the authors of the messages were going through profound crises. Additionally, some of the posts created on the *keris* controversy show that the participants do not stick to the facts and are highly emotional, such as the following examples show:

(5) Manolo: Did people in Majapahit Java just go to the field and fight half-heartedly? Come on

(6) Please, I'm Manolo – no "Mr." anything.

(7) Paulo: If we ever meet, I'd be glad to show you some examples.

43 For more information on the Enola Gay controversy, see Gloning (2005:341).

(8) Charley: [. . .] as my purpose in being here is to attempt to ensure that firstly the Melborn paper is correctly quoted, and not misrepresented, and that secondly it is addressed in a scholarly *fashion*, not an emotional one

In Example 3.5, Manolo uses a rhetorical question and ends his sentence with the expression 'come on', clearly signaling his emotional disdain for Melborn's theory. In Example 3.6, Manolo makes fun of his opponent, Charley, by using an emoticon, and does not stick to facts as he uses humor to challenge Charley's means of addressing him. In Example 3.7, Paulo refers to fighting techniques and makes a veiled challenge to David, the main supporter of Manolo. The statement appears benign, but the message implied means to provoke an emotional response since Paulo's language suggests a threat with '[i]f we ever meet'. In Example 3.8, Charley insinuates that the writing style of Manolo and David, the main contesters of Charley, is poor. This is, of course, not the case as both Manolo and David tend to write in a logical and clear way throughout the controversy.

Posting emotional responses is not restricted to the *keris* controversy on the Forum of Swords. The *nationalism* controversy on the Forum of Ethnographic Swords also shows a number of highly emotional posts:

(9) Ehud: Most of us here are enthusiastic amateurs (proud to be one!), whether we collect weapons of our ancestors or not. To pretend, however, that one is a true "academician" simply because he or she spent some years traipsing around museums in exotic places and schmoozing with the curators in a native tongue is a laughable hubris.

(10) Ehud: Please feel free to add my current posting to the file assembled by you and your Merry Gang of Attack Poodles.

In example 3.9, Ehud is referring to a moderator of the Forum of Swords, and in example 3.10 Ehud refers to the members of the Forum of Swords. The examples above show that Ehud does not stick to the facts and does not criticize his opponents in an objective way; rather, he attempts to use humor and relies on logical fallacies (in this case, a red herring and ad hominem) to distort the message he is attacking and to dissuade other members from taking the issue seriously. Moreover, he decides to mock and insult his opponents, which demonstrates that he does not take the matter at hand seriously but prefers to focus on ad hominem distortions of the topic.

The third stage of online controversies is where the moderators step in and try to mediate, such as the following example taken from the *keris* controversy on the Forum of Swords shows:

(11) Moderator: Gentlemen,
Please stay on topic and discuss only the swords.
Kind regards
Moderator

The last stage of social drama in controversies in online discussion forums is when the online community of arms and armor reintegrates. Normally, this happens when a moderator closes a controversial thread (since controversial threads do not die a natural death but have a recurring tendency), meaning the members keep posting controversial input until a moderator closes the thread. This form of 'integration' is not true re-establishment of the online sword forum community, but it is the only reliable way for this online community of participants to move away from controversy. The troubling nature of such a community is directly tied to the reluctance of many people to become involved in discussions, for they could become involved in (un)necessary controversies.

Since the members who are involved in an online controversy also contact each other via e-mail and private messages, the group dynamic and peer pressure play a major role in influencing the behavior and emotions of participants. Due to the presence of peer pressure and group dynamics, these emotions are not individual emotions but social emotions. Gross (2005:346) describes the characteristics of social emotions as follows:

a) Group belonging: In a paradigm case of a certain emotion, a person feels the physiological and psychological changes as a consequence of immediate perception; however, in social emotions, people show emotions not because they perceive intentional objection but because they belong to a certain group that should be indignant and fearful because more powerful people encourage such indignation and fear. This is also the case with the *keris* controversy in the Forum of Swords. The contenders in the controversy send different signals, showing their allegiance to a certain group or forum, such as the following example where Manolo addresses his main opponent, Charley:

(12) Manolo: Charley, surely you know that Forum of Swords is an academic forum, and in academia it is the norm for those who propose arguments to bear the burden of evidence, contrary to the position you took above when you said [. . .].

In another example, Manolo stresses that the Forum of Swords is an academic forum (in contrast to its rival forum, the Forum of Ethnographic Swords) by expressing the following:

(13) Manolo: Because this is an academic forum, we use the academic method. In the academic method, those proposing ideas – hypotheses, theories, or conjectures – bear the burden of evidence to support their proposals. Thus Melborn, in proposing his ideas, bears the burden of supporting himself (which he hasn't yet done).

Examples 3.12 and 3.13 above demonstrate that Manolo shows his allegiance to the Forum of Swords. In this case, he will do his best to portray the Forum of Swords in a positive manner and, at the same time, to attack the Forum of Ethnographic Swords. This is typical behavior of many contenders involved in controversies in online discussion forums. Group formations, defending the group, and allegiance to the group are more important than listening to the other side's arguments. This results, of course, in the usage of tactics of inclusion and exclusion, fully ignoring the aim of reaching the absolute truth in controversies as Leibniz advocated.

b) Infectious nature: Another characteristic of social emotions is that they are infectious, meaning that they spread from one member to the other, and in doing so, they keep gaining strength (Gross, 2005:347). This was also the case with the controversy on the *keris*. Nine participants and three moderators and site administrators took part in the *keris* controversy. They participated in the controversy either to defend the person who was being criticized or to defend the critic. Each thread on the Forum of Swords has a view count, which counts the number of times a thread was visited by registered members. In the case of the *keris* controversy, the thread count stands at 2,034. One should note that this does not count the number of times registered members accessed the forum without logging in, and above all, this number does not count the number of times that unregistered members opened and read the thread.

c) Global nature: Social dramas have a global nature and are all coincident with the borders of the nation state (Gross, 2005:348). Gross explains that in the Enola Gay controversy and in the recombinant DNA debate, neither the British nor the Soviets shared the American sense of crisis. Gross adds that the reason for this is that controversies stop at national borders, and, hence, other nations can react ironically towards them. This is surely one of the differences between controversies in online discussion forums and these types of controversies. Since people of many nations take part in online discussion forums dedicated to the study of arms and armor (provided they speak and write English), the ironic stance is not restricted to the nations but to a forum. The members of each forum establish a set of presumptions and attitudes that they subconsciously or consciously support, and they punish any deviations from these accepted norms and rules. In this respect, members of a forum build up a group where they feel that they belong, and they defend the ideas and principles accepted by that group, regardless of where they come from. One important factor here to take into consideration is the role of English as a *lingua franca*.[44] Not all members of the Forum of Swords and the Forum of Ethnographic Swords are native speakers of English. Many use English as a foreign language, and some use English as a second language. Hence, misunderstandings and violation of politeness principles often happen due to the usage of English as a *lingua franca*.

As Gross mentions above, social emotions tend to spread very quickly and add to the group identity of human beings. Any conflict

44 For the role of English as a lingua franca in email communication, see Bjørge (2007), for English as a lingua franca and globalization, see Dewey (2007) and Dovring (1997), also see Elder and Davies (2006).

between a subset of a group with a subset of another group can easily be spread to the entire set (Barghouti, 2005:329). Therefore, Barghouti states that a conflict that starts between two individuals with two distinct national, religious, or ethnic identities rapidly leads to a full-scale conflict between the two groups. Another important point that needs to be taken into consideration is that debating is by no means restricted to a debate with others or inter-personal debate; one is constantly engaged in intra-personal or self-debate (Dascal, 2005:34). Observing the controversies that happen in the Forum of Swords and the Forum of Ethnographic Swords, any controversy that happens between two members who are loyal to different forums eventually leads to a full-fledged controversy in both forums, where members of the two groups get involved in polemical discourse.

Controversies tend to be highly emotional activities. During involvement in any controversy, contenders show a selective perception towards the presented facts. Having a selective perception can be due to various reasons. One of these reasons is probably that, in any type of activity, people need to choose between alternatives to form opinions. Thus, debating is by no means restricted to a debate with others or inter-personal debate, but one is constantly engaged in intra-personal or self-debate (Dascal, 2005:34). Regarding this point, Dascal (2005a:35) points out that whenever people make choices between alternatives, meaning that whenever people decide something, they are consciously or unconsciously torn between different choices and, hence, are engaged in a self-debate. These mental procedures are important because they determine people's behavior, the direction of thoughts, belief systems, desires (Dascal, 2005:35), and, above all, how they interact with others.

Additionally, as human beings constantly strive to suppress their defects to maintain a pleasing self-image, they tend to apply the strategy of self-deception. One of the results of this strategy is, of course, using the strategy of 'selective perception', meaning that people tend to ignore those who are against them and concentrate on those who are favorable to them (Dascal, 2005:37). This is a feature that can be seen in different types of controversies, where the participants ignore their opponents' input and open new fronts, such as is the case with controversies in online discussion forums.

3.7 Summary

This chapter has focused on the nature of human conflict and polemical discourse. It has shown that human conflict is ubiqituous in all human activities. There are many different methods of conflict resolution, including fighting, escape, and resignation to the fact. Additionally, depending on the underlying motives of concern for oneself and concern for the other party, different conflict management patterns emerge, ranging from dominating, obliging, avoiding, and integrating to compromising. In spite of the challenge conflicts pose, one needs to develop a positive attitude towards human difference in order to further development in different fields. A culture of tolerance needs to be created where a give-and-take interaction with different ideas is guaranteed. Furthermore, one needs to attach intrinsic value to different manifestations of difference and eliminate simplistic ranking assumptions.

It is not easy to make an absolute distinction between different types of polemical discourse. Nevertheless, I presented a model by Dascal that distinguishes between discussion, debate, and controversy. The type of polemical discourse that takes place in online discussion forums dedicated to the study of arms and armor is a combination of debate and controversy. I also presented Leibniz's ideal model of how to carry out a controversy; however, as I stressed before, the contestants in controversies do not follow these principles. In religious, scientific, and medical controversies in the Early Modern Period, participants were more interested in influencing an audience or readership rather than in cooperating to find greater truth. This is important to take into consideration because it shows that Leibniz's ideas of searching for truth by cooperating with different minds in a controversy does not reflect the way controversies tend to operate. I have also shown that emotions play an important role in public controversies as controversies are highly emotional activities and take a significant toll on the participants.

In the next chapter, I will describe the concept of the République des Lettres and different media used in carrying out controversies. Before describing what kind of media was used in the Early Modern Period, I will provide background information about the members of the so-called République des Lettres who participated in the controversies in that period. I will continue with a discussion of pamphlets that served as a traditional medium used for conducting controversies in the Early Modern Period and will describe how online discussion forums are used as a new medium to carry out controversies.

4. The République des Lettres and pamphlets

4.1 Introduction

The last chapter explained the differences between different types of polemical discourse, such as discussion, dispute, and controversy, in order to make a distinction between these three types and to indicate which type took place in the Early Modern Period. As shown before, polemical discourse that takes place in an online discussion forum shares characteristics of both controversies and debates. Thus, making a clear-cut distinction between these three types of polemical discourse in practice is very difficult, just as in the Early Modern Period. The focus of the fourth chapter is to provide background information about the members of the so-called République des Lettres, who formed Europe's educational elite in the Early Modern Period and who were dedicated to the promotion and advancement of learning. The participants in several Early Modern controversies were members of this community. To understand the nature of the controversies of the period, it is necessary to describe both the people who were involved in polemical discourse and their attitudes towards being engaged in discourses of polemical nature. Hence, it will be possible to make a further step in diachronic comparison between controversies in the Early Modern Period and controversies in present-day online discussion forums, regarding the type of people who are involved in a controversy and their attitudes towards the usefulness of a controversy as a polemical discourse.

I will elucidate several topics that were the core issues of polemical discourse. I will show that although the intention of some contenders involved in controversies was ostensibly to seek truth, many controversies ended in a debate wherein the main intention of contenders was to win the contest. I will explain the general frame of a pamphlet and show that pamphlets were one of the major media used to carry out controversies in written form.

4.2 The members of the République des Lettres and their attitudes

The people who participated in Early Modern Controversies considered themselves to be members of a republic, entitled the République des Lettres.[45] Dascal and Marras (2002:3) explain that 'the learned' of Europe, from the Renaissance onwards, especially in the 17th and 18th centuries, thought of themselves as citizens of a supra-national community that shared the goal of advancing learning. Dascal and Marras add that the majority of the members of this learned society conceived of their community as a 'republic' with Reason as its sovereign. Further, the members of the community thought that under the sole rule of Reason, cooperation and freedom of thought would lead mankind into the 7th and last terrenial degree of 'light', meaning the universal *panharmonia* (Dascal and Marras, 2002:3).

Analyzing many controversies from the République des Lettres between 1680 and 1705, Dascal and Marras (2002:6) explain that public debates of Early Modern Controversies included a broad range of themes. However, Dascal and Marras state that theological and church-politics issues still dominate Early Modern Controversies. Typical features of these articles are that the authors do not hide their political perspectives or attempt to keep their emotional involvement under control, in spite of the fact that the authors/participants are supposed to keep the debate at the intellectual level, at least superficially. Dascal and Marras (2002:6–10) distinguish between

45 In an interdisciplinary project on "Controversies in the République des Lettres (1600-1800)", historical rules and principles leading different types of controversy in this period were analyzed; these included characteristic types of moves and strategies and patterns of text production (Fritz, 2005b:235). I will explain these moves and strategies more in detail in chapter six.

different types of controversies in the République des Lettres, such as scientific, literary, philosophical, historical, juridical, medical, political, and interdisciplinary (meta-controversy) debates. Dascal and Marras (2002:6) state that the vivid impression one gets from analyzing the writings of the République des Lettres is that every published article is immediately noticed and critically evaluated; most of the time, one gets the impression that participants are waiting only for the opportunity to attack their opponents whenever they write something, regardless of the contents of the publications. As I will show later, the patterns of posting behavior of contenders in controversies in online discussion forums dedicated to the arms and armor resemble the behavior of participants in controversies in the République des Lettres in that: a) participants do not try to hide their preferences for a certain forum and, hence, their political agenda, b) posts tend to get emotional quickly, c) participants try to keep the debate at the intellectual level but do not normally succeed, and d) one also gets the impression that participants just wait for opponents to start a new thread so that they can attack them.

Dascal and Marras (2002:11) explain that a significant number of the articles related to controversies in the République des Lettres were concerned with meta-polemics, meaning that they were about reflections about polemics, their nature, use, and value. The excesses that were often present in many debates were criticized; examples of these excesses include too much rhetorical punch, too much eagerness to win, and too much loyalty to one's party. These excesses were deplored because they undermined the real purpose for such critical activity, the search for truth. Dascal and Marras (2002:11) explain that some critics considered the excessive love of dispute by the *savants* as counterproductive from an epistemic point of view and also a dishonor for the République des Lettres, as it led it into a permanent state of 'civil war'. According to Dascal and Marras, other critics condemned the *esprit de secte* supported by partisan groupings, as they considered it to be an obstacle to the development of a cooperative, scientific enterprise. Other critics blamed the psychological drive of the controversialists to attempt to win at all costs, since it led to the animosity displayed in their argumentation and their readiness to use dubious rhetorical stratagems. It is interesting to see that not much has changed, in this respect, in controversies in online discussion forums. Members of both the Forum of Swords and the Forum of Ethnographic Swords show absolute royalty to their respective forum and, hence, show an *esprit de secte*. One can see clear animosity in their argumentation against their opponents and their use of dubious rhetorical stratagems and moves, as will be shown later in Chapter Seven.

Dascal and Marras (2002:11–12) state that only a few citizens of the République des Lettres categorically described polemical exchanges as an irrelevant residue of another era or as being separated from the process of generating knowledge: however, no one made any suggestions to forbid, avoid, or reduce the growing critical activity within the realm of polemics (Dascal and Marras, 2002:12). Dascal and Marras (2002:12) point out that the critics of this type of polemical exchange considered it to be a dispute, for in a dispute, the main objective of the contenders is to win over the opponent, no matter what kind of means were used. Therefore, in this type of polemical exchange, the advancement of knowledge, rational argument, clarification of the issues under dispute, reconciliation, and truth are all of secondary importance (Dascal and Marras, 2002:12). Therefore, Dascal and Marras rightly observe that the critics of this type of polemical exchange have these aims, and not victory, in mind, and, therefore, they are right in their criticism of the polemical exchanges in the dispute category. Additionally, as the critics are aware of the existence of other polemical exchanges, they do not dismiss these polemical exchanges altogether.

Dascal and Marras (2002:12) observe that some thinkers of this period took other models of debate into consideration as dispute. Based on the successes of mathematics in the period in question, one of the models considered a conflict of opinions as a type of logico-mathematical problem, meaning that if one does the proper calculations and takes all the relevant information into consideration, he could determine which of the conflicting positions was right and end the debate. Dascal and Marras name this type of polemical discourse 'discussion', and state that the model of discussion is based on a rigorous decision-making procedure by which, after weighing different alternatives, a rational being can accept the true position and reject the false one. In this model, false positions are regarded as being the result of a mistake. According to Dascal and Marras (2002:12), it seems that the Royal Society worked under the impression that the discussion model represented the appropriate way to solve scientific debates, specifically when these debates were factual rather than speculative. In such an environment, the community of scientists who are acknowledged as specialists in the subject matter would become a type of tribunal that decides which of the contenders was right. Dascal and Marras (2002:14) add that the discussion model is also implicitly advocated by those who emphasize that the usage of precise definitions related to clear and distinct ideas should hinder idle disputes and allow the solution of all worthwhile debates.

Dascal and Marras explain that this assumption led to the development of 'philosophical' or 'scientific' languages, which proliferated at the time. Leibniz realized the potential of such language to become a rational tool for the solution of debates and formulated the idea of a *characteristica universalis*. Using this idea, the contenders would be able to resolve their differences by expressing them in a formal notation and then calculating the solution (Dascal and Marras, 2002:14). However, Dascal and Marras stress that since Leibniz was a practical man, he was aware that the discussion or calculative problem-solving model could not solve all conflicts. The reason was that Leibniz realized that in a majority of cases, one could not clearly determine who was right and who was mistaken, as both parties were partially right and partially wrong, under some interpretation of their positions. Therefore, Leibniz was of the opinion that the opposition between the parties could be overcome if each could be made to recognize the 'right' and the 'wrong' parts of his own position as well as those of the opponent's position. This way, each party could weigh carefully their relative importance and be persuaded to abandon what was wrong (or unacceptable to the opponent) in his position and to accept what was right (or acceptable to him) in the opponent's position (Dascal and Marras, 2002:14).

This could, of course, not be conducted in a mechanical or formal way, nor could it be assumed that it would result in absolute certainty. Therefore, the active intervention of a 'judge of controversies', who was able to reformulate the positions in conflict and to use non-deductive types of arguments, was required. The judge would not compute arguments but would only weigh them (Dascal and Marras, 2002:14). Dascal and Marras explain that Leibniz developed an alternative model of polemical exchanges and their resolution, similar to what is called controversy, next to the strict logico-mathematical model and probably complementary to it. This model looks for rational persuasion and conciliation of the opponents rather than victory at all costs and admits that, in many important issues, one cannot reach absolute certainty. Therefore, one must conform to the use of a 'softer reason' – an expression used by Leibniz (Dascal and Marras, 2002:14). In a way of comparison, moderators of online discussion forums dedicated to the study of arms and armor act as judges of controversies when controversial threads appear in online discussion forums. Nevertheless, it seems that the degree of tolerance regarding controversial threads is very low. Controversies in online discussion forums are seen as a threat to the flow of communication, both by moderators and other participants who are not interested in getting involved in a controversy. Hence, controversial threads are locked after a while by moderators. It is clear that the discussion model suggested by Leibniz is not applied in online discussion forums.

Further, Dascal and Marras (2002:14) explain that polemics was a constitutive element of the République des Lettres and offer a two-pronged argument: historical and conceptual ones. Dascal and Marras expound that, although many consider the République de Lettres as a 17th – 18th centuries phenomenon, the République has its roots in the late Renaissance. As a matter of fact, the Reformation and the subsequent Counter-Reformation were the source of endless polemics that continued until the 18th century. According to Dascal and Marras (2002:15), the Reformation severely undermined the basis for the belief in an infallible authority, on both sacred and profane matters, that was exercised by any particular body or group within Christianity. The scientific revolution followed this trend and questioned the authority of traditional Aristotelian science and the right of the Church to intervene in the determination of scientific truth (Dascal and Marras, 2002:15). Dascal and Marras point out that, at the same time, absolute obedience to 'Reason' as another source of authority was established, and this served as the basis for the 'ideology' of the

République des Lettres. However, similar to the Reformation that had questioned absolute authority within an intra-religious context, the rise of Skepticism questioned both the power of Reason and its intra-rational affairs (Dascal and Marras, 2002:16). Consequently, Reason was not able to replace the authority of religion and become a substitute to religious authority; therefore, all sources of unquestionable authority became questionable.

Nevertheless, the role of religion could still be seen in medical and scientific discourse of the Early Modern Period. Ratia (2005:124) emphasizes that scientific and medical discourse cannot be distinguished from other discourses of the period, since medical discourse was also combined with moral and religious discourses, such as in the case of tobacco controversies. Although tobacco controversies dealt with the medical issues of tobacco, some advocated its usefulness for health, and some argued for the damage it did to one's health. In controversies in online discussion forums dedicated to the study of arms and armor, religion likely does not play a role.[46] As a matter of fact, forum rules forbid the discussion of religious topics. Nevertheless, some members show absolute obedience to some published authorities and treat them like religious figures.

4.3 Pamphlets in the République des Lettres

The contestants of the République des Lettres who were involved in controversies used the written medium as a way to carry out controversies. As a matter of fact, taking sides (con or pro) in written controversies formed a significant type of communication in 16th and 17th century Europe, with the function of settling differences or clarifying opposite views (see Gloning, 1999:86–87). Early Modern Controversies were carried out via pamphlets. Pamphlets were one of

46 Nevertheless, one should know that religion probably plays a role at the level of controlling content whenever the people in control of the content are members of religious communities.

the first media used for mass communication (Jucker, 2003:129, 132), where political and religious topics were discussed in political and religious pamphlets (see Bach 1998, Claridge, 2000). Quoting Shepard (1973), Ratia (2005:124) explains that pamphlets were a type of new media that were written for middle-class and upper-class readers and were intended to influence popular opinion by arguing a point.

Analyzing witchcraft pamphlets from the 16th and 17th centuries, Suhr (2006:27) explains that pamphlets represented one of the first types of texts that were produced to be read out loud to large, mostly illiterate audiences. On this point, Suhr's opinion differs from Ratia's opinion, who states that pamphlets were a type of new media that were produced for middle-class and upper-class readers. Generally, members of the middle class and upper class had better chances of receiving an education and becoming literate in the Early Modern Period. The purpose of the production of the large-scale printing of pamphlets was to inform and, at the same time, to influence this type of audience. Quoting Bach (1998:97), Suhr (2006:28) explains that pamphlets became one of the first types of mass media, and it was not rare that some pamphlets had a print run of up to 1,500 copies, some with multiple reprints or editions.

Pamphlets of the Early Modern Period dealt with a number of issues, such as religious, medical, and scientific topics. There were also pamphlets that were written on the health effects of tobacco. In the following, I will explain how pamphlet writing worked in this period by providing examples about pamphlets on the tobacco controversy. Ratia (2005:123) explains that the controversy about the health effects of tobacco originated in the 17th century. After three decades, when tobacco was considered as a panacea from the New World,[47] an anonymous writer using the name 'Philaretes' wrote a pamphlet called *A Warning for Tabacconists* in 1601 as a part of a longer treatise entitled *Work for Chimney-Sweepers*, where he openly attacked the use of tobacco. Ratia (2005:123) explains that in the following year, another anonymous author (later Roger Marbecke

47 Ratia (2005:123) uses the term "panacea" from the new world, based on Brooks (1952:35).

claimed that he was the author) wrote a critical reply entitled *A Defence of Tabacco*. Different sets of argumentation for and against tobacco were used as a dialog between two texts. Both texts can be classified as medical treatises and pamphlets intended to gain the attention of a larger audience (Ratia, 2005:123–124).[48] According to Ratia (2005:124), the production of medical texts expanded dramatically after 1558 with the reign of Elizabeth I, when an increasing number of texts came to be written in vernacular languages instead of Latin. Quoting Bennet (1965:179:181), Ratia (2005:124) states that this, of course, made them accessible to a wider public.

To reach a wide audience that was mostly illiterate, someone needed to read the pamphlets aloud for the audience. Based on Shepard (1973:14, 21), Bach (1998:28) explains that pamphlets were generally read out loud on a street corner or church porch, targeting a group of people who came together to listen to the news. Suhr (2006:28) explains that it is not plausible to assume that the strategies the pamphlet author and/or printer implemented were deliberate choices based on knowledge of characteristics of spoken and written language. Moreover, Suhr assumes that authors knew that their audiences were not likely to be acquainted with academic writing, and, therefore, they adapted their style of writing to their audiences. Based on Clark (1983:27), Suhr (2006:28) states that pamphlets were often produced anonymously or pseudonymously because pamphleteering was considered as an occupation of low status and bad reputation.

Ratia (2006:90) states that pamphlets can be classified as written dialogues and that they served as an influential branch of media that was intended to persuade public opinion. Further, Ratia explains that pamphlets were cheap, small (quarto size) and rather short, ranging from twelve pages up to a hundred. Ratia adds that, as a medium, pamphlets were not highly valued, in spite of the fact that they were persuasive and had a large readership. Therefore, quoting Kronick (1988), Ratia (2006:90) states that pamphleteers often wrote

48 Although the texts dealt with medical issues, they were written in a way to target the average audience, and, hence, the language was carefully chosen to target the audience accordingly.

anonymously. This is also a phenomenon online discussion forums share with pamphlets. Although many academics in the field of arms and armor read the contents in the threads on both forums in this study, many do not actively participate in the forums, since such participation is not highly esteemed in academic circles. However, one should note that in spite of the fact that the Forum of Swords has a real-name policy, one cannot be sure whether all members actually use their real names. Thus, some members could be academics who hide their true identities by using false names to take part in discussions. This, of course, is easier to do in the Forum of Ethnographic Swords, since it does not have a real-name policy.

Pamphlets were extensively used to carry out controversies, and therefore Ratia (2006:91) explains that pamphlets as a medium are generally associated with controversy. Pamphlets on the tobacco controversy that have been studied by Ratia (2006:92) seem to have two functions: first, to participate in academic discussion about tobacco and, second, to reach a wide range of individuals in order to influence public opinion. Fritz and Glüer (2001a:42) state that the pamphlets used as the medium of controversy in the République des Lettres remained a significant model of a controversy into the 19th century, in spite of the fact that other text types, such as reviews, and other media, such as journals, were gaining more and more importance. Gloning (2002:46) corroborates this statement, stating that the prototypical media type used for carrying out controversies, circa 1600, was the independently published pamphlet that was gradually replaced by other, shorter, forms in the 18th century. Gloning explains that this development was due to the creation of academic and, later, scientifically-oriented journals.

Fritz and Glüer (2001a:43) explain that pamphlets are based on the following, three-stage constellation. First, participant A makes a number of assertions, judgments, or accusations and supports them if necessary. In the next stage, participant B answers these assertions, judgments, or accusations point by point, trying to refute them or making objections to them. In the third stage, participant A tries to dismiss the refutations point by point, supporting his own statements (Fritz and Glüer, 2001a:43). Fritz and Glüer (2001a:43) explain that prototypical pamphlets are refutations, and their most striking feature is the point-by-point procedure. Fritz and Glüer add that, in the 17th century, pamphlets of this type were used as the main instrument for carrying out controversies, and prominent authors, such as Kepler, Hobbes, and Leibniz, participated in writing them as a matter of course.

Gloning (2002:46) adds that pamphlets were extensive and reached over 200 published pages (e.g. 'Verantwortung und Rettung' by Schaerers in 1611), and the critical sections of the pamphlet could be written in individual paragraphs or even whole chapters (e.g. Röslin's reaction to Kepler in his 'Mitternächtigen Schiffahrt' in 1611 that was Chapter XII and included 22 pages). The major parts of published pamphlets, such as 'Anwort auf Röslini Diskurs', are a) the title page with the indication of the topic and, where applicable, reference to the opponent, reference to the opponent's writing, and self-praise; b) the foreword, the dedication line, and, where applicable, supporting letters to the author; c) the main part of the pamphlet that is generally organized in different articles, such as different points with different lengths, possibly with an internal structure; and d) a summary or another form of a conclusion (Gloning, 2002.46). Gloning stresses that the same major component parts were also used in pamphlets in other fields, such as religious controversies. The structure of the main text, consisting of articles, is one of the main features of the pamphlets in the Early Modern Period. This structure is based on the thematic division of the pamphlets into different arguments and their related points. As the structure of pamphlets is based on articles, the answer to it is also based on articles and different points. Thus, the answer to the pamphlet follows the order of the original topics. Gloning (2002:46) explains that in answer to different textual elements, various techniques are used, such as references with help of paragraph numbers, page numbers, or thematic keywords. A second text feature is the typical two-part structure of the text, where part of the statement of the opponent is quoted and then the answer to it follows (Gloning, 2002:46–47).

According to Gloning (2002:47), the text structure of pamphlets based on articles and its corresponding point-by-point answer depends on the thematic structure of controversies. For participants in a controversy, this thematic structure presents, on the one hand, a suitable procedure for thematic structure and, on the other hand, makes it easier for the readers/audience to have an overview of the scoring of participants in the controversy and how they react and answer. Fritz and Glüer (2001a:42) expand that the pragmatic structure in exchanging pamphlets reveals certain advantages and disadvantages in carrying out controversies. The point-by-point reference to the opponent's statements can be considered as a prescribed quality standard. This means that participants in a controversy are required to refer to all points of criticism raised by their opponents in the given order. Therefore, if the points are answered incompletely or in the wrong order, these faults can be considered as criteria for success or failure in the controversy (Gloning, 1999:102; Fritz & Glüer, 2001a:43). On the other hand, the principle of point-by-point reference created the following problems[49] (Fritz and Glüer, 2001a:43–44):

Point-by-point procedure in writing pamphlets results in extremely long, complex, and confusing texts. Many pamphlet authors were aware of this fact and, hence, produced summaries and an index of contents to lighten up the texts.

Another problem with point-by-point procedure is that it ends in the repetition of arguments, leading to a purely mechanical continuation of the controversy. This, of course, prevents the further development of the *status controversial.*

This procedure also prevents the introduction of new topics and information. Fritz and Glüer (2001a:44) explain that writers try to avoid this problem by giving up the strict point-by-point principle, and by using digressions, they insert text documentation or coherent representations of their own position.

In some cases, due to the original selection or sequence of topics, unimportant topics are discussed, and this is, of course, detrimental to the thematic concentration of the texts.

The requirement of always refuting all the arguments results in a certain relentless determination, making observation of the principles of politeness and relevance difficult while, at the same time, making the atmosphere of the controversy worse. Fritz and Glüer

49 I will discuss the principles of communication thoroughly in the next chapter.

(2001a:44) point out that these and other problems made authors search for other media alternatives to pamphlets in order to carry out their controversies, such as the open letter. Fritz and Glüer (2001a:70) also agree with this and state that the disadvantages of the pamphlets in the religious controversy made Francke use other alternatives, such as writing open letters to explain himself to a third party.

The advantages of this method are, of course, that the defender can present his theological position coherently without the necessity of following a specific thematic structure, is able to participate in the controversy and play the game by his own rules, and can add further points that he considers important (Fritz and Glüer, 2001a:72). Fritz and Glüer (2001a:73) summarize the advantages of open letters in comparison to pamphlets as the following: a) the author can more easily react to the lack of transparency in the indictment and stay clear of the awkward implications of the defensive position, b) the author has more flexibility in the thematic structure, c) unlike pamphlets, the author is not restricted by the adversary's argumentation but can provide a more complete explanation of his own position, d) the author does not need to quote his adversary and can thus avoid the disadvantageous side effect of promoting his adversary's views by quoting him (a very important advantage), e) the author can more easily include passages that he considers important for his aims, such as edifying passages, f) the form of the open letters allows the author to keep a meek tone, and g) open letters are easier to read and are more coherent. Fritz and Glüer (2001a:74) point out that another method used by Francke to carry out the theological controversy was by giving a polemical sermon. This was done by combining a sermon with a contribution to a controversy. According to Fritz and Glüer (2001a:74), the advantages are that the congregation can be addressed as a whole and can also be called as a witness, and its testimony can be used as evidence. Fritz and Glüer also add that a polemical sermon enables the speaker to appeal to both the congregation and his opponents to repent and mend their ways, a feature that is typical of a penitential sermon.

As shown above, using pamphlets to carry out controversies was a popular method during the Early Modern Period. Pamphlets imposed some restrictions on their authors, as they had to follow the point-by-point principle. Due to these restrictions, participants tried to use alternative methods, such as polemical sermons and open letters. As I will show later in this volume, just as open letters offered an easier mode of addressing controversies, online discussion forums are a new medium that can be used by participants of today's controversies in an efficient and fast way to attack their opponents.

4.4 Summary

This chapter has concentrated on the contestants, belonging to the République des Lettres, who were involved in Early Modern Controversies. As I mentioned before, the members of this community considered themselves to be the citizens of a supra-national society, with the shared goal of furthering knowledge. Although the disputants were involved in controversies with the claimed intention of a rational debate, very often the polemical discourse ended in a debate where the main goal was to win.

Different media, such as pamphlets, open letters, and polemical sermons, were used to carry out these controversies. Although pamphlets were the most popular medium, they also imposed severe restrictions on their writers, such as adherence to the point-by-point principle. Therefore, to avoid this restriction, participants came to use open letters and even polemical sermons, instead. In the next chapter, I will concentrate on communication principles that regulated controversies in the Early Modern Period.

5. Communication principles from Early Modern Controversies to electronic communication

5.1 Introduction

Controversies were not an 'anything goes' type of discourse and communication where all moves were allowed. Similar to other types of communication, certain principles were expected to be followed by participants in an Early Modern Controversy. Thus, participants carefully tried to follow these principles, and although there were breaches of the communication principles, participants in controversies tried to use the moves that broke the rules in a way that would not result in accusations of rule violations. Nevertheless, accusations of breaching communication principles were as common as adhering to these same principles. Thus, controversies are interesting to study in historical pragmatics as polemical discourse of controversies of the period demonstrates a characteristic pragmatic structure, where the opponents tend to follow rather well-defined rules and principles and think about them (Fritz, 2008). Gloning and Lüsing (2002:123) explain that communication principles in controversies have normative character, meaning that communication principles are a measure of acceptance of other contributions. If a participant flouts a communication principle, other participants can accuse him of doing so.

In spite of all these rules and regulations, precisely such accusations happen very often in Early Modern Controversies. I will show later that nothing has changed much regarding this aspect in online discussion forums. Online discussion forums dedicated to the study of arms and armor are moderated environments. As shown in chapter two, the communication in online discussion forums is regulated by a set of forum rules and principles. This means that a set of rules is defined, and every new member must agree with them so that registration for a forum will be complete. Flouting the forum rules will lead to the accusation that the participant is not respecting the rules, and this will lead to the people who see a violation of rules to contact the moderating team and filing a complaint about this. These complaints of rule violations are certainly not something new as they happened very often in the Early Modern Period.

Regarding accusations in controversies, Fritz (2007) explains that, for centuries, people have accused their opponents in controversies of making chaos of rational argumentation by evading arguments, by writing incomprehensibly, by intentionally misunderstanding their opponents, by insulting them, and by committing different types of fallacies. According to Fritz, these complaints make a presupposition that ideal forms of controversy exist and relevant principles should be valid for guiding the actions of the participants involved in a controversy. Fritz (2007) defines this presupposition about ideal forms of controversy as the implicit theory of controversy followed by participants involved in a controversy as a matter of routine. Only when participants start to teach, complain, or criticize these principles do these principles become explicit.

Fritz (2007) explains that communication principles are basically maxims of conversation as proposed by Grice (1989:26). However, as far as controversies are concerned, Fritz does not fully agree with the Gricean theory, such as the cooperative principle. As far as the basic principles of communication are concerned, Fritz sympathizes more with Hinitikka (Hinitikka, 1986) and Kasher (Kasher, 1976), who stress the foundational role of some type of rationality principle. Fritz adds that the rationality principle was also mentioned by Grice (Grice, 1989:29). Fritz (2007) makes a very important observation and states that one should concentrate on the empirical study of communication principles to have a better picture of how rationality works in practice. Fritz adds that this empirical approach will probably show that there are principles that are not in any simple way connected to standard assumptions of rationality, such as principles that people inherited from earlier periods without changing them into new communicative demands. One should note that communication principles are not valid for all time periods and change over time. This means that communication principles from the Early Modern Period have changed over time, and some of them survived in the modern era as well. One should note that communication principles that are valid for online discussion forums are also in the process of change over a certain period of time. The forum charters of rules are constantly updated by the site administration so that they can better control their audience and ensure a better environment. At times, the adjustment of rules is also done to target specific needs of the forum administration.

5.2 Controversies as language games ruled by principles

From a linguistic point of view, controversies and polemics are types of communication. However, as I mentioned before, this type of communication is not an anything-goes activity as controversies are governed by certain rules and principles. Regarding these rules, Gloning (2005:263) explains some assumptions underlying a controversy: a) when one contributes to a controversy, he/she performs linguistic acts based on his/her goals in the controversy and based on the rules leading this type of communication; b) another feature of controversies is that they have a typical linguistic or pragmatic form that begins at a certain time or place in a certain field; and c) another characteristic of controversies is that the pragmatic form of controversies is subject to change and to historical development over a period of time. Taking these features into consideration, Gloning (2005:263) refers to the Wittgensteinian concept of controversies that describes them as a well-established family of language games (forms of communication). Gloning (2005:263) stresses that language games are supra-personal since they are social institutions that have emerged over time.

Fayard and DeSanctis (2005) quote Wittgenstein, who describes language games as patterns of group discourse, surrounding a particular object, idea, class, or other meaningful entity. Fayard and DeSanctis add that a language game develops as speakers generate discussion routines, including the rules of social engagement related to the community. These rules determine interpersonal relationships and mutual understanding. It is important to take into consideration that the rules of language games exercise a form of restriction on the participants in a controversy so that they are expected to behave based on the established practice (Gloning, 2005:263). At the same time, Gloning explains that the set of rules also leaves room for individual preferences and choices, such as applying different moves and strategies or using different vocabulary items. Further, Gloning (2005:263) explains that social institutions take the pressure off the individuals to find new solutions for communicative tasks and problems. Analyzing the online discussion forums dedicated to the study of arms and armor, one realizes that the communicative acts are similar to a language game. This game is regulated by different sets of rules advocated by the site owner and the moderators' team as I will show later in this chapter.

Looking at controversies as social institutions, controversies could be regarded as established procedures for handling disagreement and for confirming ideas, findings, and decisions (Gloning, 2005:263). Gloning (2005:264) also points out that language games have a historical aspect, meaning that language games change over time but not by themselves, since the historical development of the language game of controversy is a result of individuals who respond to changing circumstances. Therefore, innovative, individual practice leads to the changes in the established practice of language games. Gloning (2005:264) provides an example for the 17th century onwards when the newly established journals were used as a medium of controversy. In journals, the authors or participants in a controversy had to follow different textual conditions of journal publishing in comparison with pamphlet publishing. Fritz (2007) also recognizes this and explains that when the new scientific journals were established by the end of the 17th century, academic discussions had to comply with new principles of text production. These principles were different from traditional pamphlet writing. In producing texts, some structures are independent and other structures are dependent on the medium used. In this respect, Esser (2006:67–102) distinguishes between medium-independent and medium-dependent structures. Esser classifies medium-independent structures into words, phrases and classes, and paragraphs, and medium-dependent structures in the written medium into punctuation, orthography, and variations of characters and in the spoken medium in allomorphs of connected speech and intonation. In the same light, one should always be aware that the new medium of the Internet introduces new principles of text production that influence medium-dependent structures, such as punctuation, orthography, and variations of characters.

Analyzing the language games of Early Modern Controversies, Gloning (2005:266) explains that these language games represent a system of rules for entering into a controversy and rules for answering certain points within a controversy. In this regard, Gloning names aspects of the position represented in controversies as well as aspects of the person involved. Both aspects are important to understand the true nature of the controversy in question. He further exemplifies that a person A was 'entitled' to enter into a controversy with a person B in two ways: 1) when the position of B was incompatible with the position of A and 2) when B either attacked A personally or B attacked another participant personally, whom A wants to defend. As I will show later, the same pattern of language games is used in online discussion forums dedicated to the study of arms and armor. People enter the online controversy when the position of a person is incompatible with their own standards or when a person attacks someone else.

5.3 Classification of communication principles

Fritz (2007) explains that a number of communication principles in the Early Modern Period could be grouped into the category efficiency principles, such as the principle of brevity, the principle of non-repetition, different styles of principles of relevance, and principles of comprehensibility and perspicuity. Fritz adds that many of these principles were traditional rhetorical principles. Fritz (2007) explains that another group of principles are related to the relationship between the two antagonists. These principles include politeness principles, forbidding face-threatening acts, and principles banning irony and sarcasm.

Regarding classification of communication principles, Gloning (2002:70) distinguishes between the following communication principles in the scientific controversy between Johaness Kepler, the famous German astronomer and mathematician, and two medical men, Helisaeus Röslin and Philipp Feselius: a) the principle of truthfulness and honorableness, b) the principle of respectful and objective treatment of the opponent, c) the principle of benevolent interpretation of statements of the opponent, d) the principle of clarity, comprehensibility, and unambiguousness, e) the principle of comical presentation, and f) the principle of brevity. Gloning (2002:70) adds that these principles can be in conflict with each other. He adds that the strongest conflict of principles in this controversy is the conflict between the principle of politeness and the principle of scientific openness and directness. Gloning describes that the principle of politeness was often violated in the controversies of the 16th and 17th centuries, and participants complained about this referring to the Christian virtue of meekness.

Table 5.1: Communication principles in the scientific controversy between Kepler, Röslin, and Feselius.

Communication principles in the scientific controversy between Kepler, Röslin, and Feselius
a) The principle of truthfulness and honorableness
b) The principle of respectful and objective treatment of the opponent
c) The principle of benevolent interpretation of statements of the opponent
d) The principle of clarity, comprehensibility, and unambiguousness
e) The principle of comical presentation
f) The principle of brevity

Further, Gloning (2002:79) offers an important model for the verification of the positions in scientific activities around 1600. This model is the basis for demanding certain behavior from participants in a controversy. Gloning (2002:79–82) names the principles that are based on this model as:

a) Be prepared to construct objective criticism, and be prepared to be criticized: in science, it is an accepted procedure to expose findings to criticism. Other members of the scientific community are required to criticize other scholars' works, and this is institutionalized in the form of reviews. On the other hand, the criticized person is required to withstand the criticism, to accept it, and to make use of it.

b) Be prepared to change your position and attitude if it is necessary: Gloning (2002:80) explains that the principle of readiness to make revisions has a biographical-personal aspect and a doctrinaire aspect. Related to the personal aspect, a participant in a controversy should be open to be adaptive, and related to the doctrinaire aspect, the principle requires that a person should be open to changes and revisions of his opinion.

c) Be objective in making your opinions and do not get personal: Gloning (2002:81) states that this principle is formulated based on the principles of truth and also the difference between convincing and persuading.

Regarding the 'principles of communication' in controversies and their classification in a later publication, Gloning (2005:272) explains that many meta-polemic contributions can be regarded as attempts to get rid of certain 'aspects of the subject' in the communication or at least to have strong regulations regarding the involvement of personal aspects that were considered as not desirable in the overall goals of controversies. Further, Gloning adds that these personal aspects are regulated by a) principles governing the repertoire of moves and b) principles about communicative attitudes of controversialists. Further, he explains that moves and attitudes are closely interrelated since without analyzing the moves of a contributor to a controversy, one cannot find out about his attitude. Gloning (2005:273) offers a more detailed classification of these communication principles in the Early Modern Period:

a) Principles governing the repertoire of moves:
Gloning (2005:273) states that in Early Modern Controversies' principles governing the repertoire of moves, a super maxim was followed in a certain range of controversies that states that any person-related moves, with the exception of those related to aspects of the subject matter, should be avoided. The functional background for such a principle is due to the fact that most person-related moves do not make any fruitful contribution to the achievement of the goal of the controversy. Gloning (2005:273) adds that another super-maxim was to avoid expression of disrespect. This super-maxim was followed since the expressions of disrespect do not help to achieve the goal of a controversy and prevent the achievement of goals, such as improvement of knowledge. However, Gloning explains that there are two restrictions to this generalization: first, a group of person-related moves is admissible that is related to aspects of the subject matter as well. Gloning provides the example of accusing someone of not having linguistic competence in foreign languages, as such a lack leads to a wrong interpretation of a text used in a controversy or of lacking knowledge. Second, in Early Modern Controversies the global goal was to depreciate and to 'intellectually obliterate' the opponent. Gloning (2005:274) explains that in such situations, person-related moves were common.

b) Principles about communicative attitudes of controversialists:
Gloning (2005:274) explains that Early Modern theories of controversy often contain communicative principles specifying attitudes of controversialists, be it in the form of criticism against people violating such principles or as the portrayal of communicative ideas. As recommended attitudes, Gloning (2005:274) mentions politeness, respect, tolerance, benevolence in the interpretation of the opponent's utterances, moderation, a 'professional' spirit of criticism to criticize fairly and to accept criticism, the ability to change one's opinion, freedom from personal motives, freedom from passion, or a principle of control of emotion in public speech. As violations of the above-mentioned principles, Gloning mentions the spirit of revenge, quarrelsomeness, pride, or arrogance.

Table 5.2: A set of communication principles used in Early Modern Controversies identified by Gloning (2005:274).

Communication principles in Early Modern Controversies	
Goals	- to get rid of certain aspects of the subject in the communication
1) Principles governing the repertoire of moves	- to avoid person-related moves - to avoid expressions of disrespect
2) Principles about communicative attitudes of controversialists	Recommended attitudes: - politeness - respect - tolerance - benevolence in the interpretation of the opponent's utterances - moderation - a 'professional' spirit of criticism to criticize fairly and to accept criticism - the ability to change one's opinion - freedom from personal motives - freedom from passion or a principle of control of emotion in public speech

Other researchers have also found different communication principles in different types of controversies in the Early Modern Period. Fritz (2007) offers an open list and a mixed collection of types of communication principles that are regularly pointed out in Early Modern controversies. Fritz explains that these communication principles could be organized into different groups, such as logical principles, dialectical principles, rhetorical principles, hermeneutical principles, principles of text production, linguistic principles, and politeness principles. However, Fritz warns that these principles can only provide a vague indication of the type and background of the respective principles. Fritz (2007) provides the following list for the principles that were to be respected in Early Modern Controversies:

"a) statements should be truthful, b) claims should be given adequate backing (one should not make nudae assertiones or 'naked assertions'), c) the critic carries the burden of proof (principle of onus probandi), d) claims should be refuted point by point (principles of completeness and thoroughness), e) one should state the main question (the status controversiae) clearly and correctly, f) one should relate one's arguments to the main question, g) one should avoid irrelevant topics, h) one should avoid unnecessary repetition of arguments, i) one should be brief (the principle of brevity, amabilis brevitas), j) one should write clearly and comprehensibly (the principle of perspicuity), k) one should not use meaningless jargon (e.g. scholastic terminology), l) one should avoid formal fallacies (e.g. a particulari ad universale), m) if considered necessary, one should set out the arguments 'in form' (i.e. in the explicit form of a syllogism), n) one should not rely (exclusively) on arguments from authority, o) one should avoid personal attacks (ad hominem), p) one may (or one should) not retort in kind (retorsio), q) one should give a reasonable interpretation to the utterances of the opponent (principle of charity), r) one should take the perspective of the other party (la place d'autruy), s) one should not make fun of the opponent and should take his arguments seriously (principle of seriousness), t) one should not use rhetorical devices, such as irony or sarcasm, u) one should be polite towards the opponent (politeness principles), v) one should approach the opponent in a spirit of Christian meekness (cf. Matthew 5: 5), and w) one should be tolerant towards one's opponents."

Table 5.3: General communication principles in Early Modern Controversies identified by Fritz (2007).

Principles in Early Modern Controversies	
a) Principle of making truthful statements	m) Principle of setting out the arguments in form
b) Principle of not making naked assertions (*nudae assertiones*)	n) Principle of not solely relying on arguments from authority
c) Principle of *onus probandi*	o) Principle of avoiding personal attacks (*ad hominem*)
d) Principles of completeness and thoroughness	p) Principle of not retorting in kind (*retorsio*)
e) Principle of stating the main question (the *status controversiae*) clearly and completely	q) Principle of charity
f) Principle of relating the argument to the main question	r) Principle of taking the perspective of the other party (*la place d'autruy*)
g) Principle of avoiding irrelevant topics	s) Principle of seriousness
h) Principle of avoiding unnecessary repetition of arguments	t) Principle of not using particular rhetorical devices, such as irony or sarcasm
i) Principle of brevity (*amabilis brevitas*)	u) Principle of politeness
j) Principle of perspicuity	v) Principle of approaching the opponent in a spirit of Christian meekness
k) Principle of not using meaningless jargon	w) Principle of tolerance towards one's opponent
l) Principle of avoiding formal fallacies	

Fritz (2007) explains that a first group of principles, including the backing of assertions, the burden of proof, the point-by-point principle, the principles concerning fallacies, and a number of relevance principles, belongs to the essential core of principles that are conveyed within the tradition of academic disputation at all European universities during the Early Modern Age. These principles were also transferred and used in controversies outside university life and, hence, became the backbone of the common-sense theory of controversy (Fritz, 2007). Regarding the principle requiring the correct statement of the question under debate (formare statum controversiae), Fritz states that the principle is the duty of both participants to follow in a dispute disputation at the beginning of each round.

Pointing out to the role of communicative principles in the history of forms of communication, Fritz (2007) states the following:

a) Contributors to a controversy often violate the principles as often as they follow and mention them. Fritz explains that this has to do with the pragmatic nature of controversies as opponents have different aims and different styles of argumentation, and the presence of an audience also contributes to this phenomenon.
b) Fritz also explains that there is often a conflict of principles, meaning contributors need to find a balance between the advantages and disadvantages of following one principle or another one and, hence, reach a compromise. As an example, Fritz provides the principles of completeness and brevity.
c) Fritz (2007) also points out that some principles are valid for some types of communication or text types and not for others, meaning that a principle such as seriousness is strictly required in some parts of a controversy and less in others.
d) The principle of friendliness shows that the application of principles is to some extent negotiable (Fritz, 2007).
e) Fritz (2007) also stresses that understanding the status of certain principles requires knowing their context of justification.
f) Fritz (2007) also adds that understanding the status of communication principles also requires knowing consequences of their applications.
g) Fritz (2007) also explains that communicative principles and their ranges and modes of application are historically varied and change over time.

Gloning and Lüsing (2002:124) differentiate between the following communication principles that were expressed between J.A. Gehema and M.F. Geuder in a medical controversy in the 17th century:

a) Principles of criticizing: Gloning and Lüsing (2002:124) further divide the principle of criticizing into the following:
    i) the principle of openness towards criticism: this principle states that if someone does not react openly and positively, his behavior will not be acceptable;
    ii) the principle of the burden of proof: this principle states that if someone criticizes without being able to prove the

mistake, his criticism will not be acceptable, meaning that the critic has the burden of proof (Gloning and Lüsing, 2002:126);

iii) the principle of respect when criticizing: criticism should be done in a respectful way, and if a critic does not criticize in this manner, his criticism will not be accepted (Gloning and Lüsing, 2002:127);

iv) the principle of timeliness of criticism: this principle says that if someone does not criticize at the right time, his criticism will not be timely50 (Gloning and Lüsing, 2002:128–129); and

v) the principle of criticizing based on an important reason and principle of constructive criticism: this principle states that if someone does not have an important reason for his criticism, his critical speech act is not acceptable, and when someone criticizes without making any suggestions for improvement, his criticism will not be acceptable (Gloning and Lüsing, 2002:129–130).

b) Principle of text arrangement: this principle says that if someone does not present a topic briefly, the topic will not be clearly presented, and if someone does not explain a topic competently, the topic will be treated in an unqualified way (Gloning and Lüsing, 2002:130).

c) Principles of effectiveness: Gloning and Lüsing (2002:131) divide the principle into

i) the principle of benevolent interpretation: this principle states that if someone interprets the statements of his opponent in a narrow-minded and nit-picking way, the statement of the opponent will not be interpreted in a benevolent way;

50 This is one of the principles that have changed over the course of time. As contributions in online discussion forums are recorded on different threads, any participant at any time can revive the thread and take a critical stance towards any statement, provided that the thread has not been locked and is still open.

ii) the principle of the obligation to answer and boycott the discourse: if someone dismisses the seriousness of a factual debate in his speech, his speech will not justify an answer;

iii) the principle of waiving revenge: this principle says that if someone answers to insult/abuse with more insult/abuse, his statement will not be acceptable (Gloning and Lüsing, 2002:132); and

iv) the principle of objectivity: this principle states that if one does not remain objective in his contribution, his contribution will not be acceptable (Gloning and Lüsing, 2002:134–135).

d) Principles of argumentation: Gloning and Lüsing (2002:135) divide these principles into

i) the principle of the soundness of a claim: this principle states that if someone claims something that is not based on reason or experience, this claim will not be sound;

ii) an inductive false conclusion: this principle states that if someone uses the means that are objectionable in argumentation, his argumentation will not be valid (Gloning and Lüsing, 2002:136–137);

iii) the principle of *elenchus non causae, ut causae*: this principle states that if someone takes a coincidence as the cause in argumentation, the argumentation will not be valid (Gloning and Lüstig, 2002:137); and

iv) the principle of violation of formal logic: this principle states that if someone violates the rules of logic in argumentation, his argument will not be valid (Gloning and Lüsing, 2002:138). The following table shows the principles that were mentioned in the medical controversy:

Table 5.4: Communication principles of a medical controversy between J.A. Gehema and M.F. Geuder in the 17th century.

Communication principles of a medical controversy between J.A. Gehema and M.F. Geuder in the 17th century	
a) Principles of criticizing	i) Principle of openness towards criticism ii) Principle of burden of proof iii) Principle of respect when criticizing iv) Principle of timeliness of criticism v) Principle of constructive criticism
b) Principle of text arrangement	
c) Principles of effectiveness	i) principle of benevolent interpretation ii) principle of the obligation to answer and the boycott of discourse iii) principle of waiving revenge iv) principle of objectivity
d) Principles of argumentation	i) principle of the soundness of a claim ii) inductive false conclusion iii) principle of *elenchus non causae, ut causae*

Although it is extremely difficult to make a classification of all communication principles in Early Modern Controversies, I will suggest a model for a general classification. My model is based on the model proposed by Fritz (2007). Nevertheless, I will extend this model and add argument-related principles to it. My model consists of a) efficiency principles that ensure an efficient way for conducting controversies, b) person-related principles that prohibit personal attacks against opponents, and c) argument-related principles that make sure that participants back up their statements by references. The following table shows all communication principles I discussed in this chapter together in a model.

Table 5.5: A general classification of communication principles from the Early Modern Period.

A general classification of communication principles in Early Modern Controversies	
1) Efficiency principles	
a) Clarity principles	The principle of perspicuity, comprehensibility, and unambiguousness
	The principles of setting out the arguments in form
	The principle of not using meaningless jargon
b) Principles regarding the size of contributions	The principle of completeness and thoroughness (point-by-point principle)
	The principle of brevity (*amabilis brevitas*)
c) Principles of following a clear objective	The principle of stating the main question (the *status controversiae*) clearly and completely
	The principle of avoiding irrelevant topics
	The principle of avoiding unnecessary repetition of arguments
	The principle of the obligation to answer and boycott the discourse
2) Person-related principles	
a) Politeness principles	The principle of respectful and objective treatment of the opponent (avoiding expressions of disrespect)
	The principle of being polite
b) Openness principles	The principle of benevolent interpretation of statements of the opponent (the principle of charity)
	The principle of tolerance towards one's opponent
	The principle of approaching the opponent in a spirit of Christian meekness
	The principle of taking the perspective of the other party (*la place d'autry*)
	The principle of having a professional spirit of criticism to criticize fairly and to accept criticism
	The principle of timeliness of criticism
	The principle of having the ability to change one's opinion
c) Principles of avoiding person-related moves	The principle of avoiding personal attacks (*ad hominem*)
	The principle of being objective
	The principle of freedom from personal motives
	The principle of not retorting in kind (*retorsio*)
	The principle of not using particular rhetorical devices, such as irony or sarcasm
	The principle of being moderate
	The principle of waiving revenge
	The principle of freedom from passion or a principle of control of emotion in public speech

	The principle of seriousness
3) Argument-related principles	
	Principle of avoiding formal fallacies
	Principle of the soundness of a claim
	Principle of truthfulness and honor
	The principle of not solely relying on arguments from authority
	The principle of making truthful statements
	The principle of not making naked assertions (*nudae assertiones*)
	The principle of *onus probandi*
	The principle of *elenchus non causae ut causae*

The above-mentioned classification can be applied to the explicit and implicit rules and principles of the Forum of Swords and the Forum of Ethnographic Swords to find out what categories of communication principles are still used in communication in online discussion forums. Thus, based on the model I introduced for the classification of communication principles of controversies in the Early Modern Period, the communication rules and principles of the Forum of Swords can also be divided into three major categories as the table below shows:

Table 5.6: Communication principles of the Forum of Swords based on the classification of communication principles from the Early Modern Period.

Communication principles of the Forum of Swords	
Efficiency principles	a) Real full name for user IDs b) Real email addresses have to be provided c) Moderated environment; not all individual moves and posts are accepted d) Threads should be accurately marked with their title e) One should not waste bandwidth by using image hijacking f) One should not blat g) Principle of selective quoting h) Sword identification inquires should be done in the forums and not via private messages i) No firearms / guns pictures and posts j) User account deletion policy
Person-related principles	a) Be warm and friendly b) Trolling and abuse of forums is not tolerated
Argument-related principles	a) Posting is a privilege and not a right b) No politics; politics of other sites remain on those sites

There is one major difference between the communication principles in the Early Modern period and the communication principles in online discussion forums that shows the different nature of both sets of rules. In the Early Modern period, the communication principles had to be deduced from behavior and comments of participants. In online discussion forums, the communication principles, i.e forum rules are explicitly stated. Based on the classification of communication principles of the Early Modern Period, the principles of communication of the Forum of Ethnographic Swords can be classified as the following:

Table 5.7: Communication principles of the Forum of Ethnographic Swords based on the classification of communication principles of the Early Modern Period.

Communication principles of the Forum of Swords	
Efficiency principles	a) Discussion and interlinking to any (online) auction is forbidden b) Spamming or intentional business advertisement is strictly forbidden c) Uploading copyrighted pictures without permission and posting pornographic materials are strictly forbidden; no image hijacking d) Making public appraisals on the forum are forbidden e) Decisions made by site / forum administrators and forum moderators are not subject to public debate f) Threads should be accurately marked with their titles g) One should not waste bandwidth by using image hijacking h) One should not blat i) Principle of selective quoting
Person-related principles	a) Flames, insults, bigotry, and threats are strictly forbidden b) Posting controversial topics, such as religion and politics, and trolling are forbidden c) Enjoy the forum
Argument-related principles	a) Legal discussions: discussions about circumventing laws or regulations regarding ownership of edged weapons and their transportation or exportation are not allowed

5.4 The changing nature of communication principles over time

As mentioned in the last section, language principles change over time. Analyzing communication principles, one needs to take into consideration that communication principles are in a state of change. This means that the communication principles that were valid for the Early Modern Period might not be valid today. Although some of these principles might still be valid, some might have changed over time, and some have been abandoned. Regarding this point, Fritz (1995:483) explains that in contrast to philosophers who hold basic conversational maxims as valid, sociologists, ethnologists, and historians of dialogue form stress that many specific communication principles and their modes of application change over time and through history, and, therefore, they are not valid for all times. This change is not surprising due to the influence of new media and general changes in the culture of communication (see Fritz, 2008). Further, Fritz (2007) explains that communication principles are historically variable and subject to historical changes. Although Fritz states that there are traditions of certain principles that have lasted for a long time, such as the Aristotelian tradition of criticizing certain types of fallacies, he stresses that there are obvious changes over time that are associated with social developments, such as the development of social groups, the development of a culture of conversation, or the development of media.

Fritz (1995:483) provides the example of the principle of comprehensibility as a principle that has gone through change and explains that although the principle of comprehensibility can be taken as a very basic principle for many forms of dialogue, its use is noted in fully different ways in courtly conversations of the 17th century and in today's small talk. Courtly conversation asked for a high degree of indirectness, where suggesting and deciphering hidden meaning played an important role. Additionally, at least as far as the surface level is concerned, comprehensibility did not have priority.

Another principle that has gone through changes is the principle of politeness. Fritz provides an example that in 17th century polite conversation, contradicting an equal was a highly problematic move and needed to be combined with face-saving utterances. Further, Fritz (1995:483) explains that one of the striking examples of this is the history of forms of address. Fritz adds that the principle of politeness in regard to the use of compliments changed in the course of the 18th century. According to Fritz, polite people throughout Europe used long and frequent compliments in the 17th century. However, this practice was largely criticized during the 18th century. Not only have the principles of politeness changed over time but also the electronic media has set new demands for the politeness principle. Regarding politeness in electronic discourse, Graham (2007:742) analyzes the expectations of (im)politeness within an e-mail community and concludes that, in that community, the norms of interaction within the community of practice merge with the norms of (polite) interaction within the computer medium to establish a unique set of expectations for what distinguishes polite behavior in a computer-mediated setting. Graham emphasizes that any deviation from these norms often end in conflict, but at the same time, this situation gives the members an opportunity to (re)negotiate the group identity.

Although recent studies in politeness theory have tried to reinvestigate the influential works of Brown and Levinson (1987) and apply their refined framework to a wider range of situations, there is not an agreement on what polite behavior exactly is (Graham, 2007:742–742).[51] Graham (2007:243) stresses that different attitudes towards what constitutes impolite behavior is extremely important as it reveals how a group manages its relationships. This means that by choosing a certain type of behavior, such as polite behavior, appropriate behavior, or impolite behavior, individuals take a stance in relation to a set of community norms that are defined by the group (Graham, 2007:743). Further, Graham (2007:743) stresses that although there have been studies about what constitutes polite

51 For a detailed analysis of (im)politeness in e-community, see Graham (2007:743).

behavior, there have not been studies about what makes impolite behavior.

Graham (2007:743) agrees to some extent with Culpeper *et al.* (2003), who suggest that impoliteness happens when there is intent to attack the hearer and, additionally, that there must be consistency between the context and the interpretation of impoliteness. However, Graham states that this definition does not address situations where there are different interpretations of Speaker intent between the Speaker and the Hearer. Based on the studies of different researchers, Graham (2007:743) stresses that (im)politeness depends on both the Speaker and the Hearer. Based on Mills (2005), Graham (2007:744) emphasizes that perceptions of (im)politeness depend on both inter-actants' assessments of what is considered appropriate within a given context and the prior history that influences those interpretations.

In the study of conflict that happens across 387 messages taken from a corpus of 78,171 e-mail messages sent to ChurchList, Graham (2007:745) distinguishes three factors:

Netiquette: Graham stresses that politeness in an e-mail environment is regulated by expectations of behavior within the online community. Further, Graham (2007:745) distinguishes between three forms of netiquette in this online community:

i) accurate referencing of the content of messages in the subject line: Graham (2007:745) emphasizes that this is even encouraged via FAQ. This rule states that writers should keep their posts 'on topic' and relevant by ensuring that subject lines accurately show the content of a given message. This rule makes sure that readers read messages related to their interests;
ii) another rule of netiquette is not to waste bandwidth[52] because doing so wastes time and money. The principle of not wasting the bandwidth of other sites is also another requirement. In order not to waste the bandwidth of the site, participants are required to post related pictures only. Another rule asks the participants to post the pictures directly on the forum and not

52 Based on Shea (1994:39), Graham (2007:745) explains that bandwidth "is the information-carrying capacity of the wires and channels that connect everyone in cyberspace".

host them on another site and make them visible on the forum dedicated to the study of arms and armor; and

iii) another rule of netiquette says that one should not 'blat', which is re-posting private messages publicly without the permission of the original author. Blatting is considered impolite as it violates the privacy of the original author. All these rules are also expected to be followed by the members of online discussion forums as well. Participants are required to title each new thread accordingly. Failure to do this results in accusation of the violation of the netiquette principle and in reprimands. Participants complain that since the thread was not entitled accordingly, they opened the thread and wasted their time. This is due to the fact that participants only open the links that are of interest to them. Private messages and email should not be posted on an open discussion board, and this is also a principle that is required from members.

Lack of paralinguistic markers: Graham (2007:745) quotes Culpeper *et al.* (2003), who state that prosody can be a significant factor in the identification of a given utterance as impolite. Since prosodic markers and non-verbal cues do not exist in the communication of the e-community, the determination of intent (and impoliteness) can be difficult for the members (Graham, 2007:745).

Participation structure: Graham (2007:745) stresses that an e-mail list subscription is fluid as no subscriber knows exactly who is subscribed to the list and who will read his message. Further, Graham states that one's knowledge of one's audience affects one's behavior in a given environment, and when posting messages to a partially unknown audience, it is difficult to identify and use appropriate, polite behavior.

Additionally, Fritz (1995:484) adds that principles guiding individual types of speech acts are also subject to historical change, and as examples, he provides principles concerning self-praise and asking questions. Fritz explains that conflicting principles deriving from different traditions also existed. As an example, Fritz states that Germanic knights were frequently involved in self-praise, whereas the Christian principle of humility strictly prohibited self-praise. In today's world, the Christian tradition of humility has prevailed in Western cultures although violations of this principle are quite common amongst politicians, artists, and academics.[53] Regarding politeness principles, Fritz (2007) explains that in the Early Modern Period, at least in Germany, Christian ideas shaped an important source of principles, prohibiting face-threatening acts. However, this was used in theory. Fritz (2007) adds that religious principles did not stop priests and other Christians in the 16th century from insulting their opponents.

According to Fritz, in the 16th and early 17th century, people seem to have a higher level of tolerance regarding verbal aggression in controversies in comparison to present-day controversies among academics. As I will show later, a lot of verbal aggression and insults are also used in online discussion forums dedicated to the study of arms and armor. According to Fritz (2007), in the course of the 18th century, one became increasingly aware of inherent problems of the traditional point-by-point principle, and the new discussion of politeness principles seems to weaken the position of the disputation pattern as a scholarly form of communication and the pamphlet as its prototypical textual form.

As mentioned above, one of the principles that has gone through change is the principle of point-by-point refutation. Regarding the principle of point-by-point refutation, Fritz (2007) states that in its strict version, the principle demands that a participant in a controversy should answer a) all the points raised by his opponent, b) concentrate only on those points, and c) respond to them in a given order. Fritz adds that the objective of this principle is to avoid topical chaos. However, this strategy has both advantages and disadvantages. According to Fritz (2007), an advantage of this model is that the principle clearly stated what was expected of the refuting party, and, hence, this principle served as a standard of quality. Fritz explains that the lack of completeness and the lack of orderliness could both serve

53 Regarding the change of question-asking principles, Fritz (1995:484) states that 12th-century German epic texts of rules of etiquette forbid asking too many questions. On the other hand, Fritz (1998:494) explains that contemporaneous, didactic texts advise young people to ask questions freely so that they could overcome their ignorance.

as criteria for criticizing the quality of the opponent's contribution. There are also several disadvantages of this principle. a) In responding to an opponent, an author had to deal with points that he considered irrelevant. This had an inflationary effect, resulting in the production of very long and boring pamphlets. b) Even if the opponent changed the given order by providing arguments as it was inconvenient for him, he would still be suspected of avoiding the issue. c) If an opponent planned to introduce extra information or new claims, he had to integrate them within the existing framework of topics, resulting in rather awkward and badly structured texts. d) And it was very difficult for the readers to understand the line of argumentation if they did not have access to the original text at which the refutation was targeted. Therefore, the authors were obliged to present the opponent's position before they could begin their refutation.

Fritz (2007) explains that when rigidly applied, the disadvantages of the point-by-point procedure tend to outweigh the advantages. Fritz adds that due to these advantages, some authors chose other text types to avoid the point-by-point procedure, such as writing an open letter, addressing those points they considered relevant for their causes. Nevertheless, pamphlets continued to be written by the end of the 18th century, yet they must have appeared old fashioned to contemporaries (Fritz, 2007). Fritz states that examples of the point-by-point procedure can be seen in academic writings and its traces in controversies on the Internet. There are also other sets of rules that seem to have been created during the course of time. One of these rules is a result of the usage of the point-by-point principle in the communication on the Internet. The usage of this principle in the internet has resulted in the creation of the principle of selective quoting that is a combination of the principles of the point-by-point principle and not wasting the bandwidth. The selective quoting principle requires from participants that they should only quote the part of the post they are answering. Especially if the post is long, participants are expected to follow this principle strictly. Hence, the traditional point-by-point principle has been combined with one of the netiquette principles of not wasting the bandwidth to make up a new principle: the selective quoting principle. This principle can be added to the implicit rules of the Forum of Swords and the Forum of Ethnographic Swords shown in tables 2.1 and 2.2.

5.5 Summary

In this chapter, I have shown that controversies in the Early Modern Period were not an anything-goes activity. Moreover, they were ruled and regulated by a set of communication principles. These rules can be generally classified into a) efficiency principles (clarity principles, principles regarding the size of contributions, and principles of following a clear objective), b) person-related principles (politeness principles, openness principles, and principles of avoiding person-related moves), and c) argument-related principles. Any violation or perceived feeling of violation of communication principles would have resulted in a series of complaints and accusations from the participants involved in a controversy.

Communication principles change over time, so they are not valid for all times. Some communication principles are changed, and some new ones are added. There have been different classifications of communication principles from the Early Modern Period. These classifications do not provide a clear-cut classification of all communication principles. The next chapter will also deal with different moves and strategies used in controversies from the République des Lettres to a comparative analysis of the moves and strategies used in controversies in online discussion forums.

6. Individual moves and strategies: from the République des Lettres to online discussion forums

6.1 Introduction

To participate in controversies and to fight the opponents, one needs a set of individual moves and strategies to attack the opponents. At the same time, one needs to be prepared for the attacks of the opponents, hence a thorough knowledge of defensive moves and strategies is required to defend against an opponent's attacks. Although the requirement has always been not to attack the opponent personally and stick to logical argumentation, getting personal has always been the norm as was the case in the Early Modern Period. One needs to take into consideration that all these individual moves and strategies have been subject to rules and principles that have been required of each participant. A number of individual moves and strategies have been used in controversies from the Early Modern Period to the online discussion forums dedicated to the study of arms and armor. Originally, in the Early Modern Period, Leibniz tried to provide a formal structure for individual moves in a discussion, beginning with the initial argument (Latin: *Argumentum*) and proceeding with one or more objections (Latin: *Exceptio*). Objections may be countered with one or more repartees (Latin: *Replica*). Repartees may be answered by one or more retorts (Latin: *Duplica*) (Dascal, 2006:155–156). Fritz (2008:166–167) explains that Leibniz presents this structure in a tree-like figure, and this structure is similar to the traditional view of the course of *disputatio*; nevertheless, Fritz explains that its formalization by Leibniz is very important. In spite of this formalization, many person-related and aggressive moves were used in Early Modern Controversies. Gloning (2005:267) considers person-related moves as the most important aspect of the linguistic organization of controversies in regard to subjectivity and person.[54] Regarding person-related moves, Gloning (2005:267–272) provides a general classification and differentiates among a) aggressive moves: insults, defamatory accusation, b) inherent face-threatening potential of argumentative moves, e.g. contradicting, c) appeals to an audience/to an arbiter/to a sovereign, d) imputation of personal motives, e) moves related to epistemic states and the dynamics of controversies, and f) expression of emotions and personal evaluation.

Participants in online discussion forums use different person-related moves and strategies to explain their points when they are involved in a controversy. Generally, these moves and strategies are designed to render the opponent speechless and, at the same time, to impress the audience. This chapter will deal with different individual moves used in different types of controversies in detail. Additionally, this sixth chapter provides an overview of the moves and strategies that were used in Early Modern Controversies, both religious and scientific controversies, to have a research framework for comparative purposes. The goal of this chapter is to find out whether the moves and strategies applied in pamphlets in Early Modern Controversies are also used in online controversies.[55] This comparison will reveal to what extent the moves and strategies that were once used in Early Modern controversies are still being used in modern times and to what extent the introduction of the new medium the Internet has changed the range of individual moves and strategies and to what extent the new types of individual moves and strategies are used due to the existence of the new medium, namely the Internet. Thus, I will test the results of other studies on individual moves used in Early Modern Controversies to see whether they are also used in controversies in online discussion forums and whether they apply to wider contexts.

---

54 Frogel (2005:157) observes that the subjectivity of judgment is a main problem in philosophical thought as a philosopher should not only consider himself the superior judge of his own beliefs, but at the same time he must convince himself that his judgment shows an objective reality and not a subjective one.

55 In chapter 7, I will discuss the moves and strategies used in controversies in online discussion forums more in detail.

Hence, for the purpose of my study, I adapt this underlying typology of moves and strategies used in controversies in the Early Modern Period to make a comparison of the moves and strategies used in controversies in online discussion forums.

6.2 Moves and strategies used in the scientific controversy between Kepler, Röslin, and Feselius in the 16th century

Regarding the moves and tactics used in the scientific controversy between Kepler, Röslin, and Feselius in the 16th century,[56] Gloning (2002:44) distinguishes between different types of global targets of participants in this controversy: a) the defense of personal honor, b) pursuit of truth and knowledge where the opponent in the controversy is seen as a partner in seeking knowledge, and c) the defense and dissemination of opinion where the opponent is seen as inconvincible. According to Gloning, the goal in the latter is not to convince the opponent but to present ideas to the third party. Gloning explains that when one of these global targets comes to the fore, different types of controversies can be distinguished: a) honor controversy, b) knowledge controversy, and c) propaganda controversy. As will be shown later, the main goal of contenders involved in the two controversies of this study, the *keris* controversy and *nationalism* controversy, is to impress the audience. At the same time, there are also moves to defend personal honor. Hence, the analyzed controversies in online discussion forums are a combination of an honor controversy and a propaganda controversy. At no point does one attain the impression that the participants are interested in gaining knowledge as they keep pushing for their own viewpoints and theories.

---

56 Gloning (2002:35) explains that this controversy dealt with astrology and cosmology and took place between Johannes Kepler, the famous German astronomer and mathematician, and two medical men, Helisaeus Röslin and Philipp Feselius, in the 16th century. For a detailed analysis of this controversy, see Gloning (2002:21-85).

Generally, the moves used in Early Modern Controversies can be divided into two major types: a) the attacking moves and b) the defending moves. Analyzing the scientific controversy between Kepler, Röslin, and Feselius, Gloning (2002:45) states that, on the one hand, participants in the controversy try to present and justify their positions (defending moves), and, on the other hand, they criticize their opponent's position (attacking moves) and try to support their criticism (defending moves). Gloning explains that the prototypical text type of this criticism is the presentation of one's own ideas in the scientific paper, namely a treatise with a systematic, problem-related, thematic structure. Gloning adds that the prototypical text type for criticism and dealing with competing positions is polemic pamphlets. Pamphlets' thematic structures are generally determined with thematic guidelines of texts where competing positions are formulated. Gloning points out that both moves of presenting ideas and criticizing competing positions appear together. As will be shown later, this is also the same with the opening moves in online controversies. When a participant starts a thread to criticize a certain publication by using an opening move, he presents his own ideas and, at the same time, deals with the article or book he is criticizing by quoting parts of it, such as in the case of the opening move by Manolo criticizing the article by Melborn in the *keris* controversy.

Analyzing the scientific controversy between Kepler, Röslin, and Feselius, Gloning (2002:50) states that the range of moves used in a controversy depends on the goal a contributor wants to achieve in the polemical discourse. Gloning explains that, generally, every move that helps someone to reach one's goal is acceptable.[57] However, in spite of this freedom, Gloning explains that there is a collection of moves that belong to the communicative repertoire of a controversialist: a) to formulate a (his own or the opponent's) position, b) to support something, c) to attack the opponent's position, and d) to make a personal attack against the opponent. Gloning (2002:69)

57 Regarding the freedom of choosing every move to reach one's goal, not all of these moves are accepted and tolerated in online discussion forums. The online discussion forums dedicated to the study of arms and armor are moderated environments, which means that very aggressive moves are deleted by moderators and site administrators.

further distinguishes a clarification move as an additional move. Based on Gloning, each of these moves is explained in detail in the following:

a) Formulating an opinion/position: Gloning (2002:51) explains that these moves contain generally three sequential parts:
   i) As a part of the defense of one's own view: regarding this point, Gloning (2001:51) explains that if one wants to express his/her opinion, he needs to support his opinion with suitable means. For formulating an opinion, one needs to follow the principles of clarity and comprehensibility.
   ii) As part of the criticism of competing ideas: according to Gloning (2002:53), formulating a position is also a central part of criticism of competing positions. Gloning states that to criticize the opponent, it was common around 1600 to quote the statements of the opponent, either word by word or a summary of it, and, then, to respond to it. This method plays an important role in the point-by-point principle, where all parts of the criticism of the opponent are quoted and answered, one by one, in chronological order.
   iii) As part of the discussion of hypothetical opinions (what an opponent could say): Gloning (2002:54) states that formulated positions and opinions can also be hypothetical. These opinions are expressed to perceive the possible reaction of the opponent and, consequently, to react to them.

   The move of formulating an opinion/position is used as an opening move in online discussion forums dedicated to the study of arms and armor. In both controversial threads, the *keris* controversy and the *nationalism* controversy, the thread initiators formulate their opinions by criticizing an article, book, or idea written or expressed by their opponents. At the same time, they make use of the quoting function of the forum and criticize the statements of their opponents, point by point.

b) Supportive moves:

Gloning (2002:54) differentiates between six subgroups at the beginning of the 17th century: i) to quote parts of the Bible and their interpretations, ii) to quote old authorities (such as church fathers and physicians), iii) to quote modern authorities, iv) to formulate conclusions, consequences, evidence, and demonstrations, v) to quote experiences, and vi) to provide plausibility arguments. In terms of supportive moves in online discussion forums devoted to the study of arms and armor, the *keris* thread demonstrates a case where referring to the original texts written in Indonesian is not utilized well: there is no reference to original texts about the *keris* written in Indonesian, which is probably due to the fact that none of the participants in the *keris* controversy reads Indonesian.[58] Referring to the original sources in the corresponding language is extremely important as is the case with the Japanese swords in Nihonto[59] circles. Without reference to an original Indonesian source, then, the appeal to authority is not necessarily accurate or trustworthy. However, to refute the opponent's theory and views, Marco posts different pictures of statues from Indonesia and India of people holding daggers and provides this explanation:

(14) Marco: Another Indian depiction of Kali, with the same straight sword (I couldn't find the dates of these last two, by the way).

Marco posts the pictures of Indian deities to prove that they carry a hooked sword with a large pommel and not a sword with a symmetrical wide tip as proposed by Manolo. Confronted with the evidence, Manolo concedes and admits that he did not judge the shape properly but only in one specific way:

58 Note that the *keris* is the traditional dagger from Indonesia, and many publications on the *keris* are written in Indonesian.

59 Nihonto refers to Japanese swords made in traditional ways.

(15) Manolo: So I guess it really is a hooked sword, and not a symmetrical wide tip as I first thought! I revise my above comment on this one point accordingly. 

However, one should note that there are controversial threads in both forums where reference to old, historical texts and manuals are made. Yet references to modern authorities are often made too. For example, Charley makes reference to museum curators and researchers who also share his opinion regarding the article written by Melborn:

(16) Charley: The comments of Dr. Daru (curator of the Museum in Amsterdam) made in his publication on Keris, and of Maren in his article seemed to bear out my impression of the Melborn article.

The examples above show that reference to the Bible is substituted with the reference to modern authorities and also pictorial references. Although one might argue that there is a difference between two sets of references as the first one has a religious nature and is expected to be respected and the second is a scientific line of argumentation, one should note that the mechanisms are the same. In controversies in online discussion forums, some participants expect their opponents to accept the statements of modern authorities without any doubts and questions. If someone does not do that and tries to question the statements of an authority, he/she will be criticized for violating principles of not respecting the authorities in the field and, at the same time, of impoliteness.

c) Attacking moves:

Analyzing the scientific controversy between Kepler, Röslin, and Feselius, Gloning (2002:65) explains that next to formulating an opinion and supportive moves, it could also be a central task within this controversy to check and criticize the opinions of the opponent. Gloning differentiates the attacking moves in this controversy into i) using all types of objections (Gloning names the objection of irrelevance, the objection of untruthfulness, and the triviality of a claim among different types of objections), ii) referring to the problems, such as absurd consequences of an opinion, and iii) using different types of argumentative criticism.

The same type of attacking moves is also used in the *keris* controversy in the Forum of Swords. Charley uses the following objection of irrelevance to attack Manolo:

(17) Charley: Specifically, Mr. Rodriguez claims to have discovered a picture in Wallace's "Malay Archipelago" that completely discredits Melborn's research [. . .]

Charley states that Manolo uses the objection of untruthfulness to refer to Melborn and stresses that Manolo uses dubious and questionable claims:

(18) Charley: His [referring to Manolo's statement] dubious reasoning explained above is evidence that his commentary is questionable.

Other types of objections are also used. For example, David uses the objection of the triviality of a claim, referring to the statement by Paulo:

(19) David: No offense, but if you cannot offer an example (regardless of how awkward it may read or sound) for how millimeters make such a difference, why do you argue the point? Again, no offense.

d) Making personal attacks against the opponent:
Compared to religious controversies, making personal attacks against opponents is rare in scientific controversies (Gloning, 2002:67). Among these moves, one could identify i) the accusation of diminished intellectual capabilities without giving any reasons, ii) doubting the knowledge in a certain language to understand certain texts, iii) accusation of lacking general intellectual capabilities, and iv) lack of special knowledge in a certain field. Gloning (2002:69) describes the personal attack moves in the scientific controversy between Kepler, Röslin, and Feselius:

i) The questions of reputation and honor also play an important role in this controversy.

ii) The rude types of personal attacks used in contemporary religious controversies do not generally happen in scientific controversies, such as in the case of this controversy. If they happen, they will be sharply criticized, such as the reaction of Feselius to the word choice of Schaeres.

iii) There are also moves where personal and objective attacks are closely interrelated, such as when there is an accusation of general intellectual capabilities or when there is a question of linguistic knowledge in order to understand certain texts.

Similar to religious controversies and unlike scientific controversies, making personal attacks is commonplace in online discussion forums dedicated to the study of arms and armor as in the following example where Charley indirectly accuses Manolo of diminished intellectual capabilities:

(20) Charley: When one sets out to analyse a piece of written work, it is best that one sets oneself the task of reading and understanding that written work prior to publishing comments relating to it. Not to do so exposes one to ridicule and to the charge of diminished intellectual capacity.

e) Clarification moves:

Gloning (2002:69) explains that this move is due to the problems of understanding and interpretation in controversies, generally within the field of scientific jargon. Therefore, clarification moves serve i) to describe, in other words, what one meant or did not mean in his previous statement, ii) to characterize the type of linguistic act that describes what one wanted to do or not to do with a previous statement, iii) to modify and specify the degree of certainty, intensity, and the type of argumentation of a statement, iv) to explain the relevant context for the interpretation of a previous statement, and v) to explain central terms in previous statements (Gloning, 2002:60–70).

In the following example, Manolo uses a clarification move to modify and explain the relevant content for the interpretation of his previous statement and, at the same time, to attack the article by

Melborn again. Manolo first admits that he did not judge the picture properly and the depicted sword is, indeed, a hooked sword, but, then, he finds another point in the article to attack:

(21) Manolo: So I guess it really is a hooked sword, and not a symmetrical wide tip as I first thought! I revise my above comment on this one point accordingly. But I'm glad this has been brought up, since it allows me to introduce another difficult issue with "Origin", At the end of "Reasons for Change" we find this:

The decrease in width of the blade caused a deterioration in the capacity of the weapon to cause haemorrhage. In an effort to compensate for this shortcoming a waved form of blade came into being. This waving of the blade had the additional advantage of allowing it to be more easily withdrawn from a wound.

I've practiced stabbing my various kerisses into numerous types of target, and the wavy blades are noticeably more difficult to withdraw – each curve presents a fricative surface which retards the extraction. [. . .]

As I have shown above, some moves and strategies used in the scientific controversy between Kepler, Röslin, and Feselius are also used in the *keris* controversy. In chapter 7, I will provide a systematic analysis of moves and strategies used in online controversies.

Table 6.1: Different moves and strategies used by Kepler, Röslin, and Feselius in their scientific controversy around the 16th century.

Classification of Different moves and strategies used by Kepler, Röslin, and Feselius in their scientific controversy around the 16th century (Gloning, 2002)	
1) Formulating an opinion or position	a) Part of the defense of one's view b) Part of the criticism of competing ideas c) Part of the discussion of hypothetical opinions
2) Supportive moves	a) Quoting parts of the Bible and the interpretation of the sections of the Bible b) Quoting old authorities c) Quoting modern authorities d) Formulating conclusions, consequences, evidence, and demonstrations e) Providing plausibility arguments
3) Attacking moves	a) Using all types of objections b) Referring to the problems [in the line of argumentation or a theory] c) Using different types of argumentative criticism
4) Personal attacks	a) The questions of reputation and honor b) Rude, personal attacks are not used c) Interrelationship between personal attack and objective attacks in some moves
5) Clarification moves	a) Further description of a statement b) Characterizing the type of linguistic act c) Modifying and specifying the degree of certainty, intensity, and the type of argumentation of a statement d) Explaining the relevant context for the interpretation of a previous statement e) Explaining central terms in previous statements

6.3 Moves and strategies used in the religious controversy between representatives of Protestant Orthodoxy and the Pietists and a comparison to online controversies

As I mentioned before, next to scientific controversies, religious controversies were very common in the République des Lettres. Members of the République des Lettres participated in religious controversies in the Early Modern Period and used different strategies and moves to win over their opponents and make a better impression. The background of the religious controversy analyzed by Fritz and Glüer (2001a:56–57) is based on a controversy that was a result of a religious movement that grew around Philipp Jacob Spener, his student August Hermann Francke, and some other followers who intended to improve the practice of piety and, hence, reform the Protestant Church. The reaction of the Official Church to this movement was to enter into a public dispute with Spener and Francke by using the heresy trial. The whole purpose of the heresy trial organized by the Official Church was to excommunicate and condemn or to convert the proponents of the alleged wrong doctrine, advocated by those who were called the Pietists (the proponents of this doctrine long resisted this label) (Fritz and Glüer, 2001:45). Analyzing the pamphlet called the *Verantwortung*, written by Francke in 1707, which was produced during this controversy, Fritz and Glüer (2001a:56–57) point out the following strategies used by Francke:

a) The point-by-point method: this method is used to refute the adversary's arguments in sequence, meaning point by point. As described in chapter 4, this was one of the principles that writers of pamphlets had to follow. Francke uses this method carefully and goes through his adversary's pamphlet, Mayer's *Warnung*, thoroughly. Using this strategy, Fritz and Glüer (2001a:57) find these further applied strategies:

Reference to the writings of the opponent: using this strategy, Francke goes through his adversary's writings thoroughly and adds a refutation to each part he quotes.

The principle of thoroughness of the reply: this principle used by Francke includes both the complete processing of all the points and a comprehensive treatment of each individual point. Fritz and Glüer (2001a:58) explain that this method is very effective in a cumulative procedure; if the first argument fails to impress the reader, maybe the following ones will convince him.

Flouting the point-by-point principle: Fritz and Glüer (2001a :59) explain that many participants in controversies considered the restrictions imposed by the point-by-point principle a hindrance at least since the 16th century. Specifically, when the author's own position was considered necessary, authors disregarded the principle by adding digressions, documentation, or appendices in the proper passages. The restrictions of the point-by-point principle were also observed in other types of controversies.[60] Additionally, as described in chapter 4, to avoid the problems of restrictions imposed by this principle in writing pamphlets, some contesters used other media, such as open letters or polemical sermons.

As I will show later in detail, traces of the point-by-point method are used by participants in online discussion forums. The forums allow the users to quote the statement of another user via the quote function. This way, they can directly react to the accusations and objections of their opponents. It seems that there has been a shift in the rigidity of the point-by-point principle, resulting in a more flexible one. This function resembles the point-by-point method already used in Early Modern Controversies. However, a major difference is that the users involved in online discussion forums do not react and answer all the objections and accusations of their opponents. The fast pace of posting in online discussion forums and the information overload allow the members to avoid and escape inconvenient accusations and objections of their opponents. The following example shows how Manolo is using the quote function by partially quoting Paulo‘s statement to answer and react to Paulo’s post:

60 Gloning (2002:49) explains that from a strategic point of view, the point-by-point principle has the disadvantage: one is reacting to the choice of topics by the opponent in terms of how intensively he deals with a topic and the order of the points chosen by the opponent. Analyzing the scientific controversy over astrology between Kepler, the famous German astronomer and mathematician, and two medical men, Helisaeus Röslin and Philipp Feselius, Gloning adds that one of the strategies used by Kepler to avoid this restriction is to use excursions, such as digressions. These excursions are marked by beginning and end signals.

(22) Menolo:

Quote

That is a long list, but one could make a similarly long list of daggers used primarily in an underarm ***fashion****.*

Yes, but the point is that there's no correlation between grip choice and civilian fighting utility, which is what Melborn implied.

As the example above shows, participants pick and choose a part of the opponent's statements by using the quoting system and answer it. The point-by-point principle has changed into a selective quoting system. As a matter of fact, if a participant quotes the entire post of his opponent, he will likely be criticized by other members for wasting his reading time. It seems that the principle of not wasting the bandwidth and the point-by-point principle are combined into a selective quoting principle. If a contester directly posts after his opponent's initial post, he does not use the quoting system normally as it is clear to whom he is addressing his response. However, as many participants post on a controversial thread, the contester has to use the selective quoting system so that other members know who he is referring to.

b) Characteristic individual moves: Fritz and Glüer (2001a:60) distinguish between the following characteristic individual moves used in the religious controversy between the Pietists and the Official Church:
   i) Direct contradiction: this is a basic defensive move and is used as a direct contradiction of a claim that, if deemed necessary, is backed up by further reasoning.
   ii) Criticism of logical and dialectical defects: Fritz and Glüer (2001a:60–63) explain that these moves are deeply rooted in the tradition of the disputation and differentiate between logical defects, irrelevance, unproven assumptions, false quotations, and distributing the burden of proof.
   iii) Accusation of breaching communication principles: Fritz and Glüer (2001a:63) explain that, as a part of their controversy theory, the participants usually accept certain communication principles, such as the principle of honesty,

objectivity, and certain principles of politeness and dialectic principles (comprehensibility, brevity, or completeness of the refutation). If an opponent considers one of these principles flouted, he can make a complaint. Regarding accusation of breaching communication principles, Fritz and Glüer (2001a:63–64) distinguish the accusation of untruthfulness, which is very explosive in religious contexts. In the case of the accusation of untruthfulness in religious contexts, not only is a communication principle flouted but also one of God's commandments, one of the Christian principles in the Ten Commandments that instructs adherents not to lie, and the accusation of a want of objectivity, which is a global principle, prohibiting different kinds of 'unobjective' and ill-intentioned moves, such as personal attacks, insults, smears, and calumnies. However, Fritz and Glüer (2001a:64) state that breaching this principle is not unusual even in theological controversies.

iv) Refutation with reference to the authority of the Bible: Fritz and Glüer (2001a:66) explain that in religious controversies, the most dangerous accusation is to accuse the opponent of heresy. Therefore, it is important for the defender to show the opponent and the public that the doctrine is in strict accordance with the Bible and with accepted theological authorities (Fritz and Glüer, 2001a:66).[61]

v) Refutation with reference to theological authorities: using this strategy, the defender uses religious authorities that the opponent also respects as a source of reference.

vi) The retort: according to Fritz and Glüer (2001a:69), the retort is a strategy that is used as a counter-accusation and is a traditional move in religious pamphlets.

61 It is important to take into consideration that the use of the argument from authority was also used in a 17th century medical controversy where the traditionalist relies on classical authorities and belittles the value of modern authorities, and the modernist appeals to modern authorities and, at the same time, claims that the appeal to classical authorities is useless or even dangerous (see Gloning and Lüsing, 2002:88).

Some of these individual moves were also used in the Forum of Swords and the Forum of Ethnographic Swords. It is amazing to see these similarities in spite of the passage of time. Some of the traditional moves used in Early Modern Controversies are still used in controversies in online discussion forums. In the following, Charley uses the individual move of contradiction as a defensive move against Manolo in the *keris* controversy:

(23) Charley: What I am asking is this:- if you disagree with Melborn`s hypothesis, then construct an argument against it, and provide solid evidence that will substantiate your argument. This is what you fail to understand:- a hypothesis can never be proven, however, it can be disproven, and if this can be done then the hypothesis can be rejected as false.

In the next move, Charley uses the second move of criticism of logical and dialectical defects that were used in the religious controversy analyzed by Fritz and Glüer (2001a):

(24) Charley: Mr.Rodriguez, I suggest that you first learn about the nature of a hypothesis, and then study the formal method for its falsification. If you are unable to falsify Melborn's hypothesis, then continue your criticism of trivial matters to your heart's content.

The accusation of breaching the communication principles is very common in online controversies as will be shown in the next chapter. Here, I will give an example. In the following, David accuses Charley of breaking the communication principle or the rule of the Forum of Swords that states, 'Be warm and Friendly'. David uses the quoting function of the Forum of Swords to do this:

(25) David:

Fascinating!

Please explain why this is fascinating. I am sure you meant this literally as to do otherwise may be a violation of the "be warm and friendly" rule here at Forum of Swords.

By accusing Charley of breaching the principle of being warm and friendly, David shows that participants take these principles of communication on the Forum of Swords seriously and reprimand any breach or any perceived breach of these principles in their posts. As well, referring to published authorities and museum curators of arms and armor departments and using them as a source of authority is very common in controversies in online discussion forums. This individual move used in online controversies could be compared to the individual moves 'refutation with reference to the authority of the Bible' and 'refutation with reference to theological authorities' that were used in the religious controversy between the Official Church and the Pietists. In the following example, Charley refers to museum curators as an authority:

(26) Charley: Your assertion that I am a supporter of Melborn is very wide of the mark. I chose to involve myself in this discussion not because I carry any brief for Melborn, nor his theories, but because fatuous criticism of a paper accepted by the members of a learned society, noted academics, museum professionals, prominent collectors, and students of the keris has been subjected to carping criticism over a number of years and that criticism has been trumpeted by its author, quite falsely, as a scholarly critique.

The example above shows that some participants consider some academics and museum curators as the source of authority that they can refer to once they are involved in a controversy. Similar to religious controversies, participants in controversies in online discussion forums dedicated to the study of arms and armor use the individual move 'retort' frequently to counterattack their opponents. In the following, Manolo retorts the accusation made by Charley by using this characteristic individual move:

(27) Manolo: I am having trouble identifying your facts because you have embedded them within a framework of opinion. In your last post, even before you recited your arguments, you described my original observations as "inaccuracies", "misrepresentations", and "fatuous criticism". If you could please remove these opinions and focus on the facts, I can more effectively respond to you. Thanks.

Table 6.2: Different moves and strategies used in the religious controversy between the Official Church and the Pietists.

The moves and strategies used in the religious controversy between the Official Church and the Pietists	
1) The point-by-point method	a) Reference to the writings of the opponent b) The principle of thoroughness of the reply
2) Characteristic individual moves	a) Direct contradiction b) Criticism of logical and dialectical defects c) Accusation of breaching communication principles d) Refutation with reference to the authority of the Bible e) Refutation with reference to theological authorities f) The retort

6.4 Moves with characteristic rhetoric of individuality in 17th century controversies compared to moves in online controversies

Looking for indicators of a characteristic rhetoric of individuality in 17th century controversies[62] and analyzing the first person expressions (first-person personal pronoun 'I'),[63] Fritz (2005b:235–247) different-tiates between the following moves: 1) justifying one's entering into controversy, 2) making explicit an aspect of text organization, 3) first-person hedging, 4) contrastive (emphatic) uses (contrastive use in quasi-dialogue and anti-authoritarian use of first-person expressions), 5) self-praise or self-advertising, 6) presenting one's own observations or experiences, 7) misunderstanding and self-interpretation, 8) claiming incomprehension or incomprehensibility of an opponent's utterances, and 9) personal narrative of one's progress from error to truth. Although Fritz admits that other strategies were also used in 17th and 18th century controversies, such as personal complaints about the

62 Note that Fritz (2005b:234) took his examples from controversies in English, French, and German in the period from 1600 to 1800.

63 In chapter 8, section 8.2.3, I will explain the usage of the first singular pronoun "I" and its usage in the *keris* controversy and the *nationalism* controversy in greater detail.

uselessness of controversies, apologies, explaining one's intentions, confessions, and even prayers, he restricts his analysis of controversies to the above-mentioned points.

Some of these moves mentioned above are also used in controversies in online discussion forums. Regarding justifying one's entry into a controversy, Fritz (2005b:238) explains that as involvement in traditional controversies in pamphlets was a time-consuming and exhausting practice, participants in Early Modern Controversies felt that they had to explain why they entered a controversy. This move is also used selectively by some contenders in controversies in online discussion forums. In the following, Charley, who is a new member to the Forum of Swords, justifies his entry into the controversy in the beginning of his first post by appealing to forum members as a new member and as an opponent in this controversy:

(28) Charley: I am a new member of this discussion group, and I have joined for the sole purpose of addressing the inaccuracies and misrepresentations in the comments of Mr. Rodriguez relating to Melborn's article "Origin of the Keris and its Development to the 14th. Century". [emphasis mine]

Regarding the move of making explicit an aspect of text organization, Fritz (2005b:239) explains that this move does not express anything personal but indicates the author's awareness of his writing strategies, and it is very common in Early Modern Controversies. According to Fritz, in Early Modern Controversies, authors were expert writers with excellent backgrounds in rhetoric. This can also be seen in online controversies dedicated to the study of arms and armor. In the following, Manolo makes an aspect of his previous statement explicit by explaining in parenthesis what he meant and, then, addresses his opponent, Marco:

(29) Manolo: (I posted a reply above in between your attachments.) Where is the hooked sword in this statue? I see a straight doubl-edged one on the left (her proper right). [emphasis mine]

As the example above shows, Manolo explains why he posted within his attachments so that he will not be accused of not being patient to see all further posts by Marco. Then, he questions that the sword in the picture is a hooked sword and describes it as a double-edged sword. Fritz (2005b:239) explains that the third characteristic rhetoric of individuality, namely first-person hedging, is used to identify the personal commitment of the author to a certain belief and is an important move in a controversy. Moreover, this move is used as a hedging strategy, is applied to decrease the commitment of a person's claim from a general to a personal level, and, hence, makes the beliefs easier to justify. Personal hedging is often used in online controversies. In the following, Charley uses a hedging strategy to present his view guardedly:

(30) Charley: I suggest that the passage that I identify as the hypothesis produced by Melborn, be examined in an objective **fashion**, addressing the specifics of the proposal. [emphasis mine]

Fritz (2005b:240) differentiates between two types of contrastive (emphatic) uses, namely contrastive use in quasi-dialogue and anti-authoritarian use of first-person expressions. The first one shows contrast of opinion in the typical quasi-dialogical structure of staged polemics. In the following, Manolo uses this move by contrasting the opinion of his main contender, Charley, and his own opinion:

(31) Manolo: This is material worthy of its own thread. Let's return for now to this statement by Melborn and my response.

Melborn:

The decrease in width of the blade caused a deterioration in the capacity of the weapon to cause haemorrhage. In an effort to compensate for this shortcoming a waved form of blade came into being. This waving of the blade had the additional advantage of allowing it to be more easily withdrawn from a wound.

Me:
I've practiced stabbing my various kerisses into numerous types of target, and the wavy blades are noticeably more difficult to withdraw – each curve presents a fricative surface which retards the extraction. [emphasis mine]

Regarding the second type of emphatic use, namely anti-authoritarian use of first-person expressions, Fritz (2005b:240) explains that the formula for this move works like the following: "*Aristotle says that p, but I say that q*". Although this formula is not exactly used in the online controversies that are analyzed in this study, Manolo keeps a critical attitude towards the accepted authorities through the whole life of the *keris* controversy:

(32) Manolo: This is important because the article by Melborn is accepted without question by a certain segment of collectors; they should now be persuaded to abandon this part of the article by Melborn. I performed this analysis to demonstrate why we should not simply accept authorities uncritically – they sometimes get it wrong.

One should note that although Manolo is critical of authorities in the field, he tries to establish himself as an authority as the example above shows.

The next move that is typical of displaying individuality in the 17th century is self-praise or self-advertising. Fritz (2005b:242) explains that 17th century rules of politeness disapproved of self-praise; however, few authors could refrain from praising themselves.[64] This is also the case of controversies in online discussion forums. One should note that participants in such discussion forums spend a lot of time creating an identity and so-called expert status in a virtual world, and, therefore, they not only appreciate being praised but also become involved in self-praise as in the following move where Manolo praises his own theory, the so-called 'Armed Fashion Theory' in two different posts (note that they are separated by [. . .]):

---

64 Regarding 17th century pamphlets, Fritz (2005b:236) points out a strange textual element at that time that was used in dedications, such as formulas like "this humble booklet" ("diese meine geringe Arbeit"). Fritz states that one should not take these expressions at surface value as these expressions are not like expressions of humility; moreover, these expressions are typical expressions of polite self-deprecation that are part of the style of dedications. He further adds that humility was not one of the virtues of the authors of pamphlets of the time; on the contrary, they often praised themselves.

(33) Manolo:
I however had difficulty accepting some of the "Reasons for Change" offered at the end of the essay, and now that I have worked "Armed Fashion Theory" into an articulate form I am ready to return to my assessment of that part of the essay for a more thorough examination. [. . .]
"Armed fashion theory" demonstrated with abundant evidence that weapons change according to the needs of historical context. If the correlation proposed by Melborn above is to be supported by "armed fashion theory" principles, it must go both ways [. . .].

Another move of displaying individuality in the 17th century is presenting one's observations or experiences. Referring to scientific controversies from that period, Fritz (2005b:243) explains that in the field of science the only goal for not following the theory of classical authors was that modern-period authors stressed the importance of their own experiences and their personal observations as instruments of knowledge. In the following interaction between Paulo and Manolo, Manolo uses this strategy by stressing his own observation and theory:

(34) Manolo:
Quote

Manolo – that simply isn't true. It's like saying nobody else except Charles Darwin can ever publish material in support of evolution! In true academic methodology anybody can support or refute an idea no matter who proposed it. With greater or lesser degrees of success depending on the data they have available and their ability of course.

Paulo,
I'm afraid you misunderstood me. Charley is welcome to provide evidence to support Melborn's article if he wants. What I said was that the burden of evidence is on those who assert ideas. Melborn asserted his hypothesis/ theory/idea about keris origins; therefore it is his, or his supporters', responsibility to provide support for it. It is NOT our responsibility as critics to bear the burden of evidence; all we have to do is evaluate the idea critically. [emphasis mine].

Regarding the move of misunderstanding and self-interpretation in Early Modern Controversies, Fritz (2005b:245) states that misunderstanding and possibly intentional misinterpretations often happened in that era. This move attempts to clarify misunderstanding. Fritz (2005b:245) explains that clarifying misunderstanding by providing an interpretation of one's text is a very frequent move in his corpus. This is also the case in the controversies in online discussion forums in my corpus. In the following, Charley tries to clarify his involvement and his previous statements:

(35) Charley: I admit, I did not commence my involvement here with the intention of running a test and creating an example, but as I became aware of the style of "discussion", I realised that I had been presented with an opportunity too good to pass by. [emphasis mine].

Another move displaying individuality in Early Modern Controversies is claiming incomprehension. According to Fritz (2005b:246), on the one hand, this move is an arrogant and aggressive move, suggesting the ignorance of the opponent or that the opponent is expressing nonsense deliberately to fool his counterpart. On the other hand, Fritz explains that claiming incomprehension is also a defensive move that provides the contender in a controversy with a chance to avoid getting involved in a series of scholastic discussions. This strategy is also used in online controversies dedicated to the study of arms and armor. In the following, Charley claims that his contenders did not understand and comprehend the article written by Melborn:

(36) Charley: Some of the contributions to this thread indicate that the contributors may not have read and understood what Melborn wrote in his article "Origins of the Keris". In light of this apparent lack of understanding of the content of the article, I recommend that those who wish to comment upon this article read the article in its entirety, take time to understand what has been written, and then comment. Here is a link to the article: [. . .] [emphasis mine].

The last move showing individuality analyzed by Fritz (2005b:247) in Early Modern Controversies is a personal narrative of one's progress from error to truth. This move means that a person admits that he used to think in a wrong way, but after a while, he discovered the truth, whereas his opponents did not. This move, of course, serves propagandistic purposes. This move shows that the person is praising himself because he has found the truth. In online controversies dedicated to the study of arms and armor, this move is also used. In the Forum of Swords, Manolo constantly pushes for his own theory, called 'Armed Fashion Theory', that he developed later, and he admits that only he could do that due to his critical thinking skills. In different threads, Manolo admits that he believed in the old theories regarding arms and armor, but after having developed his own theory, he dismissed all of them as he saw their inaccuracies. This is a point that has caused many controversial threads any time Manolo is involved in a thread in the Forum of Swords as his contenders from the Forum of Ethnographic Swords feel challenged by his posts. As shown above, almost all of the moves regarding individuality used in Early Modern Controversies analyzed by Fritz (2005b) are also used in controversies in online discussion forums analyzed in this study. The following table shows different moves portraying individuality in different types of Early Modern Controversies:

Table 6.3: Moves containing characteristic rhetoric of individuality in the 17th century.

Moves containing characteristic rhetoric of individuality in 17th century controversies	
1) Justifying one's entering into controversy	
2) Making explicit an aspect of text organization	
3) First-person hedging	
4) Contrastive (emphatic) uses	a) Contrastive use in quasi-dialogue b) Anti-authoritarian use of first-person expressions
5) Self-praise or self-advertising	
6) Presenting one's observations or experiences	
7) Misunderstanding and self-interpretation	
8) Claiming incomprehension or incomprehensibility of an opponent's utterances	
9) Personal narrative of one's progress from error to truth	

As shown, the moves and strategies above show subjectivity. Fritz (2005b:247–248) explains that in the Early Modern Period, subjectivity seems to be a striking feature, and this is very surprising as this period's controversies seem to be extensively governed by traditional rules and principles, such as the principle that one should deal with *realia* and not with *personalia*, meaning that one should stick to the facts and logic and not get emotionally involved. In spite of the existence of these principles, many authors of the Early Modern Period expand on personal experiences, state personal opinions, and describe personal reflections. As with other text types of the modern era, the texts in controversies in online discussion forums show subjectivity. This is not surprising as there are no rules and principles that try to subdue expressions of subjectivity in online discussion forums in particular. The similarities between the moves related to subjectivity in Early Modern Controversy and controversies in online discussion forums are striking as, in the latter, there are rules that prescribe that one should deal with *realia* and not with *personalia*.

6.5 Moves and strategies used in a religious pamphlet war between Protestants and Jesuits in comparison to moves and strategies used in controversies in online discussion forums

Analyzing the religious controversy conducted via pamphlets between Lutheran theologian Lucas Osiander and the two Jesuits Georg Scherer and Christoph Rosenbusch, Glüer (2001:18) explains that the controversy started because of a Jesuit pamphlet that Osiander interpreted as a threat to destroy the Protestants. Both sides entered the controversy believing that their position was right. As a result, a number of aggressive moves, such as accusations, personal assaults, and calumniations, took place, followed by a number of defensive moves with the aim of refuting the opponents' claims and accusations. A striking feature of the religious controversies carried out via pamphlets is the increasing structures of repetition and rigidity of positions, meaning that there are no structures of rapprochement, such as retractions, modifications of one's original position, or showing an improved understanding of the opponent's position (Glüer, 2001:25). Glüer (2001:27) describes the moves and strategies used in this religious controversy by the end of the 16th century as follows:

a) Providing support for claims: this move is used by the accusing party to provide strong support for the charges they made. This move is also used in online controversies dedicated to the study of arms and armor. In the *keris* controversy, Manolo provides three rhetorical questions and answers his own questions himself by providing support and evidence for the charges he makes against the article written by Melborn:

(37) Manolo:

1. Why does he [referring to Melborn] propose speed to be more important for civilian fighters than battlefield fighters?

Wouldn't speed be equally as important to someone fighting in the field as someone fighting on the street? If your opponent is faster than you in making his stab, you're dead either way. In fact, you're more likely to face multiple opponents in battle, so speed would be even more important for quickly engaging opponents in succession. So to offer speed as a reason for the evolution in the civilian keris doesn't make much sense.

2. Why does he assume overarm stabbing is suited for military fighting but not for civilian fighting?

Even a cursory fashion survey shows that a large number of civilian daggers, from a great range of times and places, were used in overarm stabbing. Some examples that immediately come to mind:

* Scottish dirk
* Enga cassowary dagger (N. Guinea) [. . .]

To these we can add other weapons from Indonesia used concurrently with the keris – in Silat systems, they are used overarm to stab downward. So again, "Origin"'s reasoning fails against the factual evidence from history and fashion.

3. Was the form of the keris truly correlated to political change in Java? Armed Fashion Theory demonstrated with abundant evidence that weapons change according to the needs of historical context. If the correlation proposed by Melborn above is to be supported by Armed Fashion Theory principles, it must go both ways: The keris should have evolved back toward a buda-like form when the Majapahit Empire stabilized, at least for the military context. We have no evidence of this, though, and Melborn's argument is explicitly against it – his theory assumes the keris changed permanently.

b) Using texts and giving interpretations: using this move, the opponents quote texts or pictures as proof by using the given scope of interpretation (Glüer, 2001:30). In the controversy between Jesuits and Protestants, when the opponents used texts or pictures as proof, they subtly used the range of interpretation to their advantage. Using pictures and texts and giving interpretations is also a move that is often practiced in controversies in online discussion forums dedicated to the study of arms and armor. At one point during the controversy, Charley criticizes Manolo for not being able to distinguish between a sword with a hooked point and a *keris* based on a picture of a statue. Answering this accusation, Manolo uses the quoting function of the Forum of Swords, and refutes that it is a sword with a hooked point:

(38) Manolo:

Quote

It would appear that Mr. Rodriguez not only has failed to understand Melborn's article, but additionally is unable to distinguish between a sword with a hooked point, and keris. Not only this, but he is unable to discern the difference between the rapier grip used with a keris, and the hammer grip used with a sword intended for slashing, as employed by our Hindu diety.

The blade is not hooked; look closely, and you'll see it is symmetric with a widening near the tip. In other aspects this is very much like the other blades proposed by Melborn as proto-keris, having, in Melborn's own words, "a leaf shaped blade, with greater or lesser waist definition, a distinct central ridge, and splayed blade base". The blade length is comparable to modern keris.

Marco, one of the supporters of Melborn, who helps Charley in the *keris* controversy, posts ten different pictures of statues that hold swords to support Charley's statement that the statue is, indeed, carrying a sword with a hooked point, not a *keris*. He starts the series with the following post, coupled with the first picture of a statue:

(39) Marco: [. . .] One must be very careful in drawing conclusions about historical weapons based on Hindu religious art. The weapons (and other objects) carried by a particular god/godess are indentifying symbols called "attributes", which have a spiritual meaning particular to that god/godess (Shiva, for example, is shown carrying a trident, the implement by which he destroys the universe). Because of their highly symbolic nature, the patterns of attributes are dictated by highly conserved stylistic canons, and so change little over time and place. I located a few other depictions of Durga, and also of Kali, an avatar of Durga. Each is shown bearing a hooked sword with a large pommel,

and in the depiction of Kali, more recent than the others, the evolution of the form is clear.

c) Using sayings and quotations from the Bible: this move is used to win over the readers by using truisms and other generalizations without examination and, hence, presupposing their validity and applying them as arguments (Glüer, 2001:32). As I mentioned before, controversies in online discussion forums dedicated to the study of arms and armor do not deal with religious controversies, and, hence, references to religious books are not made. However, references to the authorities in the field, such as authors and museum curators, are made.

d) The dialectics of defense: Glüer (2001:33–35) points out that the opponents on both sides of a controversy defend their positions by using a repertoire of moves from the area of traditional logic, rhetoric, and dialectics. Glüer stresses that many moves are used in the dialectics of defense, such as direct denial, contradicting the opponent, and raising all kinds of objections against the enemy's arguments. Glüer particularly mentions the following moves: i) uncovering false conclusions, ii) retort, iii) revaluating the enemy's attack (taking on the role of a victim or even of martyr), iv) insinuating bad reasons for moves, v) defusing metaphors, vi) generalized criticism, and vii) dialectical overkill. As I will show later, many of these individual moves are also used in controversies in online discussion forums. Regarding using the move of uncovering false conclusions, Manolo states:

(40) Manolo: Once more, this is not reasonable: If the keris evolved because of political pressures which created rising social violence, it should have continued to evolve once the conditions prior to the change in question were restored. Yet Melborn says it didn't, effectively negating the very principle he stated earlier (that form follows function).

'Retort' is a move that is often used in controversies in online discussion forums. Retort is a move where the attack of the opponent is returned. Thus, retort is a counter-attack. In the following, Charley returns the attack of Manolo:

(41) Charley: It would appear that Mr. Rodriguez not only has failed to understand Melborn's article, but additionally is unable to distinguish between a sword with a hooked point, and keris. Not only this, but he is unable to discern the difference between the rapier grip used with a keris, and the hammer grip used with a sword intended for slashing, as employed by our Hindu diety.

In online controversies that I studied for this research, the move 'revaluating the enemy's attack' by playing a victim or martyr is not used. On the other hand, as I will show in the next chapter the move 'insinuating bad reasons for moves', as an attempt to show that the opponent has violated a certain type of communication principle, is used very often.

The move 'defusing the metaphors' is used when a participant in a controversy uses a negative metaphor to attack his opponent. On the other hand, the opponent defuses the negative metaphor by giving it positive meaning and emphasizing positive aspects of it. The metaphors to describe an opponent are not used in online controversies in this research. The move 'generalized criticism' to weaken the argumentative power of the contenders by stating general judgments on their credibility, reliability, or competence (see Glüer, 2001:35) is a common move. In the following, Charley doubts the credibility and competence of Manolo:

(42) Charley: Mr. Rodriguez, I suggest that you first learn about the nature of a hypothesis, and then study the formal method for its falsification. If you are unable to falsify Melborn's hypothesis, then continue your criticism of trivial matters to your heart's content. This will only strengthen the acceptance of Melborn's ideas amongst those with the ability to understand both Melborn's arguments, and your own.

The move 'dialectical overkill' is used when a participant has the basic problem of having to justify an assumption that is difficult to prove. In the following, Charley does not react to the accusations of Manolo against the article written by Melborn. Instead, Charley decides to use the move 'dialectical overkill':

(43) Charley: Mr.Rodriguez, you have referred to Melborn's "theory". A theory is a hypothesis that has been confirmed or established. Your criticism is directed at a part of Melborn's article that is hypothetical. A hypothesis is supposition. It can be conjecture put forward to account for known facts, it can be a proposition put forward as a basis for argument. A hypothesis is not a theory. I think it was Einstein who said:- "--- a hypothesis is a statement whose truth is temporarily assumed,--- ". I have also noted your objection to my use of the words "misrepresentations" and "inaccuracies". These, Mr. Rodriguez are not opinions, but demonstrable truths. Demonstrable truths, just as it is demonstrable that when somebody claims something to be hypothetical, he does not intend that his hypothesis be understood as theory.

e) Writing for the benefit of a public audience: Glüer (2001:36) explains that many controversies have very much the character of a show,[65] where participants try to weaken the opponent's position and to minimize potential damage to one's own side. Hence, the addressee in many of these controversies is not the opponent but the 'impartial reader'.[66] As will be shown later, this is also the main goal of participants who participate in controversies in online discussion forums dedicated to the study of arms and armor. They try to address a readership that reads their posts.

Table 6.4: The strategies and moves used in the controversy between Protestants and Jesuits.

Strategies and moves used in the controversy between Protestants and Jesuits	
a) Provide support for claims	
b) Using texts and giving interpretations	
c) Using statements and quotations from the Bible	
d) The dialectics of defense	i) Uncovering false conclusions ii) Retort iii) Revaluating the enemy's attack iv) Insinuating bad reasons for moves v) Defusing metaphors vi) Generalized criticism vii) Dialectical overkill
e) Writing for the benefit of a public audience	

65 Hess-Lüttich (2007:1361) defines all conversations that are staged for show and address an audience as "show controversies".

66 This was also the case in a 17th -century medical controversy between a modernist and a traditionalist (see Gloning and Lüsing, 2002:89).

6.6 Using accusations as special moves in Early Modern Controversies and their equivalents in controversies in online discussion forums

Accusations as speech acts are used frequently in different types of controversies; in the following, I will provide a detailed explanation of accusations as they appear very frequently in controversies in online discussion forums as well. According to Fritz (2005:151), accusations are a very common type of speech act that appear both in everyday life and in formal controversies. He adds that answering accusations is a sophisticated type of linguistic practice that should be analyzed from a pragmatic point of view. Analyzing a number of different types of accusations from Early Modern Controversies (such as theological and medical controversies), Fritz (2005:152) classifies accusations as part of a complex family of critical moves in dialogue that contain speech acts, such as reproaching, blaming, complaining, criticizing, objecting, and insulting. Fritz explains that accusations fulfill a number of functions in everyday life, such as disciplining one's children and teaching them the norms people consider important, showing one's moral superiority, asserting one's authority, and trying to win ground in everyday disputes. Further, Fritz (2005:152) expands that in the realm of the pragmatic study of controversy, accusations are the result of a number of remarkable properties and functions. He gives four examples:

Fritz (2005:152) explains that in controversies, accusations are often used as *opening moves*, and due to their nature, they, at times, dominate the structure of the whole controversy.

Fritz (2005:152) also considers accusations as important factors in the *dynamics of controversies* as accusations change a discussion from quiet to sharp polemics. Additionally, accusations are used to change the topic or the burden of proof.

Fritz (2005:152) states that from a dialectical point of view, accusations are considered as typical *ad hominem* moves. Therefore, he explains that the analysis of accusations and answers to accusations contribute to the study of *ad hominem* moves. Based on Walton, Fritz

(2005:152) explains that *ad hominem* moves cannot be necessarily considered as fallacies.

In the process of uttering and answering accusations, Fritz (2005:152) emphasizes the close interrelationship of questions of fact and questions of norm or of principle.

As will be shown later, accusations are used as opening moves in both threads under study in this volume. In the *keris* controversy, Manolo starts the thread by an accusation against Melborn, an author of an article about the *keris*, attacking his theories and assumptions. This is also the case with the *nationalism* controversy, where Eidel opens the thread by accusing another member of the Forum of Swords of having nationalistic ideas. Both threads turn into sharp polemics due to the nature of accusations that completely change the dynamics of both controversies from the beginning. One should note that they are threads in both forums that start as typical discussions where participants exchange information with each other. Some threads can turn into polemical discourse and controversies during the duration of the discussions. However, there is a big difference between those threads and the two threads that are analyzed for this study. The *keris* and *nationalism* controversies become sharp polemics from the beginning due to the nature of the accusations that were used as the opening moves.

Giving more information about the nature of accusations in controversies, Fritz (2005:153) explains that in making a typical accusation, a speaker A accuses the hearer B of having done some action X and at least A will be committed to two assumptions:

A assumes that the action of B was bad, meaning that A thinks that B has violated some norm or principle of action, and,

A assumes that B bears the responsibility for his action.

Based on this simple model, Fritz (2005:153) states that an accusation raises three questions: a) the question of the performance of a certain action, meaning whether a certain action was performed, b) the question of the nature of an action, whether the action was bad, and c) the question of responsibility, meaning whether the accused person was responsible for his action.

Further, Fritz (2005:154) states that answers to accusations typically address these three questions and expands that defendant B could react to A's accusation by undertaking one of the following three moves and another special move. The first three moves explained by Fritz are a) B might *deny* having performed the action, b) B might *justify* his action by making a claim that there is really no reason why he should not have performed that action, and c) B might give an excuse by making a claim that he was not responsible or bears partial responsibility for his action (meaning not being fully responsible for his action). As mentioned above, Fritz (2005:154) also differentiates a special move that is d) B might apologize for having performed the action. Further, Fritz explains that apologizing is a sophisticated move where one tends to lose some points in the accusation game in order to get out of a bad situation in a special argument and to recover one's position in the broader framework of communication.[67]

Some of the moves mentioned above are used in the *keris* controversy. As I mentioned before, the controversy begins when Manolo starts the thread by accusing Melborn of having written wrong theories in his article on the *keris*. Soon, a new member joining the Forum of Swords, named Charley, enters the controversy and claims to be someone who knows Melborn. He uses the move of justification by defending Melborn's theories in his article and states that there is no reason why Melborn should not have written that theory:

(44) Charley: The Melborn article has been lauded by some of the foremost researchers and collectors of keris. Although it would appear that not all of Melborn's ideas have been accepted without reservation, nobody has yet mounted any serious challenge to the core issues presented in this paper, nor to its conclusion. Faulty and illogically constructed criticism of the Melborn paper, such as that presented by Mr. Rodriguez, only serves to enhance the status of this ground breaking paper. For those of you who have not yet read the article by Melborn I suggest that you do so at your earliest opportunity.

In another post in the *keris* controversy, Charley apologizes in a sophisticated move to get out of a bad situation that Charley himself

67 Fritz explains that in the religious controversies he studied, "apologizing" is a rare move. Fritz (2005:154) also points to the existence of other standard moves in this context, such as asking for proof, doubting that the accuser is entitled to make a certain accusation, or making counter-accusations.

caused by using aggressive words against his main contender, Manolo, in an earlier post:

(45) Charley: I accept your objection to my use of the word "fatuous" to describe your criticism of Melborn's paper. Since your criticism on this occasion is concerned with immaterial commentary, then I consider that "fatuous" is probably an accurate word to use. However, since fatuous means "silly and pointless", and since "silly" could be considered to be opinion, I will withdraw "fatuous", with my apologies, and substitute "pointless". Pointless, because you continue to level criticism at commentary, rather than to address Melborn's hypothesis. Your criticism will cease to be pointless only when you directly address Melborn's hypothesis.

Within the framework of controversies, accusations can be both considered as destructive and productive moves (Fritz, 2005:154), meaning that in some cases, such as face-threatening acts, accusations may have destructive effects as they might endanger the continuation of communication, or, in some cases, the participants could get sidetracked by an accusation belonging to a minor part in the controversy and, hence, lose their focus on the core issue of the controversy (Fritz, 2005:154–155). In other cases, on the other hand, by challenging the defendant and forcing him to present his case in full strength, accusations move to the core of the controversy.

Fritz (2005:155) further explains that because accusations are based on (at times hidden) assumptions regarding the validity and applicability of certain norms or principles, accusations may result in important discussions of norms and principles. In some circumstances, accusations can be considered as amusing, at least to the supporters of the accuser and to parts of the audience, and they make debates more lively and attractive to the audience (Fritz, 2005:155). Fritz (2005:155) explains that accusations are frequently used as opening moves in controversies. But, at the same time, Fritz (2005:157) stresses that accusations are not only used as opening moves but are also used in the middle of the proceedings to change the topic or change the tone in an ongoing controversy.[68]

68 Regarding accusations and more aggressive moves, Glüer (2001:18) points out that the goals of the religious controversies by the end of 16th century were "*to make propaganda to harm the image of the opponent, to defeat him before*

Table 6.5: Accusations as a special move used in Early Modern Controversies.

Accusations as a special move used in Early Modern Controversies	
Characteristic moves of controversies	a) Opening moves b) Influencing the dynamics of controversies and changing the topic or the burden of proof c) Typical *ad hominem* move d) Close interrelationship of questions of fact and questions of norm or of principle
Questions regarding an accusation	a) The question of performance of an action b) The question of the nature of an action c) The question of responsibility
Answering to accusations	a) Denying the performance of the action b) Justifying the performance of the action c) Providing an excuse d) Apologizing as a special move

6.7 Summary

In this chapter, I have shown individual moves and strategies that have been used in controversies in the Early Modern Period. Different

the eyes of the public, and to win over the audience to the own side". Glüer (2001:19) adds that a number of aggressive moves, such as accusations, personal assaults, and calumniations, were used in these controversies. To defend oneself and to counter these aggressive moves, a number of defensive strategies, such as refuting the opponent's claims and accusations, disavowing or denying the accusations or resorting to counterattacks, were used. Further, Glüer (2001:19) explains that the participants in the controversy used the whole classical repertoire of moves from syllogisms (reasoning from the general to the specific or deduction) to circumstantial evidence or enthymemes (a syllogism in which one of the premises or the conclusions is not stated explicitly), and sophisms (deceptive or fallacious arguments). Glüer stresses that in this type of controversy, moves such as self-correction, accepting the opponent's arguments, or suggesting a compromise are not used and are not to be expected. Glüer points out that the controversy expands when the opponents falsify quotations, neglect evidence, use non sequiturs, introduce unrelated new propositions, and make repetitions.

researchers have identified different moves and strategies that were used in different types of controversies, ranging from religious controversies to scientific ones. Some of these moves are similar to each other. Generally, one can identify attacking moves and defensive moves.

Depending on the nature of controversies, such as an honor controversy, knowledge controversy, and propaganda controversy, the type of moves change accordingly. Further, defensive moves can be used to support someone or a certain theory. Additionally, supportive moves can be assisted by referring to authorities. Attacking moves can be used to attack the opponent's position or to construct a personal attack against the opponent. Further, other individual moves can also be identified in Early Modern Controversies, and many similar moves are used in online controversies as well. In chapter 7, I will discuss the individual moves and strategies used in online discussion forums dedicated to the study of arms and armor.

7. Individual moves and strategies in online discussion forums

7.1 Introduction

This chapter gives background information about how the *keris* controversy on the Forum of Swords and *nationalism* controversy on the Forum of Ethnographic Swords started. First, I will talk about the global structure of controversies in online discussion forums. I have chosen two threads: the *keris* controversy on the Forum of Swords and the *nationalism* thread on the Forum of Ethnographic Swords. As I will show, I have chosen these two threads as samples of controversial threads that were posted during a period of four months. One of the threads had a much longer life than the other. I will show how many participants took part in the controversy and how many times they posted on each respective forum. Then, I will offer a detailed statistical analysis on the number of posts by each participant, the average number of words per post, the average number of words in the longest post, the average number of words in the shortest post, and the total number of words posted by each participant in the controversy to show the amount of involvement of each participant in the respective online controversy and his/her frequency of participation.

Different individual moves and tactics are used in these two controversies. Participants in online controversies use these moves and strategies as strategic tools to win over their opponents and comprise a number of tactics with different characteristics. I will show that these moves include opening moves, attacking moves, defensive moves, counterattacks, deflecting moves, accusations regarding the violation of certain principles, neutral moves, the usage of rhetorical questions, and the usage of direct questions. These moves and strategies are carefully implemented to gain an advantage over the opponents and to impress the readers/audience.

7.2 Global structure of controversies in online discussion forums

The online arms and armor controversies tend to start as controversy between specialists of the related field and soon turn out to be popular controversy, at times with political and even religious emphasis. Although both forums claim not to tolerate controversial discussions on politics and religion, controversial threads with related topics to religion and politics happen from time to time. As I mentioned before, the Forum of Ethnographic Swords even has an explicit rule prohibiting discussions on politics and religion. For my research, I have collected a corpus of 23,587 words from two different controversies, the *keris* controversy on the Forum of Swords and the *nationalism* controversy on the Forum of Ethnographic Swords, including contributions posted by different members on both forums between October 2006 and January 2007. As will be shown, the nature of these controversies is not to resolve an issue and promote knowledge, thus contributing to better achievements as advocated by Dascal, but they are used to undermine the opponents' theories. Hence, when confronted with hard evidence and references, contributors to the controversies in online discussion forums simply ignore the evidence, twist the argumentation, and stress their points again. As will be shown, the online communities on arms and armor are very close-knit ones, where the members identify with their respective forum, trying to defend the academics and specialists of that forum at all costs. The goal is, then, to impress an audience that is attending/reading the forums. The purpose of this chapter is to study what kinds of tactics were implemented in this controversy and what kinds of key words were used. Furthermore, the purpose of the chapter is to find out which individual moves and strategies were used by members in this controversy.

Gloning (1999:85) describes controversies as a multiform family of different forms of communication that seeks to settle differences or to clarify opposite views. However, it is important to take into consideration that in the case studies presented below, where a long-term controversy has lasted between two online forums specialized in arms and armor, the objective was neither to settle differences nor to clarify opposite views. As this chapter will show, the objective by the majority of members involved in both controversies was to manipulate and exploit weaknesses in the line of argumentation of the opponent group and to gain a victory of ideological and economic value. Moves and tactics are carefully chosen so that a violation of rules of the respective forum does not become apparent. It is important to note that the target audience of both members were not only registered members of both forums, who consist of scholars, collectors, and martial artists, but also a huge number of people who read both forums as unregistered members. The members of this group are known as 'lurkers'. Crystal (2006:57) describes lurkers as people who access a chatgroup (in this case, an online discussion forum) and read its contents, but they do not contribute to the discussion. Crystal names different motives for lurking behavior, such as newbie [a new member] reluctance to be involved, academic curiosity, or voyeurism.[69] This is a fact that has been very well known to both groups participating in controversies in both forums. Therefore, controversies between these two online forums were not only internal fights between scholars and collectors of a small community but also were public debates, influencing the opinion of a larger community in making their buying decisions regarding certain books, published by members of both groups, and even pushing the prices of antique arms and armor of a certain culture.

Gloning (1999:85) states that pamphlets on religious topics published in Germany around 1600 have the feature of being public debates, and this is the same feature that controversies in online discussion forums share with pamphlets of the Early Modern Period.

---

69 Further, Crystal (2006:57) explains that some refer to lurking as spying and differentiates between lurking and "idling". He describes idling as an activity where the member does not try to hide his/her presence from other members of a group. In online discussion forums, registered members can also go into a lurking mode. They do not log in and simply read the posts. In this case, other members cannot tell that they are present on the forum. On the other hand, they can log in and, hence, are visible and still not post. In this case, they are idling.

Therefore, these controversies could have serious consequences, such as a drop in sales of an antique dealer, as the advocates of a certain group stop buying antique arms and armor from a dealer who is supported by another group, or even pushing the prices of a certain private collection down as collectors tend to concentrate on collecting the historical weapons of another culture. As will be shown below, these controversies have a major effect on the daily life of the participants since they spend much time online, engaged in countering and attacking the other group.[70]

As mentioned above, the objective of the controversies between the two online forums dedicated to the study of arms and armor is not to find the truth. Moreover, these controversies share the same features of controversies of German religious pamphlets written around 1600 (see Gloning, 1999:86):

Both groups who participate in controversies on these two online forums fight for an audience, for they both fear that the majority of registered and unregistered members of these two forums will be attracted to the rival forum if they lose face in an argument. This is a feature that is shared with controversies in religious German pamphlets.

Similar to German pamphlets, the participants do not act on behalf of their own convictions and beliefs. It seems that they present the interests of the group they belong to, and, consequently, they adapt themselves to the needs and the goals accepted by the whole group. Moreover, they represent the interests of the forum they belong to. It is important to take into consideration that a number of participants from each forum participate in the rival forum to answer and retort the claims they make against their own forum. It is also important to take into consideration that a certain number of participants cannot post on the rival forum as their IP accounts and addresses were banned by the staff and moderators of the rival forum. In this case, they answer the

70 It is remarkable to see that these features are also shared by religious pamphlets in Germany in 1600: Gloning (1999:86) describes that several theologians spent much of their time writing contributions to ongoing controversies or preparing polemical sermons, and active participation in a controversy could have serious consequences, such as the loss of one's profession or even expulsion.

retorts of the other forum by stating their retorts and answers directly on the forum they belong to.

Similar to German pamphlets, many contributors do not participate only in one controversy, but they are engaged in several controversies at the same time.

Moderators of the respective forums try to remain neutral, yet it is obvious that some of them try to remain loyal with the groups who belong to their forum and support them.

Some of the contributors have changed networks, and, hence, forums overtime, but this seldom happens.

Different tactics are employed to attack rival forums. Some of them are blatant, and some of them are more subtle. Normally, a controversy begins when a member starts a thread, challenging the ideas of a member of another forum that are either expressed on the other forum or written in articles. In the following, I will introduce a number of individual moves used in the *keris* controversy in the Forum of Swords and the *nationalism* controversy in the Forum of Ethnographic Swords.

7.3 Opening moves

Online controversies normally start when a member of the forum starts a thread accusing a writer or other member of the other forum (or the same forum) of something. During this tactic, the thread creator either starts the thread and his accusation move by giving a link to a thread being discussed on another forum and criticizing its contents, or he refers to a published article or book, criticizing it. As will be shown during the comparative study of two different threads, and as a matter of fact almost all controversial threads, similar to religious and medical controversies in the 17th century investigated by Fritz (2005:152), accusations are often used as opening moves, and then they tend to dominate the whole controversy. In the following, I localize and classify many individual moves used in the *keris* controversy and *nationalism* controversy into groups based on the pragmatic function they play.

7.3.1 Accusations as an opening move

In the *keris* controversy, in opening the thread, Manolo first introduces the article by Melborn by providing a link to the Forum of Ethnographic Swords. Then, he uses the citation-and-reply method (selective quoting system). This is a function of online discussion forums allowing the participants to quote parts of the post of a contributor or even place parts of an article in a quote box and answer it. In online controversies, this method is often used when the opponents engage in one forum, challenging each other's views. Referring to the writing of the opponent was also used in religious German pamphlets, which was used as a method of a counter-argument, similar to the traditional method of academic argumentation (see Schwitalla, 1999:117). In the following, Manolo uses the selective quoting principle and cites parts of the article by Melborn, first pointing out the similarities between Melborn's hypothesis and his own 'Armed Fashion Theory':

(46) Manolo:
Quote

> *The political unrest of the late classical period, prior to Majapahit, is also a possible factor in the development of the modern keris from the keris buda. In such times a light, fast, thrusting weapon would tend to be more useful than a weapon used with a slower overarm stabbing action. The lighter weight, and greater convenience of carry of the modern keris would have tended to see this longer, lighter, faster version of the Javanese personal dagger, favoured over the heavier, slower keris buda. Particularly so if the social environment was unsettled, and it was considered desirable to always have a means of defence at hand.*

This should sound familiar to readers of my recent "armed fashion theory" threads; he posits – as "armed fashion theory" does – that access to armed violence redistributes in inverse proportion to social order. He also posits an idea, supported in "armed fashion theory" and elsewhere, that weapon form follows function and that dress imposes constraints on the carry and design of weapons. So far so good, as – like I always say – good theories should reinforce each other.

In the next step, Manolo criticizes the theoretical background of the article by placing some questions and accusing Melborn. Thus, he provides strong support for the charges he makes against Melborn's article (for a similar individual move used in the religious controversies by the end of the 16th century, see Glüer, 2001:27):

(47) Manolo:
[. . .] Why does he propose speed to be more important for civilian fighters than battlefield fighters?

By questioning Melborn's approach to the development of the *keris*, Manolo answers his own question and argues that speed should be equally as important to someone fighting in the field as well as someone fighting on the street, providing further support for his claim.

(48) Manolo: Wouldn't speed be equally as important to someone fighting in the field as someone fighting on the street? If your opponent is faster than you in making his stab, you're dead either way. In fact, you're more likely to face multiple opponents in battle, so speed would be even more important for quickly engaging opponents in succession. So to offer speed as a reason for the evolution in the civilian keris doesn't make much sense.

Manolo continues in his criticism of Melborn's article by challenging Melborn's idea of claiming that overarm stabbing is suited to military fighting and not to civilian fighting. He offers a number of examples of civilian daggers from different cultures, such as Scottish dirk and Arab *khanjar*, that were used in overarm stabbing in civilian context:

(49) Manolo:
Why does he assume overarm stabbing is suited for military fighting but not for civilian fighting?
Even a cursory **fashion** survey shows that a large number of civilian daggers, from a great range of times and places, were used in overarm stabbing. Some examples that immediately come to mind [. . .] Persian khanjar, Arab khanjar [. . .].

In answering the third question and, hence, challenging the writer, Manolo proposes his own theory, namely his '*armed fashion theory*', and argues that weapons change based on the needs of historical context. Manolo claims that the writer of the article fully ignored this fact. This move, of course, bears an inherent face-threatening potential for the writer of the article (for inherent face-threatening potential of argumentative moves, e.g., contradicting, see Gloning, 2005:267). In presenting his '*armed fashion theory*', Manolo engages in self-praise (for the move self praise in historical controversies, see Fritz, 2005b:235):

(50) Manolo:
Was the form of the keris truly correlated to political change in Java?
"Armed fashion theory" demonstrated with abundant evidence that weapons change according to the needs of historical context. If the correlation proposed by Melborn above is to be supported by "armed fashion theory" principles, it must go both ways [. . .].

As I have shown above, Manolo first uses the selective quoting principle to cite parts of the article by Melborn. He partially agrees with Melborn's theory, only to criticize Melborn's theoretical framework later.

The opening move in the *nationalism* controversy is much more subtle and general. Similar to the controversy on the *keris*, the thread starter initiates the thread by accusing a moderator of another forum of having nationalistic ideas. However, the interesting point is that nowhere in his initial thread does he name the person who the accusation is directed at. This is probably due to the fact that he does not want to run the danger of being banned.[71] However, as will be shown, the members of the other forum immediately understood that they were being targeted, and one of them, named Stefano, participated to refute the claims. In spite of being a subtle accusation, the first post is, indeed, a type of accusation and serves as an opening move, and it

71 Note that a more serious danger existed during the Early Modern Controversies as being engaged in such a war of words was not without problems and had to be justified in view of the danger of being charged with instigation to riot (see Glüer, 2001:23).

tends to dominate the whole controversy (for the use of accusations as opening moves, see Fritz, 2005:152).

Another interesting feature of this accusation is that Eidel, as the thread initiator, starts the thread with an apology. This apology is not meant as a true apology: it is important consider that this apology cannot be taken at the surface value, similar to the textual element '*This humble booklet*' used in religious controversies in the 17th century (see Fritz, 2005b:235). The forum member Eidel uses these expressions of apology or hedging, such as '*I am not an expert*', just to create an opening for his opinion and provide his own analysis and criticism. Moreover, these moves can be understood as hedging strategies.

(51) Eidel: Gentlemen,
I owe you an apology for regularly bringing this issue up in a more controversial way than it should be. I also should probably define my position as precise as possible [. . .].

Eidel moves on to the main point of his accusation, namely that being a native does not mean that one can analyze the weapons better.

(52) Eidel: Indeed, the "natives" who study their weaponry have a number of advantages - they know the language, they have access to sources that might not be well known globally and they usually can acquire an access to some collections that "outsiders" do not even know about. However in the same time there is no general rule that a "native" knows his weapons better than a "foreigner". [. . .] In the end a better researcher with a solid educational background will always be a better specialist on swords, independent of his/her nationality, place of birth and so on.

In the same post, Eidel continues with a much stronger accusation, namely accusing the opponents of having accepted money to write certain publications. This, of course, is a very serious charge, which he cannot back up later. One of the key tactics used by Eidel is that he, again, admits that he used the assistance of some 'right-wing Asian political parties for searching for source documents', but he never agreed to any provisions. This is another hedging strategy used by Eidel to accuse his opponent of having accepted the offers of political parties. He does it in a very clever way. He claims that he was offered the help by right-wing political parties but refused, leaving his readers to believe that his opponents should have accepted those offers:

(53) Eidel: Now my second point was not directed for or against the exhibition, I simply referred to a new generation of "scholars" that appeared in the past 20 years. I am myself was often offered money, assistance, publications if I am to agree to promote certain national cause by writing that this nation was inventor of this weapon and was completely superior to the surrounding nations, which were always pathetic and cowardly in comparison, not to mention incapable of inventing new things. I have to admit I have used assistance of the most extreme organizations (which includes extremely right wing Asian political parties) in my search for the source documents, however I never agreed to any provisions or conditions concerning my use of these documents.

Last, Eidel closes his post by saying that talking to village elders and doing field research in the regions of weapon study is not important as one needs to concentrate on the old texts only. This, again, is another accusation and attack on the members of the other forum who have emphasized the importance of the field study and of talking to the native peoples of a given region.

(54) Eidel: Finally, I do believe that all inputs, including speaking to village elders are important, and all of them contain certain biases, but one is better off trusting XVIIth century author on the issue of use of XVIIth century swords rather than XXIst century guru, no matter how "native" the latter is.

This move is a subtle attack by Eidel against his main opponent, a moderator of the Forum of Swords. Eidel insinuates that his opponent discards the 17th century travel accounts of Europeans to Asia and only relies on 21st century accounts of the natives.

7.3.2 Justifying one's entering into the controversy

Normally, participants involved in an online controversy post by attacking and counterattacking each other. Very rarely does a new member who joins the controversy introduce himself. This, of course, can be classified as an opening move. In the *keris* controversy, this strategy was used when a new member joined the Forum of Swords to defend the author of the article, namely Melborn. In doing so, he first introduces himself and justifies his entering into the controversy, and immediately follows with an aggressive move (for the move justifying one's entering into controversy, see Fritz, 2005b:235):

(55) Charley: I am a new member of this discussion group, and I have joined for the sole purpose of addressing the inaccuracies and misrepresentations in the comments of Mr. Rodriguez [note that he uses Manolo's last name] relating to Melborn article "The Origins of Keris".

In the same post, Charley justifies his entering into the controversy by using a non-expert hedging strategy (claiming not to be an expert) that is used by some members in online discussion forums. During this move, the poster claims not to be an expert and then provides much detailed information. This strategy is, of course, used so that the poster can always avoid direct criticism of his statements by claiming that he is not an expert (see also section 7.4.3 about accusations of not having knowledge about a subject):

(56) Charley: I am not a sword collector, my collecting interest is British dueling pistols and double rifles. Until my attention was drawn to this thread I had never visited this site, although I was aware of its existence. I first read the Melborn article when I received a copy of the Journal of the Arms of Australia, in which it was initially published. Until my interest in this article was once again aroused by Mr. Rodriguez's comments my memory of the Melborn article was that it seemed to be a thoughtful and well researched piece of writing on a form of weaponry about which I knew virtually nothing.

The example above shows how Charley uses the tactic of claiming not to be an expert. This is a very clever move because he can attack his opponents through qualified remarks, and if they attack some of his statements, he can always claim that he is not an expert.

7.4 Attacking moves

In both online controversies, the attacking moves comprise a significant number of different tactics. Attacking moves can be considered as conversational violence. Similar to political discourse where politicians use conversational violence as a combined strategy of dominance, defamation, and of enhancing their image (see Luginbühl, 200/:1385), the main contesters involved in controversies in online discussion forums dedicated to the study of arms and armor use a number of strategies to dominate and defame their opponents, and, at the same time, to enhance their own image. Similar to politicians, the aim of the main contesters is to win, but they also want to look like great fighters and fair winners in front of the audience/readers. Similar to political discourse, the development of the topics discussed, the organization of the discussion, and the work on the relationship in controversies in online discussion forums are all subordinate to the goal of winning (for this subordination in political discourse, see Luginbühl, 2007:1385). A very common tactic in attacking moves is to support the criticism of the thread initiator, who started the criticism. In spite of its supportive nature, this move is a veiled attack as will be shown below.

7.4.1 Supporting the criticism of thread initiator

One of the interesting phenomena in controversies in online discussion forums is that after initiating a controversy by opening a thread, members rush to take sides either to support the thread initiator or to counter him/her. In this case, one can easily argue that one of the main differences between controversies in online discussion forums in comparison to the print media is the speed at which controversies develop. Any member involved in an online controversy should be aware that after initiating a controversy in an online discussion forum, his remarks would be immediately challenged and attacked by the members of the other party, raising the level of psychological involvement much higher. In the controversy on the *keris*, another member named Jonathan immediately posts on the thread to support the views of the thread initiator:

(57) Jonothan: [. . .] The Javanese keris in this context follow very nicely the predictions of "armed fashion theory" in that it is largely talismanic weapon directly related to social standing. Javanese society has historically been highly stratified with the strong implication that the purpose of social stratification is to maintain order. The keris was specifically displayed in support of the social hierarchy. [. . .])

His post is followed by another supportive post made by David. In this post, David enhances the level of attacks on the article in question by writing a direct attack, marking his disagreement with an authority, in this case the author of the article (for the move 'marking a disagreement with an authority' in historical pamphlets, see Fritz, 2005:235). In this post, David insinuates that the basic logic of the article is flawed and calls for 'dismantling the myth and misconception, even flat-out lies' (this move can be compared to the move of criticism of logical and dialectical defects that was used in Early Modern Controversies):

(58) David: [. . .] Manolo, These are very good points you make. Critically thinking about any given subject is the key to dismantling myth and misconception (and, sometimes, flat-out lies). In this case, one need only examine the logic of the article in question. Since when would speed of weapon use be more important in a civilian context than a battlefield context? [. . .].

Similar to the keris controversy, in the nationalism controversy, the member Ehud supports the statements of the thread initiator and attacks the members of the Forum of Swords. In one point, he quotes part of the statement of the thread initiator – "*As Eidel said, language fluency is a great plus, but that is all. Even that is not a prerequisite*" – and makes more accusations and aggressive moves, such as:
The ability to read an inscription is not that important. An amateur always remains an amateur [referring to a moderator of the Forum of the Swords, calling him an amateur]. Visiting museums and working with curators is not important [note that he uses the derogatory

statement "*schmoozing with the curators in a native tongue is a laughable hubris*"].

(59) Ehud: Nationalism is a Romanticism in sheep clothes. That is, as long as it does not degrade into jingoism. These romantic aspirations are pretty much obvious: who besides the Americans would collect Civil War swords? Most of the Moro weapon collectors are likely to trace their ancestry to the Philippines and native Iranians would sell their birthright for a true Assadollah shamshir. Nothing wrong about it: we are all trying one way or another to connect with our past. [. . .] The problem starts when one denigrates other cultures or other people: this is not romanticism anymore, just plain vileness. The other side of the same coin is the assertion of ethnic superiority in general and of the ability of only "native" person to understand a particular culture (weapons, in our case). [. . .] As Eidel said, language fluency is a great plus, but that is all. Even that is not a prerequisite: [. . .] The ability to read an inscription is just that and no more. It does not translate into academic excellence or even into academic mediocrity: an amateur always remains an amateur. Most of us here are enthusiastic amateurs (proud to be one!), whether we collect weapons of our ancestors or not. To pretend, however, that one is a true "academician" simply because he or she spent some years traipsing around museums in exotic places and schmoozing with the curators in a native tongue is a laughable hubris. Nationalism, when used wisely, is a good tool; it should be kept in check, however, to prevent its poisonous transformation.

7.4.2 Agreement with friend/friends to support own argument

This attacking move is often used when a contributor receives support from one of his friends. Then, he/she backs up the support to underpin his/her position and to intensify his/her attacks. In retorting Paulo's statements, Manolo posts two different contributions. First, he/she agrees with Jonathan and David by making an aggressive move (for person-related moves as aggressive moves, such as insults, defamatory accusation, see Gloning, 2005:267), and he/she retorts and corrects the statements by Paulo:

(60) Manolo: Thanks Jonathan and David. The impression one gets from Melborn is that this is armchair martial arts – speculating on weapon usage without the benefit of actually trying the techniques out. Every armed combat system I know of teaches knife fighting from both grip positions, for good reason: Both

> grips are used in real fighting. Anyone with even a casual exposure to knifefighting knows that many good techniques can be used with the icepick grip, including wrist and forearm locking techniques at close range. [. . .] But the idea that speed isn't so important in battle really baffles me. Did people in Majapahit Java just go to the field and fight half-heartedly? Come on . . .

It is obvious from the above-mentioned statements that the terms 'armchair martial artist', 'speculation on weapon usage', and 'failure to see the speed on the battlefield' all claim the lack of practical fighting experience of Melborn and can be easily understood as an attack and an insult.

7.4.3 Accusations of not having enough knowledge about a subject

This is a common attacking tactic used by participants in controversies in online discussion forums on arms and armor: to accuse the opponent of not having enough expert or academic knowledge to contribute to debate in an academic environment. In this case, Charley accuses Manolo of not knowing the true meaning of hypothesis. This way, Charley claims that he discovered logical and dialectical defects in Manolo's statements (for the individual move of criticism of logical and dialectical defects, see Fritz and Glüer, 2001a:60–63):

(61) Charley to Manolo: Mr. Rodriguez, I suggest that you first learn about the nature of a hypothesis, and then study the formal method for its falsification.

7.4.4 Insulting

Using direct insults is a very rare attacking move in online controversies on arms and armor due to the moderated environment of both forums. Failure to avoid making insults leads to being banned from online forums. The following aggressive post and attacking move was the main post that led to Ehud's temporary ban. Note that he calls the members of the Forum of Swords a 'Merry Gang of Attack Poodles'. At the same time, he uses the title 'Mr.' in combination with the last name of Stefano Campino to create distance:

(62) Ehud: Mr.Campino, In your comment on Amazon.com (addressed to me), you said: "...we've collected enough material to bury you with your own hate" and threatened to report me to Amazon. Please feel free to add my current posting to the file assembled by you and your Merry Gang of Attack Poodles.

7.4.5 Accusation of making a naked assertion (nudae assertiones)

In the course of the *keris* controversy, at one point David accuses his opponent, Charley, of making naked assertions (*nudae assertiones*) as David states that Charley cannot backup his statements:

(63) David: Why assume things about other people that are unprovable? What Manolo speaks of is provable. Can you offer some examples to support your assertion in terms of millimeters?

The example above shows that David accuses his opponent Charley of attacking Manolo without reasons that can be supported and proven by the audience. Hence, David accuses Charley of making naked assertions.

7.5 Defending moves

These moves include a range of defensive moves and tactics. One of them is to defend the author of the article or book who is being criticized and is under attack.

7.5.1 Defending the author of the article

This move is very common since, after a controversial thread criticizing an article or person is posted, it does not take a long period of time until another person enters the controversy to defend the author. In the next post, Paulo enters the controversy to defend the author of the article, namely Melborn. First, he starts his post by praising the level of expertise of the author of the article and tries to explain the author's line of argumentation of the text by quoting a statement from the author himself. At the end of his post, Paulo stresses that he does not consider the contributors to the controversy, meaning the critics of Melborn's article, as experts:

(64) Paulo: First of all, I think mr. Melborn is a very knowledgable person on the subject of the keris, who is unlikely to just spout off some theories. I hope he can join us in this debate. I would also like to point out that he did start the "Reasons for Change" paragraph with the following alinea: "The development of the keris buda from Prambanan I, and the modern keris from the keris buda can be supported with evidence, and accepted with reasonable confidence. However, the reasons for this development are pure hypothesis. Nonetheless, I would like to present the following for your consideration". I think he is absolutely right about that, and no one can truly claim to know exactly why the keris changed. [. . .] Evolution generally goes only one way. Especially in a rather traditional environment. Don't underestimate the power of simple fashion. [. . .] But casting doubts on a theory isn't as difficult as presenting another and more likely theory. [. . .] I would prefer this someone to be an expert in another but closely related field.

Judging the statements of the participants in the *keris* controversy, it is clear that none of them is interested in resolving the conflict or willing to accept the other's interpretation (see Dascal, 2003:281–282). In the *nationalism* controversy, Stefano, who has been engaged in a number of controversial threads against Ehud, posts an ironical statement against Eidel and Ehud to defend the person under attack:

(65) Stefano: Very interesting to know your opinions. Please keep posting the deepest feeling you have on this matter... Are enlightening.

The example above clearly shows that Stefano is not interested in the opinions of Ehud and Eidel, but he tries to attack them in an ironical tone so that the readers become aware of the *modus operandi* of Ehud and Eidel.

7.5.2 Refutation with reference to the accepted experts and authority

This defensive move is used by some participants to refer to sources of authority and defend the author of an article. Similar to the move of referring to the Bible used in religious controversies (for this individual move in Early Modern Controversies, see Fritz and Glüer, 2001a:64), Charley claims that the authorities on the subject of the *keris* all praise Melborn's article and tries to isolate Manolo and his statements:

(66) Charley: The comments of Dr. Daru (curator of the Museum in Amsterdam) made in his publication on Keris,, and of Maren in his article seemed to bear out my impression of the Melborn article. That is, until I read the comments of Mr. Rodriguez. These comments forced me to ask myself what it was that Mr. Rodriguez had read that I, and apparently Daru and Maren, had not.

7.6 Counterattacks

In online controversies, counterattacks are used to attack the opponent. Counterattacks can also be divided into different types.

7.6.1 Retorting and correcting the statements of the opponent by providing examples

In the *keris* controversy, Manolo uses a counterattack against his opponent by correcting his statements. Manolo counterattacks Charley, who tried to defend the author of the article, stresses that the hypothesis of the writer of the article is, indeed, wrong, and suggests that he has uncovered false conclusions in the article (for the individual move of uncovering false conclusions that was used as part of the dialectics of defense in Early Modern Controversies, see Glüer, 2001:27). In the following, Manolo claims that the hypothesis and the conclusion of Melborn were wrong as i) there is no correlation between grip choice and civilian fighting utility and ii) the author fails to demonstrate a correlation.

(67) Manolo: Yes, but the point is that there's no correlation between grip choice and civilian fighting utility, which is what Melborn implied. [. . .] But Melborn propose more than evoltion – he proposed correlation. The correlation is what he failed to demonstrate. [. . .] Yes, but the first step in creating a more likely theory is to sweep away the previous, bad theory, which I'm trying to do here.

Paulo posts after two hours, contradicting and counterattacking the statement made by Manolo and claims that both knife grip positions could not be used in every armed combat system. Thus, he retorts and contradicts the statement by Manolo and provides examples to support his own claim:

(68) Paulo: Except with weapons like the Buginese badik, the Acehnese rencong etc. as well as Buginese and Sumatran keris, among others. [. . .].

Manolo rejects the general statement offered by Paulo and offers his own example, and he continues by reinforcing his aggressive move and counterattack stated previously:

(69) Manolo: It might seem that "pistol" grips are always intended to be held like pistols – with the blade "pointed" like the muzzle of a pistol. But there are a number of arts which use pistol-shaped grips in reverse grip. The so-called Mughal hilt is a good example; its pommel curves downward like a pistol but it is always shown in artwork gripped in reverse.

Manolo, then, moves on and reinforces his previous accusation against the author of the article and claims that 'the armchair speculations' of the author are not supported by any evidence:

(70) Manolo: At any rate, these practical considerations are more useful than the armchair speculations in the article that clearly aren't supported by the evidence. Actual martial arts practice is a component that is well integrated into Japanese and WMA weapons research but generally lacking elsewhere, allowing erroneous ideas like Melborn's to flourish unchallenged.

7.6.2 Using the partial point-by-point method to counterattack

This strategy is used when a participant tries to counterattack the points raised by his opponent. To make sure that all points are answered appropriately and completely, the user of this strategy quotes only the points which serve his/her cause, and counterattacks them. This strategy could also be seen in religious controversies in Early Modern Controversies, where all points of attack of the opponent are quoted and counterattacked accordingly. As I mentioned before, the difference is that the participants in online discussion forums tend to quote the statements of their opponents partially and answer the points they consider important. Hence, I call this a 'selective quoting strategy' (partial quoting system). In the *keris* controversy, Charley tries to refute Manolo's arguments in sequence, meaning point by point. He clearly refers to Manolo's writings and replies to all his critical points, trying to refute them (for the usage of point-by-point refutation in Early Modern Controversies, see Fritz and Glüer, 2001a:56–57). Manolo uses three major critical points that will be presented below. Note that the point-by-point answers provided by Charley in his own post are given after each critical point by Manolo for reasons of clarity:

First accusation by Manolo:

(71) Manolo: 1. Why does he propose speed to be more important for civilian fighters than battlefield fighters? Wouldn't speed be equally as important to someone fighting in the field as someone fighting on the street? If your opponent is faster than you in making his stab, you're dead either way. In fact, you're more likely to face multiple opponents in battle, so speed would be even more important for quickly engaging opponents in succession. So to offer speed as a reason for the evolution in the civilian keris doesn't make much sense.

The first counterattack by Charley:

(72) Charley: 1) At no time does Melborn state that "---speed is more important for civilian fighters than battlefield fighters –" In fact, nowhere in his article does he mention battlefields, soldiers or military action. Conversely, he states "---

such personal weapons were carried constantly (Groenveldt)". Melborn at no time addresses the keris, nor its antecedents, as a military weapon. He only ever treats it in a civilian context. My reading of a number of opinions on the nature of the keris in Java at the time when it was employed as a weapon, indicates that it was never a battlefield weapon, but invariably a personal weapon carried at all times. Melborn suggests that "---the loss of the heavy pommel and refinement of blade form of the Prambanan daggers were changes made to allow more convenient wear of the dagger for someone in the everyday dress of a sarung.---" In other words, the form of the keris owes much to the form of dress of the people who used it.

Second accusation by Manolo:

(73) Manolo: 2. Why does he assume overarm stabbing is suited for military fighting but not for civilian fighting? Even a cursory fashion survey shows that a large number of civilian daggers, from a great range of times and places, were used in overarm stabbing. Some examples that immediately come to mind:
* Scottish dirk,
* Enga cassowary dagger (N. Guinea) [. . .]
To these we can add other weapons from Indonesia used concurrently with the keris – in Silat systems, they are used overarm to stab downward. So again, "Origin"'s reasoning fails against the factual evidence from history and fashion.

The second counterattack by Charley

(74) Charley: 2) Nowhere in the Melborn article does he compare military fighting and civilian fighting. Mr. Rodriguez asks: "Why does he assume overarm stabbing is suited for military fighting but not for civilian fighting" Nowhere in his article does Melborn state, suggest nor imply any such thing as Mr. R asserts he does.

Third accusation by Manolo

(75) Manolo: 3. Was the form of the keris truly correlated to political change in Java?
Armed Fashion Theory demonstrated with abundant evidence that weapons change according to the needs of historical context. If the correlation proposed by Melborn above is to be supported by Armed Fashion Theory's principles, it must go both ways: The keris should have evolved back toward a buda-like form when the Majapahit Empire stabilized, at least for the military context.

We have no evidence of this, though, and Melborn's argument is explicitly against it – his theory assumes the keris changed permanently.

The third retort by Charley

(76) Charley: 3) Mr. Rodriguez asks: – "Was the form of the keris truly correlated to political change in Java?" The answer to that question has suggested that the trend towards modern keris form is associated with the would seem to be that keris form was related to political change in only a very indirect way. Melborn proposes that the form of the modern keris had already started to develop, prior to the period of social unrest that preceded Majapahit. Melborn style of dress adopted by the populace of Java in the period before the 14th century. Melborn suggests that an upsurge in violence in the Javanese community could have seen the modern, lighter keris form employing the faster rapier grip method of use favoured over the older, heavier keris buda form which used the ice-pick grip.

Manolo also uses the point-by-point method to answer and counter-attack the retorts by Charley as well. He answers the main three points by using the quoting system as in the following quotation:

(77) Manolo:

Quote

1) ... At no time does Melborn state that "---speed is more important for civilian fighters than battlefield fighters –"

Please, I'm Manolo-- no "Mr." anything. I'll try to reference your comments to the relevant passages of "Origin".
Melborn implies comments about speed in this qoute: "In such times a light, fast, thrusting weapon would tend to be more useful than a weapon used with a slower overarm stabbing action". Terms such as "fast" and "slow" do refer to speed. You yourself acknowledged this later in your post, when you said, "Melborn suggests that an upsurge in violence in the Javanese community could have seen the modern, lighter keris form employing the faster rapier grip method of use favoured over the older, heavier keris buda form which used the ice-pick grip".

Quote

2) Nowhere in the Melborn article does he compare military fighting and civilian fighting. Mr. Rodriguez asks: – "Why does he assume overarm stabbing is suited for military fighting but not for civilian fighting"Nowhere in his article does Melborn state, suggest nor imply any such thing as Mr. Rodriguez asserts he does.

> The reliefs Melborn uses for discussion of early Java depict military contexts. This is evident from the subject matter (eg. Battles in the Ramayana) and from the equipment, which showns non-civilian weapons (eg. spears and shields). Moreover, he specifically says that the keris evolved to meet the needs of civilians; if it wasn't already present among civilians, it must have evolved from somewhere else – ie. the battlefield.
>
> Quote
>
> *3) ... Melborn has suggested that the trend towards modern keris form is associated with the style of dress adopted by the populace of Java in the period before the 14th century. Melborn suggests that an upsurge in violence in the Javanese community could have seen the modern, lighter keris form employing the faster rapier grip method of use favoured over the older, heavier keris buda form which used the ice-pick grip.*
>
> We already refuted this "faster" argument above. Let's look at both of these explanations. If the "style of dress" was the reason motivating change, then Melborn needs to explain what aspect of Javanese fashion changed to stimulate it. From what we know, the Javanese of the earlier period under discussion (Borobudur-era) and the Javanese of the later period (pre- and early Majapahhit) dressed essentially the same – in loincloths. What was this change in fashion that required redesigning keris hilts and using them "right-side up"?

The above exchange between Manolo and Charley shows that Manolo is using historical facts to attack Melborn's article, whereas Charley uses other facts to defend the article. However, Manolo's position seems to be more based on a strategic move, where he tries to show the weakness of the article by citing different examples, pushing Charley more and more into a defensive strategy.

7.6.3 Accusations of misrepresentation

This is a strategy in counterattacking the opponent in which the participant claims that his opponent has misrepresented the data and accuses him of carping criticism. Thus, the participant counterattacks his opponent by claiming his statements as misrepresented and, hence, irrelevant. In one of his posts, Manolo stresses his points by claiming that Melborn has erroneous views and accuses Charley of simply supporting Melborn without having any reasons:

(78) Manolo: Melborn's speculations could have easily been disposed of with only a little critical reflection. The fact that he didn't do so, and his supporters like Charley above simply take such erroneous views as given, speaks to a larger problem in our research methods: The willingness to take "experts" at face value and follow them without question.

In another post, Charley answers this accusation by claiming not to be a supporter of Melborn in spite of all the contrary evidence. He states that the authorities on the subject support the article in question and further dismisses Manolo's criticism, calling it 'carping criticism' and not true criticism. Thus, he raises all kinds of objections against the opponent's arguments and insinuates poor reasons for moves that serve to generate more ambiguity toward his assertions (for a similar move in Early Modern Controversies, see Glüer, 2001:27):

(79) Charley to Manolo: Your assertion that I am a supporter of Melborn is very wide of the mark. I chose to involve myself in this discussion not because I carry any brief for Melborn, nor his theories, but because fatuous criticism of a paper accepted by the members of a learned society, noted academics, museum professionals, prominent collectors, and students of the keris has been subjected to carping criticism over a number of years and that criticism has been trumpeted by its author, quite falsely, as a scholarly critique. A critique is a detailed analysis and assessment of something. Carping criticism does not constitute a critique.

7.6.4 Apologizing as an answer to the accusation

This move is used as a counterattack and is not a true apology. This tactic that was used in religious controversies is described by Fritz (2005a:152) as an answer to an accusation where the person apologizes for having made the accusation. In the *keris* controversy, Charley apologizes for having called the criticism by Manolo 'fatuous criticism', only to reply and substitute it with another aggressive phrase: 'pointless criticism'. It is obvious that Charley's intention is not to apologize but use the tactic of apologizing as a sophisticated move to lose some credibility in the accusation game in order to get out of a bad situation in a special argument and to recover his position in the broader framework of communication. In this case, he attacks Manolo again by identifying his criticism as pointless.

(80) Charley to Manolo: I accept your objection to my use of the word "fatuous" to describe your criticism of Melborn's paper. Since your criticism on this occasion is concerned with immaterial commentary, then I consider that "fatuous" is probably an accurate word to use. However, since fatuous means "silly and pointless", and since "silly" could be considered to be an opinion, I will withdraw "fatuous", with my apologies, and substitute "pointless". Pointless, because you continue to level criticism at commentary, rather than to address Melborn's hypothesis. Your criticism will cease to be pointless only when you directly address Melborn's hypothesis.

7.7 Deflecting moves

These moves are neither offensive nor defensive in nature and only serve to deflect and ignore the opponent's attacks and accusations. The goal is to avoid the attacks of the opponent by deflecting them without getting pushed into a defensive position and the need to justify oneself.

7.7.1 Claiming incomprehension and misunderstanding of the article by the opponent

By claiming that the opponent does not understand or even misunderstands the views expressed in an article, the participant tries to deflect and, hence, belittle the statements of his opponents. In this case, Charley claims that the contributors (the critics of Melborn's article) did not really understand and comprehend the main points of the article and provides a link to his article that is online:

(81) Charley: Some of the contributions to this thread indicate that the contributors may not have read and understood what Melborn wrote in his article "Origins of the Keris". In light of this apparent lack of understanding of the content of

the article, I recommend that those who wish to comment upon this article read the article in its entirety, take time to understand what has been written, and then comment. Here is a link to the article:

In another place, Charley claims again that his opponents did not read and understand Melborn's article:

(82) Charley: When one sets out to analyse a piece of written work, it is best that one sets oneself the task of reading and understanding that written work prior to publishing comments relating to it. Not to do so exposes one to ridicule and to the charge of diminished intellectual capacity.

7.7.2 Stressing that one is not interested in getting involved in a controversy

This deflective move was also used in Early Modern Controversies. Fritz (2005:235–236) describes this individual move as "personal complaints about the uselessness of controversies". This move is also used quite frequently in online controversies. In the following, Charley complains that he is not interested in getting engaged in any further debate. Nevertheless, he continues the debate by posting more and participating in the controversy, just like the case in religious controversies where participants complained about the uselessness of controversy, but, nevertheless, they participated in it:

(83) Charley to Manolo: In my initial post I made several remarks which expressed my own opinions. You may accept these remarks if you wish, or reject them. Either action is of not the slightest interest to me. I certainly have no intention of engaging in any debate to attempt to convince you or any other person that these opinions are valid. To do so would be to diverge from the core issue, which is to address your misrepresentation and flawed understanding of the Melborn article, and your failure to grasp the way in which a hypothesis is to be approached.

7.7.3 Giving interpretation of one's own words

This is a deflective technique that is used to insinuate that the opponent did not understand the statements of the author, and, hence, the participant provides interpretation of his own words. This tactic was also used during the controversies in religious pamphlets (see Fritz, 2005b:235–236). In the following, Paulo tries to explain what he meant in a previous post:

(84) Paulo to David: I do not say that we shouldn't question a theory. But questions are not the same as questioning someone's expertise. Alan Melborn has a huge amount of knowledge and experience, both practical and scholarly. That is not really open for debate, because the facts speak for themselves.

In the example above, Paulo uses a defensive move by interpreting his previous statements. Paulo explains that by defending Melborn, he did not mean that one should not question a theory, but he was only implying that the person and the expertise of Melborn were being unjustly criticized.

7.7.4 Using repetition

One of the strategies Charley uses not to respond to Manolo's critical points and questions is using repetition. As Manolo's main critical point against Melborn's article is targeted against its theoretical framework, Charley simply claims that Melborn suggested speculation and did not establish any theory that can be rejected:

(85) Charley: Melborn has never produced any theories to account for the reasons that caused a keris to change from the old style of keris, to the new style of keris. Most certainly he has never produced any theories, in the academic sense, to account for the development of the modern keris. He has offered some speculation, along with the invitation to think about that speculation.

Then, Charlie moves on to stress in the same post that Melborn did not propose any theory that can be refuted:

(86) Charley: I repeat: – there is no theory on the development of the keris for Melborn to defend.

In the next paragraph of the same post, Charley admits that Melborn's statement should not even be treated as a hypothesis and even claims that Melborn's statement also falls short of a formally stated hypothesis. Then, he states that Melborn's statements can be treated as a hypothesis due to the author's overarching qualification. As a matter of fact, he is using this repetition to prevent any further attacks on the article by claiming that Melborn's statements are not a part of a theory or even a clear hypothesis. By claiming that the statements of Melborn are neither theory nor hypothesis, Charley tries to fend off and deflect any attack against the article by Melborn:

(87) Charley: However, although Melborn has not produced any theories that can disproven, or proven false, he did, in my opinion, produce a hypothesis which although it falls short of a formally stated hypothesis, I believe may be treated as this because of his overarching qualification that "---the reasons for development are pure hypothesis---".

7.8 Accusation moves related to violations of principles of communication

As stated before, each forum is regulated by a set of rules that need to be followed by each participant. At times, participants accuse their opponents of a violation of agreed principles. These rules can be rules set up by the forum itself as presented before (explicit rules) or rules that are perceived by the participants as important in academic discussion (implicit rules). Sometimes, accusations are so cryptically phrased that only a small number of participants will understand the message and feel addressed.

7.8.1 Accusation of the violation of the principle of being warm and friendly

As was stated before, the Forum of Swords has a set of rules that members have to respect and follow. One of these rules is 'being warm and friendly'. It means that the participants of the forum need to keep a friendly and warm atmosphere and avoid any denigrating remarks. In the *keris* controversy, David refers to the statement 'fascinating' as posted by Charley and accuses him of having violated the principle of being warm and friendly of the Forum of Swords:

(88) David: Please explain why this is fascinating. I am sure you meant this literally as to do otherwise may be a violation of the "be warm and friendly" rule here at the Forum of Swords.

Even one of the administrators steps in during the course of the *keris* controversy and warns all participants to maintain the 'warm and friendly atmosphere' as he clearly sees a violation of this principle:

(89) Daniel: Gentlemen please try and avoid language that is personally insulting. Attacking and defending ideas, theories and opinions is fine but when the focus is on denigrating each other its not acceptable.

7.8.2 Accusation of the violation of the principle of who carries the burden of proof

As already mentioned, one of the accepted principles in Early Modern Controversies is that the critic carries the burden of proof (the principle of *onus probandi*) (see Fritz, 2007). Fritz (2007) explains that the burden-of-proof principle derives from the disputation rules and the basic rules of legal procedure. In the *keris* controversy, there is a heavy dispute between Manolo and Charlie as both have a different understanding regarding who carries the burden of proof. In line with the disputation rules and the basic rules of legal procedure from the Early Modern Period, Charlie states that Melborn does not need to prove anything, but the critic, in this case Manolo, carries the burden of proof.

As I will show in the following, Manolo disagrees and stresses that based on academic standards, the person who suggests a hypothesis, in this case Melborn, carries the burden of proof. Fritz (2007) already refers to this problem and explains that the burden-of-proof principle, as accepted in Early Modern Controversies, lowered the requirements of proof for the proponent as he could strategically use it by upholding a thesis not by proving it but by only refusing the objections of the opponent. According to Fritz (2007), this principle allowed the proponents of a theory to have the possibility to refuse proving a thesis that was seen as a generally accepted one by claiming that, in defending the thesis, one would assume the role of a respondent, meaning that one could hide behind this principle without providing any proof for one's own statements.[72]

Fritz (2007) explains that this principle tends to promote and favor traditional points of view as opposed to new points of view. This is exactly the same thing that happens during the *keris* controversy. By referring to the burden-of-proof principle, Charley defends Melborn's traditional standpoint regarding the development of the *keris* that has been an accepted theory among collectors of the *keris* for many years. The debate regarding the violation of the principle of who carries the burden of proof in the *keris* controversy starts when, in his first post, Charley claims that Manolo does not understand the true nature of a hypothesis:

(90) Charley: A hypothesis is a supposition or explanation made on the basis of limited evidence as a starting point for further investigation. If a hypothesis is to be of any use to anybody, it is important that it be clearly understood and represented as it is stated. Mr. Rodriguez has failed in his analysis of this hypothesis proposed by Melborn, because of his failure to understand what Melborn has written, which has in turn led to his misrepresentation of what Melborn has suggested.

72 Fritz (2007) explains that this move was already used by Melchior Goeze in his famous controversy with Lessing in the Early Modern Period (for more information, see Goeze, 1893:170).

Manolo retorts by saying that Charley does not respect the norms of an academic forum as, in his opinion, those who suggest arguments have to bear the burden of evidence:

(91) Manolo: Charley, surely you know that the Forum of Swords is an academic forum, and in academia it is the norm for those who propose arguments to bear the burden of evidence, contrary to the position you took above [. . .].

However, Charley disagrees with Manolo and claims that the person who introduces the hypothesis does not need to prove its truth, yet it is the task of the person who challenges and criticizes the hypothesis to prove its falsity:

(92) Charley: Since we are talking hypothesis, it would be well to remember that it is not incumbent upon the person who proposes the hypothesis to prove its truth, it is incumbent upon those who challenge that hypothesis to demonstrate that it is false. You can take issue with as much of Melborn's reasoning as you see fit, but in the end, you must demonstrate that his hypothesis, as it is stated above, is invalid.

In his following post, Manolo strongly challenges Charley's statement and emphasizes that those who make 'hypotheses, theories, or conjectures bear the burden' of evidence in the academic method:

(93) Manolo: In the academic method, those proposing ideas – hypotheses, theories, or conjectures – bear the burden of evidence to support their proposals. Thus Melborn, in proposing his ideas, bears the burden of supporting himself (which he hasn't yet done).

The next post by Charley shows that both opponents have very different ideas of what the principle of the burden of proof should be: Manolo believes that if someone suggests a hypothesis, he/she needs to prove and back up his statements, whereas Charley is of the opinion that the person who criticizes the hypothesis needs to bring evidence against it to prove its falsity. Thus, Charley follows the traditional principle that the critic carries the burden of proof. It is important to take into consideration that in religious controversies during the Early Modern Period, the principle of *onus probandi*, meaning 'the critic carries the burden of proof', was accepted as the norm:

(94) Charley: If you wish to disprove Melborn's hypothesis, then it is up to you to gather the evidence and construct the argument that will disprove that hypothesis. When you have done this, then Melborn's hypothesis can be rejected as false, but not before. It is not up to Melborn to argue in support of his hypothesis, it is incumbent upon you to argue against it, and to support your arguments with evidence.

Nevertheless, Manolo does not accept Charley's statements, and a long dispute ensues regarding who carries the burden of proof:

(95) Manolo: You also asked myself, David to prove our statements against Melborn's. Please understand that the burden of proof is on Melborn because he is the one proposing the theory, not us. He is responsible both for providing the evidence to support his claim, and for addressing weaknesses in its reasoning.

As it is obvious from the above-mentioned statements, some of the principles of the Early Modern Period, such as the principle of *onus probandi*, have survived in modern time. Fritz (2007) states above that some of these principles have become the core of academic disputation that have survived through centuries. Nevertheless, the example of different understandings of the principle of *onus probandi* above shows that participants have different attitudes regarding these principles.

7.8.3 Accusation of the violation of the principle of not making personal attacks

Similar to Early Modern Controversies, participants in online discussion forums dedicated to the study of arms and armor expect that personal attacks should not be made and, hence, should be avoided.[73] Although this principle is not written explicitly in the forum charter, participants expect that all members follow this principle. Nevertheless, the accusation of the violation of this principle is quite common. In one point during the *keris* controversy, David accuses

73 For accusations regarding *ad hominem* moves in Early Modern Controversies, see Fritz (2007).

Charley of using *ad hominem tu quoque* against Manolo, meaning that David accuses Charley of calling Manolo's statement wrong because Manolo disagrees with Charley. While this does address Charley's logic and methodology, it can also be seen as a personal attack:

(96) Quote David to Charley:

> *As can be seen from the above, Mr. Rodriguez has demonstrated his lack of understanding of the nature and meaning of the word "hypothesis". His attempts to discredit the work of Melborn lack substance, because in his criticism of Melborn's commentary, he is in fact doing exactly what Melborn invited his readers to do when he invited them to consider the suppositions that he presented.*
>
> This is not only a straw man fallacy but also an ad hominem tu quoque usage of theory is different from yours, he must be wrong). This is off topic and does not belong here.

7.8.4 Accusation of the violation of the principle of not solely relying on arguments from authority

Fritz (2007) explains that the principle that forbids relying solely on arguments from authority is particularly interesting. In Early Modern Controversies, the modernists denounced the reliance on classical authorities, such as Aristotle for physics, Pliny for natural history, and Glaneus for medicine. Nevertheless, the modernists themselves relied on the expert opinions of modern authorities, which could be held to similar status as older, accepted experts. A closer look at the *keris* and *nationalism* controversies in online discussion forums dedicated to the study of arms and armor shows that the members of both forums differ in their attitudes regarding the reliance on contemporary European travelers' accounts of Asia and Africa and also modern experts considered as authorities. The loyal members of the Forum of Ethnographic Swords tend to rely on these accounts, whereas some members of the Forum of Swords, who are involved in the controversy, believe in taking a critical approach towards these accounts. This leads to a number of controversial threads in both forums on different occasions. In the following, Manolo criticizes the attitude of some members of the Forum of Ethnographic Swords of accepting the theories of some experts without having a critical attitude in the *keris* controversy:

(97) Manolo: Let this demonstration be an encouragement to others to challenge their received "expert" knowledge and hold it accountable to historical evidence and solid reasoning. Just because someone is credible in certain aspects of weapon study doesn't mean we should automatically accept his/her conclusions about other aspects. Each assertion must be judged on its own merits, independently of the person or "expert" asserting it.

On the other hand, in the *nationalism* controversy, Eidel criticizes the accepted tenets of some members of the Forum of Swords who believe that to do research on swords, one needs to travel and understand the native cultures and, hence, criticizes the advocates of modern research:

(98) Eidel: However in the same time there is no general rule that a "native" knows his weapons better than a "foreigner". [. . .] In the end a better researcher with a solid educational background will always be a better specialist on swords, independent of his/her nationality, place of birth and so on. [. . .] In the end I believe that every weapon researcher or enthusiast should be evaluate on her/his personal merit, as well as his/her work. Comments like "he has not been to ...." "what does he know about this culture" and so on should be reserved to the last, editorial section of any critique, [. . .] Finally, I do believe that all inputs, including speaking to village elders are important, and all of them contain certain biases, but one is better off trusting XVIIth century author on the issue of use of XVIIth century swords rather than XXIst century guru, no matter how "native" the latter is.

7.9 Neutral moves

These moves are applied by participants in controversial threads who do not want to take any sides. Hence, they state their opinions in a neutral way. One of the features of controversies in online discussion forums is that, at times, participants post on a controversial thread and do not want to take either side. In this case, these participants do not want to contribute to the aggressive mode of the controversy. In his post in the *nationalism* thread, Tony explicitly addresses the moderators and stresses that he is not interested in contributing to the controversy but simply stating his opinion:

(99) Tony: Moderators: Please take note that I am not trying to rock the boat. The following post is just another view and opinion of one person, or one nation.

Tony, then, moves on to explain that he is critical of the actions of colonial powers against the natives. Although this might be understood as a subtle criticism of Eidel's and Ehud's ideas, one should note that the post is so carefully written that neither Eidel nor Ehud sees the necessity to retort to this post.

(100) Tony: Nationalism is taking pride in the fact that your peoples history is properly documented. Ask the Native Americans if their history has been properly described and documented by the intruders of their land. They have been described as savages, and worse, in history books and in the movies. All they were doing was fighting to keep their land, but get labeled as an enemy. The same can be said about the Filipinos and the Moros. I keep them seperated, because they are seperate. The Filipinos fought to keep their land, but gave in to the Spanish. The Moros fought to feep their land, but never gave in to the Spanish. There were a separate entity throughout the Spanish rule. They followed the Sultan of Sulu, not some King half a world away. The history the Spanish wrote about the Philippines is half truth. Pigafetta was a historian with a penchant of over exagerrating events. Lapu-Lapu had more then 1500 men fighting Magellan's 49 men???? And thats why they lost??? It sounds better to report back to the King that you were outnumbered so greatly as for the reason of your lose.

The way Tony closes his post shows clearly that he does not want to be labeled as non-American, anti-American, or someone who favors local people. Hence, he emphasizes this fact:

(101) Tony: (FYI: I am American born and am very proud to be American. I am in no way demeaning this great country we live in, I just want the written history of my ancestors to be correct).

Tony states explicitly that he is an American so that he can avoid the possible attacks of some members of the Forum of Ethnographic Swords who tend to be very nationalistic. This way, Tony tries to avoid getting involved in the controversy.

7.10 Using rhetorical and direct questions in controversies

Questions in different communication settings play different roles as they have different discourse functions in different situations. For example, questions in advertising discourse are used to challenge and persuade consumers into purchasing certain products, and, therefore, questions in such a communication setting have a rhetorical function (see Leech, 1966:111–112). On the other hand, questions in the courtroom also have a different function as they are not meant for seeking information but for leading up to a final decision (Stenström, 1988:310). As communication in an online discussion forum resembles a dialogue in written form and, hence, all participants can ask questions, the questions asked during controversies in online discussion forums are not like the questions asked in the courtroom discourse and the discourse of news interviews, in which only the examiner and the interviewer are allowed to ask questions (see Stenström, 1988:310 and Jucker, 1986:100). In online discussion forums, each member can ask questions and respond to them.

Surely, different questions can be asked during the course of a controversy. Gloning (2005:270) states that as controversies are communicative events, questions of meaning and mutual understanding are crucial as well. Problems such as questions of word usage, problems of the proper interpretation of utterances, problems of mutual knowledge, problems of vagueness, problems of ambiguity, problems of misunderstanding, and problems of individual language use as opposed to established usage, occur in controversies as well (Gloning, 2005:270–271). At times, participants involved in controversies in online discussion forums ask questions when there is a problem of vagueness or ambiguity and problems of misunderstanding. However, questions also have a fully different function in online discussion forums. Participants ask questions the way politicians do, meaning that they use them to attack their opponents. Regarding questions asked by politicians, Lüginbühl (2007:1386) states that politicians stage cooperative behavior by performing inoffensive speech acts, such as giving advice and asking questions. In spite of the fact that these speech acts look inoffensive on the surface, they often have the implication of serious attacks on the integrity of the opponents, enabling politicians to behave in a competitive way. This is the same with controversies in online discussion forums.

An analysis of the nature of questions and their pragmatic function in controversies in online discussion forums shows that contesters use questions deliberately as a tool to attack, defend their positions, and even avoid answering a previous question. Additionally, moderators and administrators use questions to stimulate conversation in a thread and encourage further participation but are susceptible to the same tactics of participants in a controversy. In respect to the former point, questions asked by moderators and administrators resemble teachers' questions, as teachers' questions have a stimulating function for the students' thought processes, and, at the same time, these questions are used to encourage students' participation and keep the class discussion going (see Dillon, 1988:104).

There are different classifications of the types of questions proposed by different researchers, such as Athanasiadou (1994:562), who distinguishes between a) questions requesting information, b) questions requesting action, and c) unanswerable questions; Freeborn *et al.* (1993:137), who differentiate between three forms of interrogative mood (questions), namely a) yes/no questions, b) wh-questions, and c) tag questions; and Quirk *et al.* (1985:803) and Weber (1993:23), who distinguish between two forms of interrogatives, namely a) yes/no questions and b) wh-questions. Biber *et al.* (1999:203–210) classify interrogative clauses into a) wh-questions, b) yes/no questions, c) alternative questions, and d) question tags.

But for the purpose of this study, I will analyze the questions used in online discussion forums dedicated to the study of arms and armor from a pragmatic point of view and their use in discourse function. Therefore, any type of classification of questions should serve the purpose of how the questions are used in the online discourse. As I mentioned before, communication in online discussion forums is a written dialogue. Thus, in such a setting, questions serve as natural indicators of turn-taking and interaction. This function of questions in pamphlets is already identified by Suhr (2006:29). For her research of witchcraft pamphlets, Suhr (2006:29) tests the hypothesis about whether reporting speech, such as using direct speech and/or dialogue, was used often in the witchcraft pamphlets to increase interaction with the audience. To test her hypothesis, Suhr (2006:29) analyzed four features of spoken language: a) first-person pronouns, b) second-person pronouns, c) discourse markers (including interjections), and d) direct questions. Regarding questions, Suhr (2006:32) explains that direct questions are natural indicators of turn-taking and interaction, and, therefore, a part of spoken language because they normally demand a response from the hearer.

Based on Yule (1996:77), Suhr (2006:32) states that questions and answers make a typical adjacency pair for structuring conversation. One should note that not all types of questions demand an answer from the hearer. Rhetorical questions do not demand an answer from the hearer as, according to Suhr (2006:32), rhetorical questions serve as assertions rather than questions.[74] In her study, Suhr (2006:33) makes a distinction between direct and rhetorical questions because only direct questions have a feature closely linked with speech situations. Davis and Brewer (1997: 141) explain that rhetorical questions may be asked so that their recipients could respond with 'yes' or 'no'. Further, Davis and Brewer state that, depending on how rhetorical questions are framed, rhetorical questions

74 Quirk et al. (1985:825) also state that although rhetorical questions are interrogative in structure, they function as strong assertions. Thus, a positive rhetorical yes/no question resembles a strong, negative assertion, whereas a negative rhetorical yes/no question is similar to a strong, positive assertion, such as *Is that a reason for despair*? (*Surely that is not a reason . . .*) and *Isn't the answer obvious*? (*Surely the answer is obvious*). Davis and Brewer (1997:142) explain that the complexity of rhetorical questions is not because of their form but because of their illocutionary force. This illocutionary force can be an assertion, a prediction, an apology, a request, or a directive.

can invite answers as well, such as 'yes, but', 'yes and no', and 'moreover' or 'no, but'. Nevertheless, Davis and Brewer (1997: 141) also emphasize that the recipient of a rhetorical question is not expected to answer, but the questioner is the one who is supposed to answer the question in case there is an answer. According to Davis and Brewer (1997: 142), a classification of rhetorical questions should include whether the question surely expects an answer, is likely to have an answer, is not likely to have an answer, or is likely under no foreseeable circumstances to have an answer.

For analyzing the role of questions in online controversies, I distinguish between rhetorical questions and direct questions. As mentioned above, the third classification of questions by Athanasiadou (1994:562) is the category of 'unanswerable questions'.[75] Unanswerable questions can further be divided into other categories. Driver (1988:247–248) divides unanswerable questions into a) rhetorical questions and b) vain questions. Rhetorical questions are used by a questioner as rhetorical devices, and although they are answerable, the questioner does not expect any answer; on the other hand, vain questions cannot be answered at all for different reasons, such as in the question *How many drops of water are there in the Atlantic Ocean*? (Driver, 1988:247–248). In my analysis, there is no occurrence of a vain question, and for the purpose of my study, I classify the questions into rhetorical questions and direct questions only.

From a pragmatic point of view, both types of questions, namely rhetorical questions and direct questions, have different functions in the *keris* controversy and also in the *nationalism* controversy. First, rhetorical questions are generally used when the poster does not look for any real answer to his question and uses them

75 Blakemore (1992:114) also points to the existence of unanswerable questions and states that not all interrogative utterances operate as requests for information. Regarding this point, Blakemore (1992:114) quotes Wilson and Sperber, who distinguish between different forms of questions that cannot be answered: a) exams questions, which are meant to assess the examinee's/candidate's knowledge, b) expository questions which are answered by the questioner himself, c) rhetorical questions, which do not expect any answer, d) speculative questions, which do not expect an answer since no one knows the answer yet, and e) guess questions, which ask respondents to take a guess.

as an assertion. Moreover, the poster uses this type of question either to support his/her position or the position of his supporters in a given controversy. Further, I differentiate between two different types of these forms of rhetorical questions. The questioner either answers the question himself/herself (AP = answer provided) or does not provide any answer (NA = no answer). The latter example leaves the reader in suspension, and the recipient is invited to think about the answer himself. Nevertheless, both types of rhetorical questions are used as assertions and do not have the function of information seeking as is the case of direct questions. The following example shows how Manolo uses the first type of rhetorical question, namely the AP type to attack Melborn's article:

(102) Manolo: Why does he assume overarm stabbing is suited for military fighting but not for civilian fighting?
Even a cursory fashion survey shows that a large number of civilian daggers, from a great range of times and places, were used in overarm stabbing.

In the following example, David uses a number of rhetorical questions of the second type (NA) without providing any answers to support the criticism of Manolo:

(103) David: Otherwise, what is the answer? Battlefield participants were not interested in speed? The "evolved" weapon would not be used in overhead stabbing attacks in a civilian context? The weapon would cease to change? One can step back and see problems with such assumptions.

As I analyze my corpus from the point of view of controversies, it is necessary to analyze the function of each type of questions used by the contesters involved in the *keris* and *nationalism* controversies. Each type of rhetorical questions discussed above, namely AP and NA, can be used either to support one's own position in a controversy or a supporter's position in the controversy, or they can be used to attack the position of the opponent. In the following, I will introduce different types of questions and their related functions in each controversy.

7.10.1 Using rhetorical questions to support one's own position or a supporter's position

One of the pragmatic functions of rhetorical questions in controversies in online discussion forums dedicated to the study of arms and armor is to support the original critical idea of the poster or to support the statement of supporters. In this function, rhetorical questions are used to foment and underpin a certain theory. In the following example, Manolo uses a rhetorical question and provides an answer to support his own theory, 'Armed Fashion Theory'. The theory developed by Manolo clearly presupposes that the form of the *keris* was not correlated to political change in Java. This is, of course, a critical approach and against the theory suggested by Melborn's article. To criticize Melborn's article, Manolo formulates his theory by using a rhetorical question and answers the question himself to underpin his own theory:

(104) Manolo: Was the form of the keris truly correlated to political change in Java? Armed fashion theory demonstrated with abundant evidence that weapons change according to the needs of historical context. If the correlation proposed by Melborn above is to be supported by Armed Fashion Theory principles, it must go both ways: The keris should have evolved back toward a buda-like form when the Majapahit Empire stabilized, at least for the military context. We have no evidence of this, though, and Melborn's argument is explicitly against it – his theory assumes the keris changed permanently.

At the Forum of Ethnographic Swords, rhetorical questions with answers are used in the *nationalism* controversy. In the following, Tony uses a rhetorical question and provides an answer to support his own theory. As Tony is critical of the colonial European powers and their exaggerations, he criticizes the statement that the Portuguese sailor in service of the Spanish court, Magellan, only lost to the native Moro king warrior Lapu Lapu because he was heavily outnumbered. Note how he answers his own rhetorical question to underpin his own theory:

(105) Tony: Lapu-Lapu had more then 1500 men fighting Magellan's 49 men???? And thats why they lost??? It sounds better to report back to the King that you were outnumbered so greatly as for the reason of your lose.

Rhetorical questions without providing an answer are also used in the *nationalism* controversy to support one's own position. In the following, Tony uses two rhetorical questions without providing an answer to support his own position:

(106) Tony: How would you like to be told that you are owned by someone you have never heard of? Especially since the Spanish never owned the Moros in the first place?

7.10.2 Using rhetorical questions to attack the opponent

One of the special functions of rhetorical questions in controversies in online discussion forums is to attack the position of the opponent. In this case, a rhetorical question is used to undermine the theory or the line of argumentation of the opponent and leaves the audience to ponder the answer. Rhetorical questions have a very strong critical force. The user either answers the questions himself or does not provide an answer. In the following example, Manolo uses one type of these questions with the function of undermining Melborn's position. The context in the example demonstrates that Manolo is not looking for an answer to this question, but he just wants to show that Melborn's position is wrong (in Manolo's opinion). Note that in his article, Melborn claims that *keris budda* (a keris that has its handle and blade made in one piece and, hence, is a sturdy dagger) was used for overarm stabbing on the battlefield, where speed was not as important as in civilian fighting. Manolo disagrees with this statement by using a rhetorical question without providing a real answer:

(107) Manolo: But the idea that speed isn't so important in battle really baffles me. Did people in Majapahit Java just go to the field and fight half-heartedly? Come on.

In the *nationalism* controversy, Ehud uses rhetorical questions to attack a moderator of the Forum of Swords, who maintains that one needs to be acquainted with the native culture to study the respective weapons. Ehud does not provide any answer either:

(108) Ehud: What innate advantage does, say, Turkish ancestry offer to the ability to study the evolution of Kilijes?[76] Or Moro to kampilans?[77] Or any other to whatever weapon one wishes to designate?

The main contester of Manolo, Charley, also uses a rhetorical question without answer, insinuating that Manolo does not conduct an intelligent and objective discussion in a scholarly way and, hence, attacks Manolo directly:

(109) Charley: Based upon what I have learnt of Melborn, I believe that he would welcome intelligent and objective discussion, conducted in a scholarly fashion, of his ideas. Why do you not attempt to do this?

After providing a number of examples of daggers with large pommels that were used in a downward grip position throughout history that should refute Melborn's hypothesis, Manolo asks a rhetorical question without providing an answer to support his own position:

(110) Manolo: Shall I continue? I can... But it would belabour this already obvious point: The "hypothesis" Melborn proposes regarding the need to eliminate the large pommel to accomodate this **fashion** is unsupported by comparative evidence.

7.10.3 Using direct questions to seek information

Direct questions that generally are meant to ask for answers are also used in different functions in the *keris* controversy and the *nationalism* controversy. One of the functions of direct questions is its general use to seek information. Although direct questions to seek answers are

---

76 Note that a *kilij* is a Turkish type of saber. For a study of Turkish sabers, see Astvatsaturjan (2002).

77 Note that a *kampilan* is one of the traditional swords used by Moros in the Philippines. For more information on traditional weapons used by Moros, see Cato (1996).

posed in the *keris* controversy, they are rare. In the following, Jonathan asks direct questions to ask for clarification and information:

(111) Jonathan: Was there a significant change in metalurgy between the older keris and the "modern" style ? If so stronger metals would allow a thinner longer blade to still have the strength to be used and not deform or break. Wasn't there an evolutional change in blade geometry when weapons went from bronze to iron and steel?

Direct questions to seek information are also used in the *nationalism* controversy. Their occurrence is also rare in this controversy. Only three direct questions with the function of seeking information were asked in the *nationalism* controversy. All three were asked by the member Manuel:

(112) Manuel: Were there any foreign observers at the time? Brits, Spaniards, Dutch and Asians were still active in the region. Are there no accounts from them? You could take them with a somewhat higher degree of impartiality no?

However, in the controversies analyzed for the purpose of my study, the majority of these questions are generally asked from one's own supporters, meaning that a person involved in a controversy asks one of his/her supporters a direct question to underpin his/her own position. In the following example, Manolo asks Jonathan a direct question with the function of seeking information:

(113) Manolo asking Jonathan: Jonathan, you do Silat. Doesn't your system use weapons like tombaks and kujangs in blade-down position?

7.10.4 Using direct questions to challenge the opponent's statements

Direct questions are also asked to challenge the opponent's statements. In this function, direct questions are used to seek information and, at the same time, weaken the position of the opponent:

(114) Manolo to Marco: Where is the hooked sword in this statue? I see a straight doubl-edged one on the left (her proper right).

At times, a number of direct questions are posed at the opponent to challenge all his previous statements as the examples below show. Paulo asks,

(115) Paulo: Was the keris you used sharpened? Were keris historically sharp? Do you think there may have been differences between the various regions and the various keris in themselves whether they were meant to be used as a weapon or as a dress accessory or as a talisman?

The examples above clearly show that Paulo asks different direct questions so that his opponent is forced to answer these questions. The questions are carefully chosen to support the theory of Melborn.

7.10.5 Using direct questions to divert attention

One of the functions of direct questions is to divert attention and, perhaps, to change the course of discussion in polemical discourse. This strategy is generally used by moderators and administrators to divert attention of the participants and influence them to answer other questions with the intention of calming down a conflict situation. In the following examples regarding the *keris* thread, the moderator asks four different direct questions with the function of diverting attention:

(116) Moderator: How did empus hardened the edges of keris? I mean did they use differential heat treating? Is the body of a keris soft and the edges hard? How did the empus forge the blades to adjust to the fighting?

The questions above are basic questions about the Indonesian *keris*. By asking these questions, the moderator hopes that the participants would answer these questions and not concentrate on the polemical discourse.

The following table shows the individual moves and strategies used by different members who were involved in the *keris* controversy on the Forum of Swords and the *nationalism* controversy on the Forum of Ethnographic Swords:

Table 7.1: Different moves and strategies used in controversies in online discussion forums.

Different moves and strategies used in controversies in online discussion forums	
Opening moves	Accusations as an opening move
	Justifying one's entering into the controversy
Attacking moves	Supporting the Criticism of Thread Initiator
	Agreement with Friend / Friends to Support own Argument
	Accusations of Not Having Enough Knowledge about a Subject
	Insulting
	Accusation of making a naked assertion (*nudae assertiones*)
Defending Moves	Defending the author of the article
	Refutation with reference to the accepted experts and authority
Counterattacks	Retorting and correction of the statements of the opponent by providing examples
	Using the point-by-point method to counterattack
	Accusations of mispresentation
	Apologizing as an answer to the accusation
Deflecting Moves	Claiming incomprehension and misunderstanding of the article by the opponents
	Stressing that one is not interested in getting involved in a controversy
	Giving interpretation of one's own words
	Using repetition
Accusation Moves Related to Violations of Principles of Communication	Accusation of the violation of the principle of being warm and friendly
	Accusation of the violation of the principle of who carries the burden of proof
	Accusation of the violation of the principle of not making personal attacks
	Accusation of the violation of the principle of not solely relying on arguments from authority
Neutral Moves	
Using Rhetorical and Direct Questions in Controversies	Using rhetorical questions to support one's own position or a supporter's position
	Using rhetorical questions to attack the opponent
	Using direct questions to seek information
	Using direct questions to divert attention

7.11 Summary

In this chapter, I have shown that controversies in online discussion forums share some characteristics with controversies that were conducted via pamphlets during the Early Modern Period. In spite of the similarities of some individual moves, due to the nature of the medium, the Internet, the speed of online controversies is much higher than in Early Modern Controversies. Participants can post at any rate and as fast as they wish as long as the controversial thread in question is not locked by moderators and administrators. I have shown that different members have different interests when they get involved in an online controversy. They either try to attack a person, an article, a book written by a rival from another forum or simply by someone they do not like or they consider their work as not good, or they try to defend someone who is being criticized. Opening moves are generally accusations. They can also be moves of other kinds, such as justifying one's entry into a controversy.

Other moves are attacking moves, which range from supporting the criticism of the thread initiator, agreement with supporters, accusing the opponent of not having sufficient knowledge, and insulting. Surely, there are also a number of defensive moves that are used to defend against attacks. Defensive moves used in both the *keris* and *nationalism* controversies include defending the author of the aricle and refutation with reference to authorities.

A number of moves are counterattacks, which are chosen by members who either, instead of defending, switch to counterattacks or are used after defensive moves. Counterattacks include retorting and correction of the statements of the opponent, using the partial point-by-point method to counterattack, accusations of mispresentation, and apologizing as an answer to the accusation. Next to attacking and defensive moves, they are certain moves that are used to deflect the attack of opponents. Deflecting moves include claiming incomprehension and misunderstanding, stressing that one is not interested in getting involved in a controversy, providing interpretation of one's own words, and using repetition.

As I mentioned before, online discussion forums dedicated to the study of arms and armor are governed by a set of explict rules. Additionally, there are some implicit rules as well. Any violation of these rules result in accusations of violating certain rules and principles. These accusations in both the *keris* and *nationalism* controversies include accusation of the violation of the principle of being warm and friendly, accusation of the violation of the principle of who carries the burden of proof, accusation of the violation of the principle of not making personal attacks, and accusation of the violation of the principle of not solely relying on arguments from authority. There are also neutral moves that are posted between controversial posts.

Rhetorical and direct questions are also used as special individual moves in controversies. Rhetorical questions are used to support a certain position or to attack the position of the opponent. Additionally, direct questions are used to seek information, to challenge the position of the opponent, or to divert attention.

8. Stylistic choices in controversies

8.1 Introduction

The purpose of this chapter is to demonstrate which stylistic choices participants in controversies in online discussion forums have made. Similar to other fields of communication, participants in online discussion forums have their own individual styles of addressing each other, choosing words, and using different types of expletives in the form of emoticons. Before analyzing the individual styles of participants in online controversies, one should determine what the notion of style means. Enkvist (1973:11) describes that it is difficult to describe what style exactly means. Different approaches to describe styles have been proposed, but even the description of style as a matter of choice cannot be a workable concept as one can never be sure what choices were available and present to the author of a certain text (Enkvist, 1973:13). Enkvist (1973:15) states that all stylistic analysis is based on one of the following three approaches: the first approach to analyze style is to consider style a departure from a set of patterns which have been described as a norm (Enkvist, 1973:15). Thus, based on this principle Enkvist states that stylistic analysis should compare features in the text to be analyzed and features in the body of a text as a norm and therefore considered as a relevant background. Another approach for the definition of style is to consider style as an addition of certain stylistic features to a neutral, styleless, or prestylistic expression. Thus, based on this approach, expression becomes a stripping process in which the stylistic layer is removed to reach the stylistically neutral or unmarked core (Enkvist, 1973:15). The third approach to analyze style is to consider style as connotation, where each linguistic feature attains its stylistic value from the textual and situational environment. Thus, linguistic analysis in this approach is a study of the relationships between certain linguistic units and their environment (Enkvist, 1973:13). However, Enkvist (1973:15) states that these three approaches may well be seen as complementary rather than as contradictory or mutually exclusive.

Mukherjee (2005:1043) groups a multitude of stylistic factors in a pool of different choices selected by language users into a) user-bound factors, such as the speaker's or writer's age, gender, idiosyncratic preferences, and regional and social background, and b) factors referring to the situation where the language is being used, such as the medium (spoken vs. written), participation in discourse (monologue vs. dialogue), attitude (level of formality), and field of discourse (technical vs. non-technical fields). Regarding the user-bound factors in online discussion forums dedicated to the study of arms and armor, one should note that members belong to different age groups, both men and women (although men outnumber women), with different idiosyncratic preferences and different regional and social backgrounds. This, of course, leads to a variety of choices of style in online discussion forums. One should also note that many members use and speak English as a second or a foreign language. Esser (1993:9) rightly observes that no language is a fully homogeneous system and certainly, the language used in online discussion forums is no exception. Thus, a homogeneous corpus collected in an online discussion forum environment cannot be expected. Regarding factors referring to the situation where the language is being used, the communication in online discussion forums is a written form, a dialogue, in some subforums formal (such as the Nihonto Forum on the Forum of Swords) and in some subforums informal (such as the General Forum in the Forum of Swords), and the language is, in most forums, a technical language.

Cherney (1999:25) explains that within the realm of research on CMC (computer-mediated communication), style is usually used to refer to features of language, such as 'oral' versus 'written' features. There is a long-standing debate between researchers whether the language used on CMC has oral or written features as some CMC has characteristics of oral language in a textual medium (Cherney, 1999:25). Of course, the stylistic choice of participants regarding different linguistic forms is also reflected in online controversies; hence, there is evidence of an individual style of participation in controversies. As the online forums are moderated environments, exposed to a set of rules and norms, the participants adjust themselves to a certain linguistic style. Therefore, the determination of the individual markers of style is not an easy task since one cannot easily determine how far an individual is imitating the other participants.

As social animals, human beings interact with each other in groups and may use linguistic features peculiar to a group.[78] Thus, one has to take into consideration that an individual creates his/her systems of verbal behavior to imitate those common to the group with which he/she interacts and wants to be identified with (see McMenamin, 1993:51). Therefore, it is not easy to distinguish between linguistic features of an individual and a group. Nevertheless, for the purpose of this study, the determination of these individual or group style markers will reveal much about the nature of conducted controversies. The purpose of my study in this chapter is not to determine what the individual style of each participant is. Rather, my intention is to show how these stylistic markers are used in a controversy and possibly change its course. The communicative style in online discussion forums is similar to the conversational style. One should note that identifying differences in linguistic utterances in conversation is not a new source of study. Tannen (1984:1) describes conversational style as the choice of the basic elements of how people talk, which differs from one person to the other. She identifies different variables that might influence the individual choice of these elements, such as gender, ethnicity, class, and regional background.

As online discussion forums are dialogic in nature, they can be considered a type of written dialogue. A linguistic study of the texts in online discussion forums should reveal which types of linguistic structures and features are indicative of the dialogic nature of written communication. Mukherjee (2003:121) explains that in spoken language, speakers create linguistic structures that defy the merely syntactic description because intonational means may intertwine with

78 As social animals, people are not self-regulating creatures. Agamanolis (2006:308) states that human physiology is at least partly regulated and stabilized by people around them via a number of channels, such as facial expression, physical touch, and hormonal signals.

syntactic structures that are otherwise unrelated. Although the communication in online discussion forums does not have intonational means, a number of other choices, such as emoticons, are available to the users that substitute facial expressions and intonational means and co-join with syntactic structures.

Written texts that are dialogic nature are not a new phenomenon as pamphlets from the Early Modern Period already shared this feature. According to Ratia (2006:88), pamphlets have traditionally been considered dialogic in nature. Analyzing the medical texts on the controversy on tobacco, including treatises, pamphlets, and a herbal (a herbal text), published between 1577–1621, Ratia (2006:87–88) explains that the texts are dialogic regardless of the genre.[79] Ratia explains that this is evident due to the direct and indirect references to other texts, in the borrowed ideas, and also the frequent references to the reader. Ratia (2006:87) uses the term 'dialogue' in a broad sense, meaning texts as dialogic contributions in their own right. Additionally, the texts are in dialogue with the academic community, which consisted of close, professional circles. According to Ratia (2006:99), involvement with the hearer (or reader of the text) is shown by the usage of the second-person pronoun in subject and object positions that have the same amount of affective quality (Ratia adds that only the genitive form is excluded). The typical interactive question-answer patterns also show involvement with the hearer.

The contributions of participants in online discussion forums dedicated to the study of arms and armor are also highly dialogic in nature. One can find frequent uses of the second-person pronoun, question-answer patterns, and direct addressing of other participants. In the following, I will show the linguistic features that show that the contributed texts in online controversies are dialogic in nature: the written contributions of the members involved in controversies resemble oral communication.

---

79 Ratia (2006:99) explains that pamphlets have the quality of involvement. Further, Ratia adds that involvement is associated with the concept of affect, emotive language use, regulating the relationship between the writer and the audience, and the intensity of discourse. Ratia explains that pamphlet-like texts show more "involvement with the hearer", whereas other texts (referring to herbals and treatises) show more "ego involvement".

8.2 Style markers in online controversies as written dialogue: audience interaction and addressing other participants

To show the stylistic markers which show the dialogic nature of the communication in online discussion forums, I introduce a model proposed by Esser in the following. Regarding dimensions of variation of a language, Esser (1993:11) distinguishes between three general categories:

a) speaker/writer, which is relatively permanent, b) relation between speaker/writer and hearer/reader, and c) what the speaker/writer wants to communicate. Further, Esser subdivides each of these general categories into the following: a) speaker/writer into time (such as Old English: a temporal dialect), region (such as Scottish English: a regional dialect), intelligibility (such as Standard English: a standard dialect), individuality (such as an individual's English: an idiolect), and interference (such as German English: a learner's dialect);
b) relation between speaker/writer and hearer/reader into medium (spoken/written English), participation in discourse (monologue /dialogue), explicitness (elaborated/restricted code), and attitude (such as formal English); and
c) what the speaker/writer wants to communicate into field of discourse (such as legal English), intention (such as the language of advertising), and appropriateness of form to purpose (the style of a postcard, a lecture, a monograph).

First, I will apply the above-mentioned model to the communicative context of online discussion forums to have a better grasp of the communicative situation and the stylistic variation in online discussion forums. The factor time plays a partial role in some communication in online discussion forums. Although the participants use Modern English to communicate, very often they use old words and terms from Middle English and Early Modern English written in swordsmanship manuals. This, of course, leads to a communicative setting where encoding the posted messages requires an understanding of the meaning of words used in old texts. Different participants from different English-speaking countries take part in online discussion forums and also get involved in online controversies. Thus, the dimension 'region' also plays a role in the communication in online discussion forums. There are participants from the USA; UK, Australia, New Zealand, and South Africa. The 'dimension' social group also plays a role in online discussion forums and participants from different social and educational backgrounds take part in online controversies. Additionally, as each individual uses favorite words and has tendencies to use certain structures, the 'dimension' individuality (idiolect) can also be applied to the study of the language used in controversies in online discussion forums. As there are members of both forums who are not native speakers of English, and use English as a second language or a foreign language, the dimension of interference from another language, specifically the native language into English plays a role in communication in online discussion forums. In this respect, one should take the role of English used as lingua franca into consideration.[80] There is surely an interference of norms and principles deriving from other cultures of people who use English as a lingua franca in controversies in online discussion forums. Esser (1993:11) explains that the dimensions of the general category of speaker/writer are relatively permanent. In the following, I will not analyze the dimensions of this category as they are related to the individual. For the purpose of this study and to show the dialogic nature of controversies in online discussion forums the second general category of the above classification, namely relation between speaker/ writer and hearer/reader, is important and I will analyze these dimensions in my work.

80 Quoting Crystal (2003:619), Bjørge (2007:61) reports that the estimation of native speakers of English is between 320-380 million, the estimation of the number of people who use English worldwide is 1120-1880 million. Thus, many speakers of English use English as lingua franca. This way, non-native speakers outnumber native speakers (Dewey, 2007:333). For more information on the role and assessment of English as a lingua franca (ELF), see Elder and Davies (2006) and Dovring (1997).

The second general category of dimensions of variation identified by Esser (1993:11), namely relation between speaker/writer and hearer/reader, is especially important for showing the dialogic nature of communication in online discussion forums. Esser (1993:19) explains that certain lexical and grammatical features are considered as typical of spoken English, such as filled pauses like *em*, and phrases such as *sort of*, *you know*, and *I mean*. There are plenty of lexical and grammatical features in controversies in online discussion forums that can be considered as typical of spoken English. Similar to written texts, in the medium of the online discussion forum, there is a time lag between the encoding and the decoding of a message. However, participants generally do not spend much time in writing a careful piece of work. The writing is very casual and generally ridden with mistakes. The dimension of the participation in the discourse in online discussion forums dedicated to the study of arms and armor is a written dialog, where posts appear in asynchronous way. At times, participants in a controversy complain that their opponents conduct a monolog in their posts and do not react to their postings. The dimension of explicitness in online discussion forums is evident in the restricted code of the communication. By using many specialized terms and information on historical background, participants in online discussion forums assume that the meaning is shared, i.e. that the communication cannot be universally understood. This, of course, leads to the state where in specialized subforums, such as the Nihonto forum in the Forum of Swords, many participants do not dare to post and prefer to read the posts as lurkers. The dimension attitude reveals the social relationship between an addresser and an addressee, i.e. using formal or informal language.

The third general category of dimensions of variation proposed by Esser (1993:11) is what the speaker/writer wants to communicate. The dimension of field of discourse covers communicative purpose on the one hand and subject matter on the other (Esser, 1993:27). Subject matter is reflected in language through a specialized vocabulary as is the case in online discussion forums. The communicative purpose of controversies in online discussion forums is to impress an audience and the subject matter is revealed by the usage of many technical terms in the field of historical arms and armor. The dimension of intention is about describing what language is being used for in the situation, i.e. what form of speech acts. The intention of communication in controversies in online discussion forums is to make propaganda against opponents and to impress and persuade an audience. The dimension of the appropriateness of form includes making choices of a certain medium. Esser (1993:30) states that to communicate subject matter in the written medium one can select a letter, a postcard, a telegram or a memo. Of course, in today's electronic world one can choose email or in case of online discussion forums, one can post in such forums.

In the following, I will analyze the *keris* controversy and the *nationalism* controversy with the following dimensions of variation: medium, participation in discourse, and field of discourse. The dimension of variation of medium and participation in discourse reveal the dialogic nature of controversies in online discussion forums. One of the ways to show that the dimension of medium in online discussion forums is dialogic in nature is to explain the usage of vocatives and how participants address each other during the *keris* and *nationalism* controversies. I will explain when and why they choose to use the last name instead of the first name. Further, I will explain how the pronouns *we*, *I*, and *you* are used to interact with the audience or opponents.

8.2.1 The dimension of medium: the usage of vocatives and signature lines

In this section, I will analyze the types of vocatives that are used in the *keris* controversy in the Forum of Swords and in the *nationalism* controversy in the Forum of Ethnographic Swords. As forms of address, vocatives show how the participants interact with each other and with the audience. Hence vocatives show the dialogic nature of the medium of online discussion forums. According to Biber *et al.* (1999:1108), vocatives are important in defining and maintaining social relationships between participants in a conversation. Leech (1999:108) emphasizes that 'vocatives' and 'forms of address' are closely related themes that are easily confused. According to Leech, in syntactic terms, a term of address represents a device used to refer to the addressee(s) of an utterance. On the other hand, Leech explains that a vocative is a special type of address term, a nominal constituent loosely integrated with the rest of the utterance.

Biber *et al.* (1999:1108–1110) and Leech (1999:110–112) distinguish between the following types of vocatives: a) endearments used to address close family members (but not usually male to male), sexual partners, and other 'favorite' people (Leech, 1999:112), such as *baby* and *darling*, b) family terms, such as *mummy* and *mum*, c) familiarizers that show the relationship between speaker and addressee as familiar rather than a more distant and respectful (Leech, 1999:112), such as *guys* or *man*, d) familiarized first names used not only to address friends and family members but also in speech among colleagues and casual acquaintances (Leech, 1999:112) (shortened and/or with the pet suffix -y/-ie), such as *Tim* or *Kackie*, e) first names in full, such as *Paul* or *Jennifer*, f) titles and surnames, such as *Mr. Graham*, g) honorifics that denote an uncommon category, such as *sir* or *madam* – Leech (1999:112) explains that the relation of respect is seldom marked by such vocatives in present-day English – and h) others (including nicknames), such as *boy* or *everyone*. Biber *et al.* (1999:1108–1110) further explain that group 'h' covers a wide range of nominal structures that have the function of vocatives, containing some quite complex noun phrases, such as

> Those of you who want to bring your pets along, please sit in the back of the space ship.

Regarding the application of this model to the type of vocatives that are used in controversies in online discussion forums, one notes that endearments are not used in the *keris* controversy for obvious reasons as the *keris* controversy is a controversial thread, and on controversial threads, endearments are not used. But there are, indeed, threads on some subforums where endearments, such as 'Dear Joe', are used at the beginning of the post. For obvious reasons, family terms are not used for communication in online discussion forums since participants there are typically not related to one another and would probably find the use of family terms as awkward in what is supposed to be a professional environment. Familiarizers are used among some members in some subforums, especially a subforum as the Pub in the Forum of Swords that is dedicated to casual talk about non-sword related topics. The category of familiarized first names is not used in the *keris* controversy, but there are threads where this type of vocative is used. First names are used quite often. Only Charley uses the title and the surname of his opponent Manolo to refer to him as I will explain in detail later. To calm down the heated discussion, the site administrator Daniel and the moderator use the honorific 'gentlemen' in the *keris* controversy, such as the following example used by Daniel:

(117) Daniel: Gentlemen please try and avoid language that is personally insulting [emphasis mine].

In the *nationalism* controversy, first names are, at times, used although most members use Internet names/Internet hangers.[81] This is an indication that members know each other in spite of Internet names and use each others' first names to address each other on the forum. Further, the title and surname is used by Ehud once to attack his opponent Stefano Campino:

(118) Ehud: Mr.Campino, In your comment on Amazon.com (addressed to me), you said: "...we've collected enough material to bury you with your own hate" and threatened to report me to Amazon [emphasis mine].

Addressing the opponent by using the title together with the last name is a common tactic used in online controversies. This tactic is used to create distance with the opponent before attacking him/her. Additionally, Eidel uses honorifics once in the course of the *nationalism* controversy in order to appear apologetic and introduce his opinion:

(119) Eidel:
Gentlemen,
I owe you an apology for regularly bringing this issue up in a more

81 As mentioned before, the Forum of Ethnographic Swords does not have a real-name policy as the Forum of Swords.

controversial way than it should be. I also should probably define my position as precise as possible [emphasis mine].

The usage of honorifics in the example above in opening a controversial thread shows a very interesting phenomenon in online controversies. By using honorifics in this manner, the participant addresses the whole registered members of the online community in a polite way before moving to his accusation and attack against a certain person. Addressing and naming moderators directly when one is not sure about the violation of a certain principle is a common move in online discussion forums dedicated to the study of arms and armor. In the following, Tony uses the vocative 'moderators' that can be classified in the category of 'others' suggested by Biber *et al.* (1999:1109):

(120) Tony: *Moderators: Please take note that I am not trying to rock the boat* [emphasis mine].

As I have shown above regarding the functions of vocatives, a more specific classification of vocatives based on their pragmatic function needs to be introduced for the study of vocatives in online discussion forums since vocatives in this environment seem to have a different pragmatic function. To start with, I will make a short introduction of the types of vocatives that are used in another online environment, namely chat rooms, and compare them to the types of vocatives used in online discussion forums. Regarding the types of vocatives used in the chat rooms and their pragmatic functions, Anglemark (2006:296) concludes that the usage of vocatives in Internet chat forums is different from the vocative usage in spoken communication. According to Anglemark (2006:296), language users use vocatives for different functions in a conversation and quotes Leech (1999), who, based on the analysis of the spoken section of the Longman Spoken and Written English corpus (LSWE), identifies three pragmatic functions of vocatives in spoken dialogic use: a) vocatives are used for calling for the attention of someone who is not listening, b) vocatives are used to identify and designate the addressee among a group of people, and c) vocatives are used to establish and keep social relationships by using the first name or titles. Anglemark (2006:296) explains that the third group of vocatives is the most varied and contains usages as endearments, such as to children or lovers, honorifics such as 'sir', and general exclamatory remarks, such as 'you're mean!'

Anglemark (2006:298) states that the three pragmatic groups described above were not quite suitable for the study of vocatives on chat rooms and suggests the following four pragmatic functions for the study of vocatives: a) the attention-summoning vocative, b) the greeting, c) the social vocative, and d) the designatory vocative. Anglemark (2006:298) states that in spoken language, the vocative is often used for the purpose of calling for a person's attention; however, in Internet chat rooms, vocatives are seldom used in this function. The reason for this is that, in chat rooms, no one knows exactly whether another participant is actively looking at his screen. On the other hand, Anglemark (2006:298) states that the use of vocatives for greetings and saying goodbye is very common in chat rooms. Anglemark stresses that the vocatives in this category that would normally be classified into the functional category 'establishing and maintaining social relationships' have more than a social function. Moreover, vocatives in this group signal 'that the speaker is aware of the new interlocutor's entrance or impending exit, a signal that would not be necessary in face-to-face communication" (Anglemark, 2006:298). Another category identified by Anglemark (2006:298) is the social vocative, which is similar to Leech's 'social relationships' category. Anglemark states that this type of vocative is used frequently in chat room conversation, such as 'oh well done sir'. The category of designatory vocative is used frequently in chat rooms to state whether a particular remark is targeted to one particular person, a group of people or the whole group. It is usually separated from the rest of the text by brackets, such as in '[I mean you, Chin]'.

Vocatives in online discussion forums are not used to greet or say goodbye as the communication in online discussion forums is asynchronous. Similar to chat rooms, vocatives are not used to summon people for attention as no one knows whether the other person is looking at his/her screen. I divide vocatives used in online discussion forums for the purpose of this research into a) vocatives used to identify and designate the addressee among a group of people and b) vocatives used to establish and keep social relationships. In the following, I will show how Manolo uses a vocative to identify and designate Paulo among the readers:

(121) Manolo:
Paulo, Yes, but the point is that there's no correlation between grip choice and civilian fighting utility, which is what Melborn implied.

In the next example, Charley uses the second type of vocative by using the title 'Mr.' to create distance:

(122) Charley:
Mr.Rodriguez.
I have clearly stated the reason for which I chose to [. . .] [emphasis mine].

Normally, the participants in an online controversy use the first names to refer to each other. At times, in controversies, they use the title 'Mr.' to create distance and, at the same time, to insult their opponents. This is also the case in the *keris* and *nationalism* controversies. Throughout the whole threads, all participants use the first name to communicate with and address each other, such as 'Paulo', 'Thanks David and Joe', and 'Thank you Stefano'. In the course of the *keris* controversy, only one participant, namely Charley, constantly uses the title 'Mr.' in combination with the last name to refer to his main opponent, such as 'Mr. Rodriguez'. He does this to create distance from his opponent. The role of vocatives in this case is not necessarily to address the main opponent. Moreover, the person using this strategy is addressing the audience and only signals the distance to his main opponent. At one point, Charely also uses the title 'Mr.' in combination with the first name of his second main opponent, David, to refer to him as 'Mr. David':

(123) Charley to Manolo and David: I have found Mr. Rodriguez's, and Mr. David's comments very useful in more ways than one.

In answering Charley, Manolo insists in being called by the first name, clearly stating that he does not want to abide by this rule set up by Charley:

(124) Manolo to Charley: Please, I'm Manolo – no "Mr." anything. I'll try to reference your comments to the relevant passages of [the article].

However, Charley continues to use the title 'Mr.' to refer to Manolo in his other posts. At this point, Manolo starts to belittle this tactic:

(125) Manolo to Charley: [. . .] PS: Charley, I kindly asked you earlier to refer to me as "Manolo". However, if you are determined to use "Mr.", I ask that you please make reference to my capacity as fashion critic. The following are acceptable:
* Mr. "Armed fashion theory", The People' Champion and Author of the People's Theory
* Mr. Fashion Conscious
* Mr. Custom-Fitted
* Mr. To-the-Nines
* Mr. Pieced-up-Creased-up
* Mr. Je-ne-sais-quoi
* Mr. Arbiter-of-Good-Taste

The above post was surely considered as provocation. Charley does not comply with Manolo's request as he considers him as an enemy and not someone he wants to cooperate with. Moreover, Charley is more interested in influencing the audience that is reading the posts in the *keris* controversy. Therefore, Charley keeps using the title 'Mr.' in combination with Manolo. Charley's answer to Manolo reveals that he wants to put distance between the two and does not take Manolo's suggestions seriously:

(126) Charley to Manolo: *Mr.Rodriguez, regarding your request to address you by your given name. I address family and close friends by their given name. I address strangers with whom I feel some affinity by their given name. You are neither a member of my family, a close friend, nor do I feel any affinity with you. Under these circumstances I deem it quite improper for me to address you by your given name. I leave your standards in matters of personal address to yourself* [emphasis mine].

On the other hand, Charley calls the members who support and help him on the thread by their first names. This is a true signal for those who Charley considers his friends and his supporters. On the other hand, he uses the title 'Mr.' to refer to his opponents. Throughout the whole *nationalism* thread, all participants use the first name to communicate with and address each other, such as 'Tony', which indicates that they feel close to each other and prefer to have an informal communication among themselves. Only in one instance, Ehud uses the last name of Stefano to create distance and attack him personally:

(127) Ehud: *Mr. Campino, In your comment on Amazon.com (addressed to me), you said: "...we've collected enough material to bury you with your own hate" and threatened to report me to Amazon. Please feel free to add my current posting to the file assembled by you and your Merry Gang of Attack Poodles* [emphasis mine].

Regarding signature lines, some of the participants end their posts without any signature as Manolo does. Others use their first name as the signature, such as 'Joe', and others use their first name with the first letter of their last name, such as David M. As the Forum of Swords offers members the function of a signature line at the end of each post, some members use this function either to include a link to their websites or even some lines of their favorite quotes from books and even some lines of poetry. Only a few members involved in the controversy use this function.

8.2.2 The usage of the pronoun we *to address group identity*

There are certain linguistic features, such as personal pronouns, that carry ideological distinctions. In studying controversies, Ratia (2005:124) points out that differences in the variation of linguistic features are not arbitrary as they carry ideological distinctions that are central in polemical discourse. For example, talking about tobacco controversies, Ratia adds that at the base of health issues, there can be religious and moral issues that might be more effective in argumentation. The religious and moral issues are reflected in ideologies, and ideologies can be expressed by using different linguistic features. One of the linguistic features that can be analyzed in this respect is the study of pronouns that reveal the ideologies. Quoting van Dijk (1995), Ratia (2005:124) explains that ideologies influence group relations and interest and can be analyzed by looking at personal pronouns. Further, according to Ratia (2005:125), pronouns carry authority claims and express the inter-personal relationship between the author and the audience. Personal pronouns also reveal the emotive aspect of communication. Ratia (2005:126) stresses that emotive language is used in argumentative texts for persuasion. Ratia adds that emotive language is frequently used in argumentative texts and is described as 'affect'. According to Ratia (2005:126), personal pronouns play an important role in marking an affect because of semantic and linguistic changes. Affect can best be researched in the relationship between the two interlocutors *I* and *you*. Ratia (2005:127) stresses that all personal pronouns in her study of the language of tobacco controversies appear to have affective quality under certain conditions. In the following sections, I will study the types and effects of the pronouns *we*, *I*, and *you* to find out the interrelationships between the people involved in controversies in online discussion forums. This, of course, reveals the dialogic nature of the dimension of medium of online discussion forums.

Wales (1996:36) explains that the actual discourse referents for the pronoun *we* seem to be limitless and adds that the precise interpretation of the pronoun *we* depends on the particular context of use and the inferences based on the mutual knowledge of speaker and interpreter. Biber *et al.* (1999:329) also state that in contrast to the pronoun *I*, which is unambiguous in referring to the speaker/writer, the pronoun *we* is often vague as it is not clear whether it refers to the speaker/writer and the addressee (inclusive *we*) or to the speaker/writer and some other person or persons associated with him (exclusive *we*). Regarding this point, Ratia (2005:126) explains that the pronoun *we* is especially interesting due to its complex nature. The pronoun *we* is complex as it cannot be described by the inclusive and exclusive uses of the pronoun only. Ratia adds that this pronoun is useful in polite interaction between oneself and another as "in theory it minimizes benefits to self, and maximizes benefits to the addressee", but in other contexts, it could mean different things. Based on Wales (1996:58–59), Ratia (2005:126) explains that in a social and ideological sense, *we* has another meaning as 'more than one' of the same, meaning that the addressee can be included in the same group and share the speaker's views (inclusive *we*) or the addressee can be excluded from the group (exclusive *we*).

Quoting Wales (1996:58, 65–66), Ratia (2005:126) distinguishes between five kinds of the uses of *we*: a) rare *we* [+ ego] [+ voc] (i.e. 'you and me together') signals joint activity or involvement; b) 'authorial *we*' that commonly appears with verbs of saying, showing, thinking, and other actions, frequently in the preterit such as 'We have already discussed …', and with verbs of anticipating, returning, postponing, such as 'We deal with some cases below'; c) 'workshop *we*' [+ voc] that can be easily replaced with *you* and co-occurs with verbs of seeing, looking and modals of obligation, such as 'Already we can see …' and 'we shall at some stage need a term'; d) specific exophoric *we1* within a larger context that has immediate reference to the context of situation; and e) the generic *we2* has specific reference to a cultural context. According to Ratia (2005:126), both have egocentric tendencies. Based on Wales (1996:58), Ratia adds that the difference between specific exophoric and generalized references is not precise but rather continuous, meaning that making a clear-cut separation is not possible.

In her study of tobacco controversies, Ratia (2005:126) uses *we* to refer to a group of people in a narrower context, for example to physicians, as a specific exophoric *we*1, and *we* to refer to a group of people in a larger context, such as to people in generic *we*2. Ratia (2005:133) states that the most common use of the first-person plural in *A Warning for Tabacconists* is in the generic sense of *we*2. Further, Ratia adds that references to *our* and *vs* [*us*] in relation to the inclusive 'our bodies' are striking and explains that these forms identify the author with the addressee as a member of the same group.

One of the striking features of the *keris* controversy is that there are no occurrences of the generic *we2* referring to people in general. The pronoun *we* is used as the specific exophoric *we1* to refer to the participants in the controversy 32 times. In his posts, Manolo uses the exophoric *we1* to refer to the community of the Forum of Swords and, at the same time, to distinguish them from the other community, the Forum of Ethnographic Swords. This, of course, reveals a certain degree of loyalty to the Forum of Swords and corresponding social identity. Compared to other members, Manolo uses the exophoric *we1* the most (15 occurrences) and applies it to convey a certain tactic of inclusion and exclusion. By using the exophoric *we1*, Manolo attempts to demonstrate that the members of the Forum of Swords follow academic principles in contrast to the Forum of Ethnographic Swords. Then, Manolo paves the way by using the personal pronoun *we* to include the whole community, including the opponents, to accept academic standards. He attempts this by stating the following sentence in four different posts:

(128) Manolo: *Because this is an academic forum, we use the academic method* [emphasis mine].

Then, Manolo expresses himself explicitly by referring to himself and his supporters at the Forum of Swords as 'true academics' by using the exophoric *we1*:

(129) Manolo: Paulo, I invite you to join us in accepting the academic standard which the Forum of Swords promotes, so that we can make genuine progress in our research [emphasis mine].

Manolo even goes so far as to assert that his theory is valid for the whole community and regards his own theory as 'the People's Theory'. Manolo posted this to retort to Charley, his main opponent in the thread, who calls Manolo by his last name and the title 'Mr. Rodriguez'. Manolo asks Charley to use his first name, and as Charley does not follow, he starts making fun of Charley by saying that he should use the title 'Mr. Armed Fashion Theory, The People's Champion and Author of the People's Theory'. In a later post, he uses the exophoric *we1* to reinforce his theory and by calling his supporters 'The People':

(130) Manolo: We are happy to believe those who say Melborn is a gentleman, and in a gentlemanly spirit offer him our advice and look forward to a friendly collaboration in which we work together on a revised version of "Origin" that will satisfy The People [emphasis mine].

Further, Manolo states that Melborn in his article and his main supporter Charley could not offer a single supporting fact for their claims, and in another post invites Melborn to join the discussion on the Forum of Swords and to accept advice to re-write his essay. This, of course, is pure speculation and something that Manolo cannot really expect to happen. In both cases, Manolo uses the exophoric *we1* to refer to his supporters at the Forum of Swords:

(131) Manolo: Neither Melborn nor Charley have offered one single supporting fact to bolster their claims, while we have provided a mountain of refuting evidence.
Manolo: [. . .] so we continue to invite Melborn to make an appearance so we may advise him on ways to re-write his essay and make it consistent with the evidence [emphasis mine].

The 'workshop *we*' [+ voc] is used in the *keris* controversy 16 times. At one point, Manolo uses the 'workshop we' [+ voc] to indicate that all his supporters agree with his theory of 'Armed Fashion Theory' that proves the inadequacies of the article 'The Roots of Keris'. Thus, Manolo attempts to show a collective identity behind his theory and its validity. Note that the 'workshop *we*' [+ voc] can be substituted with the pronoun *you*:

(132) Manolo: So we see from this brief Armed Fashion Theory analysis that "The roots of the Keris" does not present a reasonable argument for keris evolution [emphasis mine].

Rare *we* [ego] [+ voc] is used four times. In the following example, Manolo uses rare *we* [+ ego] [+ voc] to refer to himself and his main rival Charley.

(133) Manolo: I invite you to revise your comments accordingly before we continue [emphasis mine].

Manolo uses the authorial *we* twice. In the following, I will provide an example of this type:

(134) Manolo: We already refuted this "faster" argument above [emphasis mine].

All in all, Manolo uses the pronoun *we* 29 times to refer to his own group and distinguishes it from the opponents on the other forum. Thus, he tries to reinforce the sense of belonging in his group and distinguish it from his opponents. The high frequency of the usage of the word *we* in the posts of Manolo in comparison to other members shows that Manolo often uses the tactic of referring to his own group. When one compares the frequency of usage of the pronoun *we* used by Manolo to the occurrence of the personal pronoun *we* in the posts of Charley, his main opponent, a difference becomes clear. In his 5 posts consisting of 6,470 words, Charley uses the personal pronoun *we* only ten times compared to 25 posts of Manolo consisting of 4,686 words, where Manolo uses the personal pronoun *we* 29 times.

In the *nationalism* controversy, there are no occurrences of the rare *we* [+ ego] [+ voc] and authorial *we*. On the other hand, there are six occurrences of 'workshop *we*' [+ voc], seven occurrences of specific exophoric *we1*, and 16 occurrences of the generic *we2*. In the following example, Tony uses the 'workshop *we*':

(135) Tony: We can't rewrite the history that has already been written. All we can do is put out for everyone to read, is the other side [emphasis mine].

In his first post in the thread on the *nationalism* thread, Ehud makes use of the pronoun specific exophoric *we1* to refer to the group of his supporters on the Forum of Ethnographic Swords, attempting to set it apart from the other rival community members of the Forum of Swords and appear as a part of a unified group:

(136) Ehud: Nothing wrong about it: we are all trying one way or another to connect with our past [emphasis mine].

The specific exophoric *we1* is also used to refer to the group to refer to the cluster of collectors and people that are participants of the Forum of Ethnographic Swords and specifically those involved in the *nationalism* controversy. Donald uses the specific exophoric *we1* to refer to this group:

(137) Donald: It seems to me that we are entering into a debate which has no definitive "black or white" answer [emphasis mine].

The generic *we2* is used to refer to people in a larger context as shown in the following examples:

(138) Tony: When the Americans "won" the Philippines after the Spanish-American War, they told the Moros that we own you now [emphasis mine].

As the examples above show, the usage of the pronoun *we* provides the participants involved in a controversy in an online discussion forum with a number of strategies and tactics to defend themselves, such as by using *we*1 to refer to their own group and attribute positive features to themselves. Additionally, they can use the authorial *we* to feign humbleness and modesty. Further, the usage of the pronoun *we* shows the dialogic nature of the dimension of the linguistic variation of medium.

8.2.3 Different functions of the pronoun I

As the examples above show, the usage of the pronoun *we* provides the participants involved in a controversy in an online forum to establish and maintain social relationships. According to Palander-Collin (2006:339), people reflect and build up social hierarchies and relationships through language use. By using different address terms, politeness strategies, or pronominal choices, an individual expresses and shapes hierarchies and social relationships. Similar to Early Modern English personal letters, the first- and second-person pronouns are used as pragmatic devices to address the writer-addressee relationship. Palander-Collin (2006:339–340) explains that first- and second-person pronouns create a communicative situation for the writer and the addressee, establishing addressee-oriented styles and social interaction.[82]

82 Further, Palander-Collin (2006:340) quotes Fairclough (1992:8-9), who states that in many situations, language does not simply transfer objective information, but it shapes and keeps social relationships showing and establishing personal identities and hierarchies between the participants. According to Bell (2001:143, 145), speakers change style due to the change in their audience, reflecting the variation between speakers on the social dimension.

Based on Biber *et al.* (1999:333), Suhr (2006:32) states that personal pronouns are used more often in spoken conversations than in written language due to the fact that first- and second-person pronouns serve as markers of involvement and interaction, which are features that occur more often in spoken language than in written language. Chafe (1985:117) claims that the use of first-person pronouns can be associated with ego involvement, such as the involvement of the speaker with himself, and the use of second-person pronouns with the speaker's involvement with the reader.

Regarding the personal pronoun *I*, Ratia (2005:128–137) distinguishes between the following: a) the multifunctional *I* and b) the authorial *I*. Ratia explains that the multifunctional *I* has four different functions: first, it is a hedge and a cautious note where the author is conscious of the maxim of quality. This means that the author admits the possibility of having made a mistake in his/her reasoning and expects possible criticism of his/her arguments will follow. Second, *I* is implemented to increase the writer's authority and convincing the reader of the author's expertise, such as 'I am not ignorant that . . .' and 'I read in Gallen [that…]'. Third, *I* is also used neutrally in an authorial phrase, such as 'I mean' and 'I refer'. Fourth, *I* is used to persuade the audience, e.g. 'I pray you' and 'I assure you'. In the *keris* controversy, a number of personal pronoun *I* examples is used. Multifunctional *I* as a hedge, indicating caution towards the public, is used 29 times. The main contesters in the *keris* controversy, namely Manolo Rodriguez and David, do not use any multifunctional *I* as a hedge. On the other hand, Charley uses 4 multifunctional *I* examples as a hedge to praise the work of Melborn:

(139) Charley: I believe may be treated as this because of his overarching qualification [. . .] [emphasis mine].

A close look of the multifunctional *I* as a hedge used by other participants in the *keris* controversy shows that it is used as a signal that the participant is not exactly sure about his own statement and anticipates criticism as is the case with the statement by Joe below:

(140) Joe: I have never fought an armored opponent so if I am wrong please say so [. . .] [emphasis mine].

Multifunctional *I* as a hedge is used 18 times in the *nationalism* controversy. One of the examples of this type of the pronoun *I* is:

(141) Manuel: I am not sure that we as a spieces are actually capable of looking at ourselves and our actions from a completely objective position [emphasis mine].

In the *keris* controversy, a number of personal pronoun *I*, a total of 136 occurrences, are used to increase the participant's authority and to convince readers of the forum of the posters' expertise. Manolo uses this type of *I* 15 times during the course of the *keris* controversy, such as:

(142) Manolo: I was reading from Alfred Russel Wallace's famous Malay Archipelago this morning, and was surprised to find, on p.78, [. . .] [emphasis mine].

His main opponent Charley uses this type of pronoun *I* 21 times. In many of these cases, he refers to the article of Melborn as a source of authority and asks other participants to read the article. At the same time, he insinuates that the opponents of Melborn's article have not read the article carefully:

(143) Charley: I recommend that those who wish to comment upon this article read the article in its entirety, [. . .] [emphasis mine].

The pronoun *I* used to enhance the authority of the participant in the *nationalism* controversy is used 13 times. One of the examples is:

(144) Eidel: I have never collaborated with Harvard researchers of Caspian project and I think their knowledge of Azerbaijan/Caucausus is extremely shallow [...] [emphasis mine].

The pronoun *I* is also used neutrally in authorial phrases in the *keris* controversy very often (the total number of occurrences is 136). Manolo Rodriguez uses this type of authorial *I* 20 times, such as:

(145) Manolo: I happily grant that all these points you raise would need to be considered in a real test, which would be of a scientific nature and could be measured with a good degree of control and variable isolation [emphasis mine].

The pronoun *I* in its neutral function is used 31 times in the *nationalism* controversy. One of the examples is:

(146) Tony: i am still trying to find it so i can post a link [emphasis mine].

The pronoun *I* in the persuasive function (emotive use) is also used in the *keris* controversy. Manolo uses this type of *I* six times in the *keris* controversy:

(147) Manolo: I kindly ask that you clarify this earlier comment of yours: [. . .] [emphasis mine].

The pronoun *I* in the persuasive/emotive function is used nine times in the *nationalism* controversy. One of the examples is:

(148) Tony: I praise our famous writter, Mark Twain, [. . .] [emphasis mine].

Quoting Pearce (2001:219), Ratia (2005:129) explains that the main function of *I* is authorial, indicating that the author assumes responsibility for his work because it will expose him to criticism. Ratia (2005:129) states that the authorial *I* is used in epistemic phrases and mentions the following epistemic verbs: 'know, say, think, see, and confess'. Ratia adds that *I think* makes an exception in this group since it can express either certainty or uncertainty. The authorial *I* is also used in the *keris* controversy often (a total of 35 occurrences). Manolo uses this type 48 times, such as in the following example:

(149) Manolo: [. . .] like I always say – good theories should reinforce each other [emphasis mine].

The authorial *I* is used 23 times in the *nationalism* controversy. One of the examples is used by Shahin as shown in the following example:

(150) Shahin: I think *nationalism* tends towards emphasizing the positive in order to an imply a negative about everyone else [emphasis mine].

8.2.4 Different functions of the pronoun you

Another pronoun which shows the interaction between participants and hence the dialogic nature of online controversies regarding the dimension of linguistic variation of medium is the pronoun *you*. Biber *et al*. (1999:330) explain that the pronoun *you* resembles the pronoun *we* as it is used with different intended referents. It is not clear whether the pronoun *you* refers to one or more people. Ratia (2005:130) distinguishes between two types of the pronoun *you* in her analysis of tobacco controversies: a) *you* addressing the reader and b) *you* attacking the opponent and addressing the audience. Ratia (2005:130) quotes Pearce (2001:220), who states that studies of political discourse put forward that the pronoun *you* is used effectively to express solidarity with the reader. In the *keris* controversy, *you* is used to express solidarity with the participants who are in line with thinking like the poster. In the following, David, who is a supporter of Manolo, uses *you* in this function, addressing Manolo Rodriguez directly:

(151) David: These are very good points you make [emphasis mine].

In general, I distinguish between two types of *you* addressing the reader. Either *you* is used to address the whole audience/readership of the threads, such as the following, where Manolo addresses the whole participants and also readers:

(152) Manolo: If your opponent is faster than you in making his stab, you're dead either way. In fact, you're more likely to face multiple opponents in battle, so speed would be even more important for quickly engaging opponents in succession [emphasis mine].

On the other hand, *you* is used to address one specific participant in the thread, such as the following example where Manolo addresses Stefano:

(153) Manolo: My e-mails never seem to reach you, my friend [emphasis mine]!

The usage of the pronoun *you* to attack the opponent is very frequent in the *keris* controversy. From the total number of the pronoun *you* used in the controversy, namely 178, *you* is used 144 times to attack the opponent as shown in the examples below:

(154) Manolo to Charley: I am having trouble identifying your facts because you have embedded them within a framework of opinion [emphasis mine].

(155) Charley to Manolo: Pointless, because you continue to level criticism at commentary , rather than to address Melborn's hypothesis [emphasis mine].

(156) David to Charley: So while you are defending Maisey, his proposals, and his conclusions (which you claim you are not doing but, based on a review of your posts, are doing), you are attacking criticism of his work, which has been "accurately quoted and addressed in an objective and scholarly **fashion**" [emphasis mine].

(157) Paulo to David: You and Manolo are quick to dismiss his article and, more importantly, his expertise [emphasis mine].

An analysis of the pronoun *you* in this function shows that four main contesters involved in the controversy are not only the ones who use the pronoun *you* to attack each other but also are the only ones to use the pronoun *you* in this function. Charley uses the pronoun *you* to attack 40 times, David 39 times, Manolo 31 times, and Paulo 25 times.

In the *nationalism* controversy, all types of the pronoun *you* mentioned above are used as well as the following examples show:
You addressing an individual:

(158) Donald to Manuel: The historical perspective that you are raising here is indeed tragic, but can we tie this into the topic? [emphasis mine].

You addressing the group:

(159) Manuel: How would you like to be told that you are owned by someone you have never heard of? [emphasis mine].

You attacking the opponent:

(160) Ehud to Stefano: In your comment on Amazon.com (addressed to me), you said: "...we've collected enough material to bury you with your own hate" and threatened to report me to Amazon. Please feel free to add my current posting to the file assembled by you and your Merry Gang of Attack Poodles [emphasis mine].

There is also another category of the pronoun *you* that is used in this controversy, and this is exophoric *you*, addressing a group outside the members of the discussion board as in the following example where *you* refers to the Moros:

(161) Manuel: When the Americans "won" the Philippines after the Spanish-American War, they told the Moros that we own you now.

8.2.5 Discourse markers

As I mentioned before, one of the features of communication in online discussion forums in general and in online polemical discourse in particular is that the discourse resembles dialogue, and, hence, it can be considered a written dialogue. One of the particular areas for the analysis of the discourse in online discussion forums (consisting of written dialogue) is the existence of discourse markers. Hence discourse markers show that the dimension of variation of the medium is typical of spoken language. The analysis of some discourse markers in controversies is important as it reveals the dialogic nature of online controversies. It is important to take into consideration that discourse markers do not only occur in spoken language. Most research on discourse markers has been done on speech data and has concluded that discourse markers occur primarily in speech. However, discourse markers also appear in the written medium (see Müller, 2005:6–7 and Jucker & Ziv, 1998). Nevertheless, there are some types of discourse markers that are used in controversies in online discussion forums that reveal the dialogic nature of online controversies. In the following, I will concentrate on and analyze certain types of discourse markers that are used in the *keris* controversy and the *nationalism* controversy that reveal the dialogic nature of controversies.

Müller (2005:1) explains that discourse markers contribute to the pragmatic meaning of utterances and are very important for the pragmatic competence of the speaker. Further, Müller (2005:8) explains that most researchers emphasize that discourse markers are used to facilitate the hearer's task of understanding the speaker's utterances. Müller also explains that discourse markers are analyzed from two basic frameworks: coherence and relevance theory. However, at the end, both approaches reach very similar conclusions. Quoting Schiffrin, Müller explains that discourse markers function as contextual coordinates for utterances and, hence, serve as coherence in communication. From the Relevance Theory point of view, discourse markers help the hearer to constrain the number of possible interpretations that is provided by the linguistic form of a sentence or an utterance (Müller, 2005:8–9). Based on Brinton (1990:47), Müller (2005:9) distinguishes the following functions of discourse markers:

- to initiate discourse
- to mark a boundary in discourse (shift/partial shift in topic)
- to preface a response or a reaction
- to serve as a filler or delaying tactic
- to aid the speaker in holding the floor
- to effect an interaction or sharing between speaker and hearer
- to bracket the discourse either cataphorically or anaphorically
- to mark either foregrounded or backgrounded information

Opinions of researchers regarding the number of pragmatic markers differ from a dozen to five hundred (Schmied, 1998:59). Quoting Brinton (1990 and 1996), Schmied (1998:59) explains that the often quoted types comprise *actually*, *anyway*, *I mean*, *now*, *so*, *then*, *well*, *you know*, and *you see*. Fraser (1998:301) states that discourse markers are lexical expressions, such as *nevertheless*, *after all*, *moreover*, *so*, and *incidentally*. Fraser (1998:302) explains that in spite of the fact that discourse markers are mainly taken from the syntactic classes of conjunctions, adverbials, and prepositional phrases, they do not have the function in a sentence that their classes would propose. Jucker and Smith (1998:171, 174) explain that discourse markers are not only used to convey information or to express social relations but also help each person shape models of each other's presumed knowledge. Further, Jucker and Smith (1998:172, 174) distinguish between the following types of discourse markers that help each person shape models of each other's presumed knowledge: a) reception markers, such as *yeah*, *oh*, and *okay*, that are used to indicate that one received the incoming material, b) presentation markers that are subdivided into information-centered presentation markers, such as *like*, that serve to modify the information itself, and c) addressee-centered presentation markers, such as *you know* and *I mean*, that relate the information to the presumed knowledge state of the addressee. Unlike other research in the past, in their study Jucker and Smith (1998:172) analyze discourse markers not as units of discourse that serve as guides to coherence, but they suggest a model that deals explicitly with the function of discourse markers in negotiations.

A very interesting finding is that reception markers such as *yeah*, *okay*, and *oh* are neither used in the *keris* controversy nor in the *nationalism* controversy. Although these discourse markers happen in some other threads, they do not happen very often in online discussion forums as the communication is asynchronous and participants do not see a need to use such signals in their communication as their postings are visible to other members. The information-centered presentation marker *like* is used only once in the *keris* controversy. There are, of course, other occurrences of *like* in both *keris* and *nationalism* controversies, where *like* functions as a verb, preposition, and suffix. However, these functions are not interesting for the purpose of this chapter here. Regarding addressee-centered presentation markers, the discourse marker *you know* occurs four times, and the marker *I mean* appears four times in the *keris* controversy.

There are also occurrences of the discourse marker *I mean* in the *keris* controversy. The following example shows the occurrence of the addressee-centered presentation marker *I mean* in the keris controversy:

(162) Moderator: *I mean* did they use differential heat treating?

None of these addressee-centered presentation markers occur in the *nationalism* controversy.

Based on Biber *et al.* (1999:1086), discourse markers are inserts that have a tendency to appear at the beginning of a turn or utterance and have two roles: a) to signal a transition in the ongoing process of the conversation and b) to signal an interactive association between speaker, hearer, and message. Biber *et al.* (1999:1086) add that words and phrases as discourse markers, such as *well* and *now*, are often ambiguous because they share the discourse marker function with an adverbial function. Further, Biber *et al.* (1999:1086) emphasize that the items considered 'discourse markers' are open to debate and mention *well*, *right*, and *now*, including the finite verb formulae *I mean*, *you know*, and *you see*. There are also less frequent types, such as *mind you* and *now then*, that could be considered discourse markers. Biber *et al.* (1999:1086) add that some inserts, such as *oh* and *okay*, can also be considered discourse markers.

Suhr (2006:32) states that discourse markers are, at times, called 'pragmatic markers' and are mainly elements of spoken language. Discourse markers do not have a meaning and do not have a grammatical function in an utterance, but they are still an integral part of spoken language (Suhr, 2006:32). Further, discourse markers function as turn-taking signals, the changing of a topic, or the repairing of one's own or someone else's discourse (Suhr, 2006:32). Based on Brinton (1996:33–38), Suhr adds that discourse markers express a reaction to preceding discourse or express intimacy between speaker and hearer by confirming shared assumptions. Further following Taavitsainen (1995:439), Suhr explains that interjections are often classified as discourse markers because they, at times, have the same functions as discourse markers. However, in her study, Suhr (2006:32) does not differentiate between interjections and discourse markers and puts them into one category. Suhr (2006:38) identifies the following discourse markers in her study of witchcraft pamphlets that she identified by checking manually through close readings: *ah*, *alas*, *ha*, *ho*, *lo*, *marry*, *nay*, *now*, *o*, *oh*, *pray*, *see well*, *what*, *why*, and *yes*. One should note that Biber *et al.* (1999:1083) identify *oh* as an interjection and explain that interjections have an exclamatory function, expressing the speaker's emotion.[83]

Some of the discourse markers used in the *keris* controversy are the following. Manolo uses the discourse marker *now* as follows:

(163) Manolo: Now again, our goal here at SFI is to increase academic understanding, so we continue to invite Maisey to make an appearance [emphasis mine].

Jucker (1993:436) states that one of the interesting features about *well* as a discourse marker is that it has a remarkable number of homonyms, such as a manner adverb, a degree word, a noun, and a verb. David uses the discourse marker *well* in the following:

(164) David: Well, I would look forward to reading that [emphasis mine].

Another example of discourse markers used in the *keris* controversy is shown below:

(165) David: Yet even this is not a guarantee, right [emphasis mine]?

Another discourse marker that is used in the *keris* controversy is *surely*. Downing (2006:39) explains that *surely* is a pragmatic marker of an epistemic stance that shows the speaker's attitude towards the proposition in which it happens and also shows the state of knowledge or intentions of the addressee. In the following example, Manolo uses the discourse marker *surely*:

(166) Manolo: Charley, surely you know that SFI is an academic forum, and in academia it is the norm for those who propose arguments to bear the burden of evidence, [. . .] [emphasis mine].

None of the discourse markers mentioned above occur in the *nationalism* controversy. Only Eidel uses the discourse marker *now* once:

---

83 Biber *et al.* (1999:1083) explain that *oh* is by far the most common interjection that appears in combinations, such as *Oh well*, *Oh God*, *Oh I see*, and *Oh right*. They also identify *Oh wow*, *Ooh*, *Oops*, *Whoops*, *Ugh*, *Aargh*, and *Yippee* also as interjections.

(167) Eidel: Now my second point was not directed for or against the exhibition, I simply referred to a new generation of "scholars" that appeared in the past 20 years [emphasis mine].

However, this does not mean that the language on the *nationalism* controversy is not dialogic in nature. As a matter of fact a large number of emoticons used there are an indication of how participants try to communicate with each other in an informal way, similar to oral communication.

8.3 Lexical choices

It is obvious that being engaged in any type of a controversy requires the usage of a certain type of lexical terms, and, additionally, when the polemical exchange ends in a heated discussion, different types of polemical terms are used. Gloning (2002:71) points out that to participate in a scientific controversy, one needs to be able to use appropriate and related lexical terms. Gloning adds that the lexical profile of contributions in a controversy depends on two factors: first, on the topic of the controversy and, second, the functional requirements of the type of the presentation. To deal with a certain topic in a controversy, one needs to know specific vocabulary, e.g. depending on the controversy, religious or political terms, technical terms, philosophical terms, or astrological-cosmological terms (Gloning, 2002:71).

The thematic vocabulary is used to deal with the topic, and it contains technical terms and terminology, but it also has lexical terms that help to deal with the topic as well. Gloning (2002:71) explains that the thematic vocabulary in the astrology controversy includes all types of terms for celestial bodies (fixed star, comet), names of the planets (Venus, Jupiter), names of zodiac signs, terms for astronomical constellations (sextile, quartile), components of the cosmos, terms for astronomical instruments, terms for devices, terms for observable phenomena (new moon), and terms for all types of astronomical incidents (Gloning, 2002:71).

Gloning (2002:71) explains that parts of the thematic vocabulary depend on the convictions and theses that are presented in a controversy. As an example, Gloning explains that Kepler believes in the correlations between heaven and earth, and, therefore, he uses a number of expressions, such as *Vereinigung* [association], *Verknüpfung* [linkage], *Verwandtschaft* [relationship], *verbunden sein* [to be connected], *verknüpft sein* [to be linked], *vereinigt sein* [to be united], *regiert werden* [to be governed], *etwas wirken* [to act upon], *bewegen* [to move], etc. There is a variety of thematic vocabulary and topics in controversies. Gloning (2002:72) explains that the internal structure of thematic vocabulary follows the structure of topics in controversies. Gloning adds that the relationship between the thematic structure and the structure of thematic vocabulary is not specific for controversies, but it is a general principle of thematic conversation. Gloning adds that in scientific controversies around 1600, not all areas of vocabulary were developed enough to be sufficient to deal with the topics. Therefore, the authors were forced to build new terms or to resort to Latin counterparts. Gloning provides, as an example, *species immateriata* that was used by Kepler in 'Tertius Interveniens'. As mentioned before, regarding the dimensions of variation, Esser (1993:27) explains that the dimension of field of discourse covers communicative purpose on the one hand and subject matter on the other. Thus, subject matter is reflected in language through specialized vocabulary regarding arms and armor in online discussion forums. This, of course, was also the case with Early Modern controversies. Given the different nature of controversies in online discussion forums dedicated to the study of arms and armor, the types of vocabulary and expressions should also be of a specific nature. In the following, I will show what kind of thematic vocabulary and expressions are used in the *keris* and *nationalism* controversies.

8.3.1 The usage of jargon and technical terms

As mentioned above, to deal with a certain topic in a controversy one needs to know specific/thematic vocabulary (Gloning, 2002:71). This specific vocabulary includes jargon and technical terms used to describe different types of arms and armor. In the *keris* controversy, a number of technical terms are used that require special knowledge of the subject. This specialized vocabulary can be divided into:

Terms describing a specific weapon: in the following, I will show the examples that occur in the *keris* controversy, such as '*keris*' (an Indonesian or Malay weapon with an endless variety of blades, hilts, scabbards, and decorations),[84] 'Enga cassowary dagger' (a dagger from New Guinea), 'Medieval ballock dagger' (a dagger from Medieval Europe with a handle that resembles ballocks – this dagger is also know as kidney dagger),[85] 'Arkansas toothpick' (the Arkansas Toothpick is a heavy dagger with a pointed, straight 30–50 cm blade; this dagger is balanced and weighted for throwing and can also be used for thrusting and slashing), 'Italian stiletto' (a stiletto is a long, narrow-bladed dagger used for stabbing)],[86] 'Tuareg *telek*' (a double-edged straight-bladed knife with a cross pommel used by Tuaregs in North Africa),[87] '*khanjar*' (a curved, double-edged Persian dagger),[88] 'Cossack *kinzhal*' (or *kindjal*, a double-edged short sword from the Caucasus[89]), '*kujang*' (a dagger fitted with a spearhead from West Java), '*tombak*' (also *tumbak*, a collective term for all types of spears from Indonesian archipelago), [90] and '*bendho*' (actually *bendo*; this is a machete in the shape of an axe, mostly used for harvesting the *aren* palm),[91] '*Keris Buda*'[92] (considered as the earliest type of *keris*, where the handle and the blade were made of one piece], 'Buginese *badik*' (*badik* or *badek* is a knife with a large variety of shapes and sizes from Indonesian archipelago),[93] and '*rencong*' (a dagger with a sharp blade with a slightly convex back from Aceh, Gayo, and Alas).[94]

---

84 For more information, see van Zonneveld (2001:62).
85 See Stone (1999:355).
86 For more information, see Stone (1999:584).
87 For the description, see Stone (1999:608-610).
88 For more information on *khanjar*, see Moshtagh Khorasani (2006:219-229).
89 For more information, see Stone (1999:358).
90 For the translation, see van Zonneveld (2001:148).
91 For the description, see van Zonneveld (2001:35).
92 Note that the technical term for this type of *keris* is *keris majapahit* (see van Zonneveld, 2001:69).
93 For the description, see van Zonneveld (2001:27).
94 For the description, see van Zonneveld (2001:113).

Terms that describe a certain school of swordsmanship or martial arts or smiths, such as the following examples that occur in the *keris* controversy: '*Silat*' or '*pencak silat*' (a Southeast Asian martial art), '*pesilat*' (practitioner of silat), and '*empu*' (traditional smith of *keris*).

Terms that describe the way of holding or using a specific type of weapon or techniques, such as the following examples taken from the *keris* controversy: 'pistol-shaped grip' (in this grip the dagger is held with the tip of the blade pointing forward), 'reverse grip' (in this grip the dagger is held with the tip of the blade pointing downward), and 'icepick grip' (the same as the reverse grip).

Terms that describe the specific shapes and parts of a certain weapon, such as the following examples from the *keris* controversy: 'played blade base' [the base of the blade is sloped], 'wavy blade' [a blade with waved edges], 'large-pommeled dagger' [a dagger with a big knob on its hilt], 'the heavy pommel' [dagger with a heavy knob on its head], 'hooked point' [a dagger with a hooked tip], 'rectangular tang' [a tang is the end of the blade that is fitted into the handle and has different shapes, such as round or rectangular], and 'asymmetric grip' [the grip of a dagger that is not symmetric].

Terms describing the apparel and way of dressing of a certain culture, such as the following example from the *keris* controversy: '*sarong*' or '*sarung*' [a garment that consists of a length of cloth wrapped around the waist that is worn by men and women in Malaysia, Indonesia, and the Pacific Islands].

Terms describing (historical) locations, deities, and dynasties, such as the following examples taken from the *keris* controversy: 'Majapahit' [Majapahit was the last Hindu Empire on the Indonesian archipelago from 1293 to the beginning of the 16th century], 'Prambanan' [Prambanan is the biggest Hindu temple in Indonesia and is located circa 18 km from Yoyakarta on the Java island], 'Durga' [God of victory in Hinduism], 'Kali' [a goddess in Hindusim], and 'Vishnu' [God of preservation].

Contrary to the *keris* controversy, the *nationalism* controversy does not contain much specialized/thematic vocabulary as the *nationalism* controversy concentrates on the topic of nationalism and not so much on an edged-weapon-related topic. Nevertheless, in the *nationalism* controversy, a number of technical terms are used that require special knowledge of the subject. This is, of course, the restricted code of the communication that can be traced back to the dimension of explicitness in online discussion forums. By using many specialized terms and information on the historical background, participants in online discussion forums suppose that the meaning is shared, i.e. that the communication cannot be universally understood. The following are terms that describe a specific weapon, such as a *shamshir* [Persian sword], *tabar* [a Persian axe], Moro *kris* [a short sword used by the Moros on the Philippines], *barong* [a dagger with a leaf-shaped blade used by the Moros], and a term that describes the usage of a certain technique as 'hooking thrust' [a thrust that is done with a curved blade].

8.3.2 Person-related terms

These words are used to refer to a member of the other group or his actions in the controversy. These are normally personal attacks against the opponent, such as the following examples taken from the *keris* controversy: *armchair martial artists* (Manolo, 2nd post); *misrepresentation* (Charley, 1st post); *diminished intellectual capacity* (Charley, 1st post); *the inaccuracies and misrepresentations in the comments of Mr. Rodriguez* (Charley, 2nd post); *fatuous criticism* (Charley, 2nd post); *carping criticism* (Charley, 2nd post); *Your diatribe directed at Melborn's hypothesis*, addressing Manolo (Charley, 2nd post); *pointless criticism* (Charley, 3rd post); *his lack of understanding*, referring to Manolo (Charley, 4th post); and *his attempts to discredit the work of Melborn lacks substance*, addressing Manolo (Charley, 4th post),

These person-related terms are also used to attack the members of the opponent group in the *nationalism* controversy, such as *romanticism in sheep cloths*, referring to a member on the Forum of Swords (Ehud, 1st first post); *jingoism* [referring to a member on the Forum of Swords (Ehud, 1st post); *romantic aspirations*, referring to a member on the Forum of Swords (Ehud, 1st post); *plain vileness*, referring to a member on the Forum of Swords (Ehud, 1st post); *schmoozing with the curators in a native tongue* , referring to a member on the Forum of Swords (Ehud, 1st post); *laughable hubris*, referring to a member on the Forum of Swords (Ehud, 1st post); *poisonous transformation*, referring to a member on Forum of Swords (Ehud, 1st post); and *Merry Gang of Attack Poodles*, referring to the members of Forum of Swords (Ehud, 1st post).

8.3.3 Polemical terms and phrases towards theories, arguments, and ideas of the other group

These terms and phrases are used to attack and criticize the theories, arguments, and ideas of the opponent. These terms could be the result of the principle of warfare, a communication principle that was used in the religious controversy between the Protestants and the Jesuits and dominated by aggressive moves. Glüer (2001:21–22) states that the aggressive mode of controversy in the religious debates in Early Modern Controversies is based on principles of warfare, meaning that the goal of inflicting pain in the controversy substitutes doing physical harm. Glüer (2001:22) explains that, as a result, the vocabulary of aggressive actions is used in this type of controversy, such as *bezüchtigen* (to charge), *greiffen an* (to attack), *schelten* (to scold), *drewen auff die hohen Potentaten und verhetzen sie wider mich* (they menace the high potentates and stir them up against me), *toben* (to rage), *gar hässig reden* (to talk hatefully), *gifftig stechen* (to prick with poison), *calumnirn und liegen* (to culmniate and to lie), *fabulirn* (to fabricate facts), *mit Schalcksnarrenbossen, spitzigen dröworten, gifftigen Scorpionstichen* (with rogue buffoonery, crotchety threats, poisonous stings of scorpions), and *trotzig läugnen*, *spotten* (defiant denial, mockery). Glüer also explains that the disputants use interjections, such as *pfui*, *ey*, and *auweh* (fie!, ah!, and alas!) to appeal to the emotions. Further, Glüer adds that, at times, the mode of expression resembles the tone of an interrogation, such as the frequent usage of short wh-questions in asyndectic order. Being engaged in such a war of words was not without problems and had to be justified in view of the danger of being charged with instigation to riot (Glüer, 2001:23).

Similar aggressive terms attacking the theories and statements of opponents are used in the *keris* controversy, such as *bad theory* (Manolo, 3rd post); *armchair speculations* (Manolo, 4th post); *incorrect conclusions* (Manolo, 5th post); *unsupported in the historical records* (Manolo, 6th post); *Melborn's essay looks weaker than ever* (Manolo, 6th post); *Melborn's speculations* (Manolo, 9th post); *Melborn's hypothesis isn't supported* (Manolo, 15th post); *All of Melborn's speculations fail against comparative evidence, practical evaluation, and simple critical reflection* (Manolo, 18th post); *his [Melborn's] arguments are not falsifiable, but simply false* (Manolo, 19th post); *the original idea is so poorly reasoned*, referring to the article by Melborn (Manolo, 21st post*); Melborn's article is a poorly reasoned, factually unsupported explanation that does not pass even superficial criticism* (Manolo, 21st post); *Melborn's article lacks evidence and must be rejected by any standard, academic or not* (Manolo, 23rd post); *he does not understand the distinction between hypothesis and theory,* addressing Manolo](Charley, 4th post); *he does not understand that the scientific method does not allow for any hypothesis to be proven*, addressing Manolo (Charley, 4th post); *myth and misconception* (David, 1st post); *wrong assumptions* (David, 1st post); *dubious reasoning* (David, 3rd post); *questionable claims* (David, 4th post); *red herring*, referring to the argumentation of Charley (David, 5th post); *fallacy of special pleading* (David, 5th post); *straw man fallacy*, referring to Charley's arguments (David, 7th post); *ad hominem tu quoque* (*because Manolo's usage of theory is different from yours, he must be wrong*), and t*he lack of evidence for certain surmises*, referring to Melborn article (Ward, 2nd post).

At times, polemical phrases are written as ironical remarks towards the opponent. These remarks, such as 'Come on' in the following example, increase the intensity of the controversy, such as *But the idea that speed isn't so important in battle really baffles me. Did people in Majapahit Java just go to the field and fight half-heartedly? Come on* (Manolo, 2nd post). Sometimes, the polemical terms and phrases are directed against the history accounts and not necessarily against a participant, such as in the following statement from the *nationalism* controversy: *National pride at its worst*, referring to history accounts on General McArthur (Tony, 3rd post). These types of moves and aggressive terms are also used in the *nationalism* controversy, such as [*It] may be just as biased as that of Ancient*

Iranian Circle[95] (Eidel), *their knowledge of Azerbaijan / Caucausus is extremely shallow* (Eidel), *a complete idiocy of Said-like 'post-orientalist approach'* (Eidel), *romantic aspirations* (Ehud, 1 post), *[He] denigrates other cultures or other people* (Ehud, 1 post), and *just plain vileness* (Ehud, 1 post),

8.4 Emoticons

Participants in both forums have the opportunity to use a different set of emoticons and integrate them in their messages. These emoticons, also called smilies, add a personal touch to the messages and integrate a certain type of emotion to messages. Janoschka (2004:97) explains that the term 'emoticon' is made up of the notions *emotion* and *icon*. Janoschka adds that by using certain icons, one can express certain emotions, such as 'enjoyment' and 'pleasure' (☺), or 'sadness' and 'disapproval' (☹). Emoticons substitute extralinguistic cues, such as gestures and facial expressions used in interpersonal communication. Chats on the Internet lack gestures and facial expressions because of the missing physical presence of interlocutors and eye contact (Janoschka, 2004:97, Kresic, 2000:72). Emoticons play the same role in online discussion forums dedicated to the study of arms and armor.

The Forum of Swords has the possibility to use different emoticons in an online environment, where people cannot see each other and mostly can only communicate with words. Thus, this is an environment without prosodic and non-verbal markers. Regarding the usage of emoticons in the e-community environment, Graham (2007:745) states that in spite of the fact that emoticons are applied to come close to facial expressions, the range of emoticons conveyed by these symbols is normally humorous rather than representative of the full range of emotion. Graham claims that one would unlikely use the emoticon for sadness (☹) in case of the death of a relative. However, practical experience shows that the members of both forums dedicated

95 The name of the organization is changed due to privacy reasons.

to the study of arms and armor take these signs seriously in a given context. Some of them, indeed, are used in humorous ways in some contexts, but some are used in some contexts to express sadness. The following emoticons (facial expressions) can be used by the members of the Forum of Swords. Sixteen different types of emoticons are available to participants as the following tables show. However, it is important to take into consideration that there is no difference in appearance between the sign for a smile and a big smile as is evident in the following table:

Table 8.1: Different emoticons with their related meanings and functions from the Forum of Swords.

Symbol	Meaning	Function	Symbol	Meaning	Function
	To have a big smile :-)	To signal that someone is very happy		To drool	To show deep admiration for something
	To eek	To express mild alarm, disappointment, or surprise		To be confused	To signal confusion regarding a certain statement
	Rolleyes	To be sarcastic		To be mad	To stress that one is angry about a certain statement
	:p	To laugh		To be cool	To signal that something is first-rate or excellent
	To wink	To signal something		To gag	To refrain or stop from exercising free speech
	To grin	To smile broadly, often baring the teeth, as in amusement, glee, embarrassment, or other strong emotions		To smooch	To kiss

	To blush	To signal embarrassment, modesty, and shame.		Ninja	To suggest something sneeky or covert
	To be sad	To convey a sad feeling		To smile :)	To signal that someone is happy about something

Figure 8.1: The following figure shows different emoticons in their original form on the Forum of Swords.

Standard Smilies			
	:drool:		:-)
	:confused:		:eek:
	:mad:		:rolleyes:
	:cool:		:p
	:gag:		;)
	:smooch:		:D
	:ninja:		:o
	:)		:(

As shown above, sixteen different types of emoticons or facial expressions are available to the members of the Forum of Swords. Four participants in the *keris* controversy used nineteen emoticons altogether. These emoticons consist of ten smiles, four winks, three signs of being cool, one laughing, and one being sad. Thus, the members used four different types of emoticons altogether.

The Forum of Ethnographic Swords also allows its users to use a set of emoticons to express their feelings and add a personal touch to their posts. In contrast to the sixteen different types of emoticons in the Forum of Swords, participants of the Forum of Ethnographic Swords can choose from twelve different types of emoticons, as the following table shows:

Table 8.2: Different types of emoticons used on the Forum of Ethnographic Swords.

Symbol	Meaning	Function	Symbol	Meaning	Function
	big grin	To smile broadly, often baring the teeth, as in amusement, glee, embarrassment, or other strong emotions		wink	To signal something
	Confused	To signal confusion regarding a certain statement		frown	To regard something with disapproval or distaste
	Embarras s-ment	To signal embarrassment, modesty, and shame		rolls eyes (sarcastic)	To be sarcastic
	Smile	To signal that someone is happy		shrug	To raise the shoulders, as a gesture of doubt, disdain, or indifference
	Mad	To stress that one is angry about a certain statement		Cool	To signal that something is first-rate or excellent
	Stick out tongue	To show spite, arrogance, or rebellious behavior		eek!	To express mild alarm, disappointment or surprise.

Figure 8.2: The following figure shows different emoticons in their original form on the Forum of Ethnographic Swords.

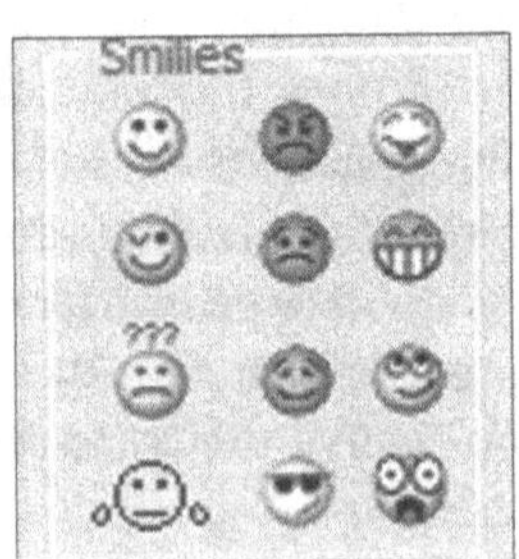

There is some overlapping between the two forums regarding the function of emoticons. However, one should note that the Forum of Ethnographic Swords does not have the following functions that are offered by the Forum of the swords: a) to have a big smile, b) to laugh, c) to drool, d) to gag, e) to smooch, and f) ninja. On the other hand, the Forum of Ethnographic Swords offers two other emoticons that do not exist in the set of emoticons offered by Forum of the Swords: a) to shrug and b) to stick out tongue. Similar to the Forum of the Swords, the participants on the Forum of Ethnographic Swords use the above-mentioned emoticons to express certain feelings.

Analyzing the usage of these emoticons should be done from a pragmatic point of view and taken in their related context. For example, a sign for laughing and happiness in combination with the criticism of the opponent easily becomes a sign of ridicule. In the following, I will distinguish the emoticons based on their intended usage. I will distinguish between emoticons that are used for their intended meaning or in a neutral way and emoticons that are used sarcastically and are meant to attack the opponent.

8.4.1 Emoticons used for their intended purpose or in a neutral way

As mentioned above, emoticons can be used for their intended purpose, but at times, they are also used sarcastically. From 10 signs of smiling used in the *keris* controversy, 9 are not used for their intended purpose as they are used sarcastically to attack the opponent. Marco is the only one in the *keris* controversy who uses the smiling sign for its intended purpose and not to attack the opponent as is shown in the following:

(168) Marco: There is a great mural in a Thai temple (forget the name) that includes Dutch soldiers in Mara's army. I guess it was OK to be more true to life when showing the bad guys.

There are four wink signs that are used in the *keris* controversy. Two of them are used for their intended purpose and are not meant to attack the opponent, such as the following:

(169) Paulo: We use it in both grips, and even do occasional grip changes in the middle of a technique (not recommended for actual combat but nice for the spectators).

The cool sign ( ) is used three times in the *keris* controversy. One of them is used in its intended purpose as the following example shows where Manolo praises the editorial skills of his main supporter David:

(170) Manolo: As always, David's editorial skills allow him to extract the underlying issues from a given posting. Truly The People's Editor.

The sign of being sad is only used once. Although this emoticon here does not mean true sadness, it shows that the user is disappointed. This is not meant to be sarcastic or to attack anyone:

(171) Paulo: *I realize this probably won't help you much . . .*

8.4.2 Emoticons used sarcastically to attack the opponent

Emoticons can also be used sarcastically to attack an opponent as in Manolo's following statement, which criticizes Melborn's article. It is obvious that the emoticon standing for laughing does not mean happiness but is meant sarcastically:

(172) Manolo: Did people in Majapahit Java just go to the field and fight half-heartedly? Come on...

This is the same with the following statement by Manolo criticizing Melborn's article and calling it a bad theory and ending the sentence with a wink sign:

(173) Manolo: Yes, but the first step in creating a more likely theory is to sweep away the previous, bad theory, which I'm trying to do here.

At one point, he invites Melborn to join the Forum of Swords, knowing exactly that he would not join and ending the sentence with a sign of coolness ( ). This is, of course, meant in a sarcastic way:

(174) Manolo: I hope to see him do that, and welcome him to come to this forum so that the many critical thinkers here can offer their help.

Manolo also uses the smilie face to be sarcastic towards his main opponent Charley in the *keris* controversy:

(175) Manolo: I'm feeling generous today (as a People's Champion should), so I'll reciprocate and use "hypothesis" in place of "theory" if it so pleases you.

In the Forum of Ethnographic Swords, emoticons are also sarcastic and attack an opponent, such as in the following example:

(176) Ehud: Most of the Moro weapon collectors are likely to trace their ancestry to the Philippines and native Iranians would sell their birthright for a true Assadollah shamshir

8.5 Summary

This chapter has shown that the communication in online discussion forums is dialogic in nature and can be considered as dialogue in written form. The dimensions of linguistic variation indicating the dialogic nature of communication in online discussion forms are the medium, participation in discourse, and explicitness. There are many indications for the texts being dialogic, such as the interaction and addressing other participants by using titles and last names or addressing by the first name, the usage of the pronoun *we* to address the group identity, different functions of the pronoun *I*, and different functions of the pronoun *you*.

I have shown that, normally, participants use the first name to communicate with each other. They use the last name to create distance towards their opponents. Different types of the pronoun *we* are used in the discourse, such as rare *we* [+ ego] [+ voc], 'authorial *we*', c) 'workshop *we*' [+ voc], d) specific exophoric *we1*, and e) the generic *we2*. There are also different usage of the pronoun *I*, such as the multifunctional *I* and the authorial *I*. The multifunctional *I* can be used as a hedge and a cautious note, it can be used to increase the writer's authority and convincing the reader of the author's expertise, it can be used neutrally and it can be used to persuade the audience. The pronoun *you* can be used to address the reader and to attack the opponent.

Different lexical choices are used during controversies in online discussion forums dedicated to the study of arms and armor. They are specialized vocabulary ranging from jargon and technical terms, person-related terms to polemical terms, and phrases towards theories, arguments, and ideas of the opponent group. Different types of emoticons are also used on both discussion forums. These emoticons can be used for their intended meaning, or they can be used sarcastically to attack the opponent.

9. Conclusion

9.1 Summary

I have shown in my research that communication in online discussion forums has opened up new ways of interaction among different people with different backgrounds from different nations. Not all communication goes in a smooth way in online discussion forums. As a matter of fact, as participants do not feel restricted by the rules of social etiquette and rules that they all face in their everyday lives, the conflicts and controversies seem to occur very often due to the nature of the new medium, the Internet, where participants can hide their true identities. As is the case with real communities, virtual communities that are built as a result of interaction among different members in online discussion forums have their conflicts and controversies as well. This is, of course, not surprising as human beings have their conflicts, and the corresponding polemical discourse in all spheres of their lives and online communities are no exception to this. Nevertheless, in spite of the existence of the forum rules, it seems that conflicts and controversies in an online environment tend to turn out aggressive very fast.

Participants in controversies in online discussion forums make up an online community with typical characteristics of social networks. I have studied two controversial threads, the *keris* controversy from the Forum of Swords and the *nationalism* controversy from the Forum of Ethnographic Swords. The Forum of Swords is the biggest online discussion forum dedicated to the study of arms and armor. It has different subforums with different areas of specialties. Each subforum is dedicated to the study of a special field of arms and armor. The Forum of Ethnographic Swords consists of three subforums. Each forum has a set of explicit rules that are described in the charter of rules of the forum. Next to these, there are implicit rules that participants follow. These rules are partly rules that are based on traditional rhetorical principles, and some are individual principles. Other forms of collecting information about arms and armor also exist in the field of arms and armor, such as specialized books and articles.

To gain a better understanding of controversies in online discussion forums, I examined different types of polemical discourse, namely discussion, dispute, and controversy. All three types existed in polemical exchanges in religious, scientific, and medical controversies in the Early Modern Period. As I have shown, discussion is a type of polemical exchange where participants use rational argumentation to reach a common consensus. On the other hand, rational argumentation plays a marginal role in debates and a broadly conceived role in controversies. Further, a discussion has a well-defined topic. In discussions, participants have the chance to find solutions and correct mistakes. On the other hand, disputes are a type of a polemical exchange with a well-defined divergence that can dissolve or be dissolved. Controversies are a type of polemical exchange that is between a discussion and a dispute. In controversies, contenders collect arguments to raise the weight of their positions against their adversaries' objections. Nevertheless, making a clear-cut differentiation between these categories seems to be an impossible task as controversies in online discussion forums dedicated to the study of arms and armor have both the characteristics of disputes and controversies.

To take part in controversies, participants are expected to follow certain rules and principles since controversies are not 'anything goes' activities. Leibniz was one of the firm believers of setting up communication principles for a procedure of a controversy to arrive at more knowledgeable positions for all parties involved. Leibniz believed that the growth of knowledge required the co-operation of many minds, and he naively believed that by specifying a set of communication principles, one could establish a framework where people with differing ideas could argue and debate with each other without bringing in the aspects of subjectivity and personal emotions. However, in reality, controversies were carried out very differently even in the 'Golden Age' of controversies in the 16th to 18th centuries. The goal of participants was to win and to impress the audience. This is also the case in controversies in online discussion forums. The goal of participants is not to resolve an issue, but they try to impress readers by making their opponents speechless. This is not surprising as controversies have an existential dimension (opponent's reputation: their career and their intellectual and personal prestige) and a public dimension (the addressee).

The features of controversies are that they do not stay restricted to the initial questions that originate them. Further, in controversies, participants question their adversaries' basic factual, methodological, and conceptual presuppositions to undermine their positions and viewpoints. Controversies also have a hermeneutical aspect, as contenders in controversies accuse each other of misinterpreting their data and of not responding to the objectives. Further, controversies have the character of being open since no one can predict the outcome. No one knows how a controversy ends when he/she gets involved in it. Being involved in a controversy is highly emotional, shown by the way participants in online controversies complain about getting involved in them and the emotional toll they take.

Another feature of controversies is that getting involved in controversies is a highly emotional activity. The individual emotions are surely affected by the group emotions due to the influence of group dynamics. These are what can be called social emotions. Social emotions play an important role in controversies in online discussion forums as well. Participants complain about the emotional toll that they face when involved in public controversies. A controversy in an online discussion forum starts when a breach of accepted principles or norms, such as harsh criticism of a book or an article, happens. This leads to a state of crisis when participants rush in to side with the thread initiator or to attack his/her comments. The next step in this highly emotional activity is when moderators of online discussion forums step in and mediate. Only when the controversial thread is closed, does the online community reintegrate and go back to its original status.

An important factor in analyzing any type of controversy is to find out some background information about the type of participants who participated in controversies. In the Early Modern Period, members of the République des Lettres considered themselves members of a republic and citizens of a supranational community with the goal of advancing learning. Members of this society promoted conducting different types of polemical discourse. Although they established different sets of rules and communication principles, they got very emotional, attacked each other, and could not hide their political perspectives. One of the most important media used by members of the République des Lettres to carry out controversies was pamphlets. Pamphlets were read out mostly to illiterate people and were dialogic in nature. Further, pamphlets were an early form of mass communication. Nevertheless, as a text type, pamphlets had their restrictions as well. One of these restrictions was the point-by-point principle, which forced people to answer the accusations of their opponents point by point. Therefore, some contesters decided to use polemical sermons or open letters instead.

Controversies were not 'anything-goes' activities. Therefore, to carry out controversies, different communication principles were set up. These communication principles changed over time, meaning that communication principles that were valid for the Early Modern Period are not valid for communication principles of today's discourse. One of the reasons for this change is due to the change of the type of media that is used to carry out controversies. This is partly due to medium-dependent structures in the written medium, such as punctuation, orthography, and variations of characters. Additionally, one should always be aware that the new medium of the Internet introduces new principles of text production that influence medium-dependent structures, such as punctuation, orthography, and variations of characters. For example, being involved in online controversies, such as communicating in online discussion forums dedicated to the study of arms and armor, requires the participants to follow the principles of the netiquette (accurate marking of the content of messages in the subject line, not wasting bandwidth, and not blatting). Similar to communication principles from the Early Modern Period, any violation of netiquette principles will lead to conflicts and controversies.

Next to these principles, there are certain communication principles that have gone through change, such as the principle of point-by-point refutation. Combined with one of the principles of netiquette, this principle has changed into the selective quoting principle. Using this principle, participants selectively quote parts of the statements of their opponents and answer them. They do this to save the bandwidth and not be restricted by the traditional point-by-point principle. There are different communication principles from the Early Modern Period that were used in religious, scientific, and medical controversies. These principles ranged from efficiency principles/traditional rhetorical principles (the principle of brevity, the principle of non-repetition, different types of principles of relevance, and principles of comprehensibility and perspicuity) and the principles related to the relationship between the two antagonists (politeness principles forbidding face-threatening acts and principles banning irony and sarcasm).

Although it is very difficult to make a general classification of communication principles from the Early Modern Period, I classified them into efficiency principles, person-related principles, and argument-related principles. Based on these communication principles, participants in controversies from the Early Modern Period used different moves and strategies. These moves ranged from formulating an opinion or position, supportive moves, attacking moves, personal attacks to clarification moves, and other characteristic individual moves, such as using accusations. Some of these moves are also used in controversies in online discussion forums. Different moves and strategies are used in controversies in online discussion forums. These moves can generally be divided into a) opening moves, b) attacking moves, c) defending moves, d) counterattacks, e) deflecting moves, f) accusation moves related to the violations of principles of communication, g) neutral moves, and h) using rhetorical and direct questions in controversies.

Different dimensions of linguistic variation can be used to analyze the stylistic markers of a text in online discussion forums. In this volume, I studied the dimensions of medium, participation in discourse, explicitness, and field of discourse to show the dialogic nature of online controversies. Participants in controversies in online discussion forums use a number of pragmatic markers to communicate and interact with other members, showing that the texts are dialogic in nature. Different types of vocatives, such as first name, titles and surnames, and honorifics, are used to refer to other members. Further, different types of the personal pronoun *we*, such as rare *we* [+ ego] [+

voc], authorial *we*, 'workshop *we*' [+ voc], specific exophoric *we*1, and generic *we*2, are used to address the group identity.

The pronoun *I* is also used to address the writer-addressee relationship in controversies in online discussion forums. The pronoun *I* is generally used as a multifunctional *I* and an authorial *I*. The pronoun *you* is also used as a pragmatic marker to address the audience or to attack the opponent. Different types of discourse markers, such as *well*, *now*, *for now*, *right*, *I mean*, and *you know*, are used in online controversies showing the dialogic nature of written texts in such controversies. Different lexical choices are made to take part in controversies, such as the usage of jargon and technical terms, person-related terms, and polemical terms and phrases towards theories, arguments, and ideas of the other group. These lexical choices show the type of subject matter of the linguistic variation of the field of discourse where an understanding of the technical terms is required to take part in controversies.

Different types of emoticons are used in online controversies to replace the lack of facial cues and expressions. Emoticons are either used for their intended purpose or in a neutral way, or emoticons are used sarcastically to attack the opponent. Emoticons add special force to written statements in online controversies as they replace facial expressions in an environment where paralinguistic markers are lacking. Nevertheless, the determination of intent of emoticons can be difficult for members, and, hence, the emoticons can serve as another source of misunderstanding in online controversies.

9.2 Future steps in terms of research into online controversies

As I have shown, online discussion forums seem to be a modern substitute for pamphlets to carry out controversies. Controversies in online discussion forums tend to be very aggressive and only end by the mediation of moderators who close the threads. Although some academics get involved in online controversies dedicated to the study of arms and armor, generally, they prefer to stay out of them due to the emotional pressure such an involvement affects its participants with. Further research of other online controversies is required to find out more about the nature of online controversies, the principles applied there, and other moves and strategies implemented. Such an analysis will enable researchers to analyze the nature of online controversies in more detail.

As participants in online controversies act in an environment without paralinguistic markers and facial expressions, misunderstandings and conflicts are commonplace. Moderators and administrators of online discussion forums constantly revise and develop rules and principles of communication in online discussion forums to meet the challenge of providing a friendly online atmosphere. The dangers are clear as any online discussion forum that is not moderated well and properly runs the danger of losing members. Such forums are doomed to fail, meaning that the number of active participants dwindles until almost no one else takes part in the forum. Further future research of the rules and principles of communication of online discussion forums should reveal how these principles work in online communities and similarities in pattern and nature of communication principles.

Very often, participants who become involved in online controversies claim that, in the real world, they would not have had problems with some of their opponents. Although this is a claim that needs to be substantiated, further research needs to be done to find out what exactly contributes to the frequency of controversies and conflicts in online discussion forums. Linguists need to find out whether there are similarities of behavior between online communication behavior and the communication behavior of the same people in real life. To do so, one could set up different test studies of test persons who are willing to cooperate in different communication settings.

As participants in online discussion forums with English as the language of the forum come from different countries, there is interaction among native speakers of English, speakers with English as their second language, and speakers with English as a foreign language. This also leads to cultural and linguistic misunderstanding and, hence, controversies in some cases. In this respect, one should take the role of English as lingua franca into consideration. At times, native speakers of English use English as a weapon against their opponents who are not native speakers of English, claiming that their opponents do not understand the statements properly due to not being native speakers. Further linguistic research should reveal how the interaction between these three groups takes place and how they affect each other. Further, a comparative study of communication principles and forum rules of other discussion forums with different topics and different cultural and language background will reveal more about similarities and differences of online culture of communication in general and online controversies in particular.

Another field of special interest for the analysis is how handling controversies and conflicts is discussed in moderator forums of online discussion forums. As I mentioned before, moderator forums are not visible to other members. Only moderators with moderating status have access to these private forums. At times, even moderator forums experience conflict situations among moderators who do not agree on how to handle a certain person or situation. Thus, meta-communication about polemical discourse in the moderator forums results in controversies as well. This is a fascinating phenomenon that arises in some of these moderator forums. Discussing how to handle controversial threads leads to controversies among moderators themselves. At times, this is due to the fact that some moderators are friends with some members who were involved in a controversial thread, and, hence, they want to support them accordingly. So in discussing how to handle controversies, there are formal and informal groups that influence the decision-making process of moderators in how they should handle controversial threads in online discussion forums. This needs to be analyzed from a linguistic point of view in future research about controversies in online discussion forums.

At this stage, I would like to stress that further future research on controversies in online discussion forums will shed more light on what extent the new medium, the Internet in general and online discussion forums in particular, has changed the nature of carrying out controversies. Surely, one can already observe in my research that through the introduction of the new medium, some new communication principles have been introduced, and some old communication principles have also been changed and adapted. A further linguistic study of controversies in online discussion forums will show how and why this new medium has taken up such an important role in some circles, such as the arms and armor community, and, above all, whether this new medium will find acceptance in other academic circles in the future.

References

Agamanolis, Stefan 2006. Beyond Communication: Human Connectedness as a Research Agenda. In Patrick Purcell (ed.) *Networked Neighbourhoods: The Connected Community in Context*. London: Springer, 307–344.

Allan, James & Brian Glimour 2000. *Persian Steel: The Tanavoli Collection*. Oxford: Oxford University Press.

Andersen, Gisle 1998. The Pragmatic Marker *like* from a Relevance-theoretic Perspective. In Jucker, Andreas H. / Ziv, Yael (eds) *Discourse Markers: Descriptions and Theory*. Amsterdam and Philadelphia: John Benjamins, 147–170.

Anglemark, Linnéa 2006. "well folks im signing off here"– Vocatives in Chat Room Conversation. In Taavitsainen, Irma / Härmä, Juhani / Korhonen, Jarmo (eds), *Dialogic Language Use*. Mémoires de la Société Néophilologique de Helsinki. Helsinki: Société Néophilologique, 295–303.

Astvatsaturjan, E.G. [Аствацатурянб Э. Г.] 2002. *Турецкое оружие в собрании государственного исторического музея* [*Turkish Weapons in the Collection of the State Historical Museum*]. Санкт Петербург Д. А. Фебурин [Saint Petersburg: D. A Feburin].

Athanasiada, Angeliki 1994. The Pragmatics of Answers. *Journal of Pragmatics*.4:4, 561–574.

Bach, Ulrich 1998. Early Mass Communication: Political Pamphlets from 1642 to 1647. In Borgmeier, Raimund / Grabes, Herbert / Jucker, Andreas H. (eds), *Historical Pragmatics*. Reprinted from Anglistentag 1997, Gießen Proceedings. Trier: WVT Wissenschaftlicher Verlag, 97–111.

Barghouti, Omar 2005. Ethical Implications of De-Dichtotomization of Identities in Conflict. In Pierluigi, Barrota / Dascal, Marcelo (eds) *Controversies and Subjectivity*. Amsterdam and Philadelphia: John Benjamins, 325–336.

Barrotta, Pierluigi / Dascal, Marcelo 2005. *Controversies and Subjectivity (Controversies)*. Amsterdam and Philadelphia: John Benjamins.

Bell, Allan 2001. Back in Style: Reworking Audience Design. In Eckert, Penelope / Rickford, John R. (eds) *Style and Sociolinguistic Variation*. Cambridge: Cambridge University Press, 139–169.

Bell, Chris and Fei Song 2005. Emotions in the Conflict Process: An Application of the Cognitive Appraisal Model of Emotions to Conflict Management. *The International Journal of Conflict Management*. 16/1, 30–54.

Bennett, H.S. 1965. *English Books and Readers 1558 to 1603: Being a Study in the History of the Book Trade in the Reign of Elizabeth I*. Cambridge: Cambridge University Press.

Bernhard, Hans 1998. Konfliktbewältigung im Führungsalltag. In Kälin, Karl / Müri, Peter (eds), *Sich und andere führen*. Thun: Ott-Verlag, 154–180.

Biber, Douglas / Johansson, Stig / Leech, Geoffrey / Conrad, Susan / Finegan, Edward 1999. *The Longman Grammar of Spoken and Written English*. Harlow: Longman.

Bjørge, Anne Kari 2007. Power Distance in English Lingua Franca Email Communication. *International Journal of Applied Linguistics*. 17/1, 60–80.

Blake, R.A. / Mouton, J.S. 1964. *The Managerial Grid*. Houston: Gulf.

Blakemore, Diane 1992. *Understanding Utterances: An Introduction to Pragmatics*. Oxford: Blackwell.

Blöchliger, Karl 1999. Funktion und Bedeutung der Gruppe im Unternehmen. In Kälin, Karl / Müri, Peter (eds) *Sich und andere führen*. Thun: Ott-Verlag, 115–128.

Boning, Uwe 2000. Verhalten in Konfliktsituation. In Uwe Böning (ed.) *Interkulturelle Business-Kompetenz: Geheime Regeln beachten und unsichtbare Barrieren überwinden*. Frankfurt: Frankfurter Allgemeine Buch, 235–242.

Brinton, Laurel J. 1990. The Development of Discourse Markers in English. In Jacek Fisiak (ed.) *Historical Linguistics and Philology*. Berlin: Mouton de Gruyter, 45–71.

Brinton, Laurel J. 1996. *Pragmatic Markers in English: Grammaticalization and Discourse Functions*. Berlin-New York: Mouton de Gruyter.

Brooks, Jerome E. 1952. *The Mighty Leaf: Tobacco through the Centuries*. Boston: Little, Brown and Company.

Brown, Penelope, and Stephen Levinson 1987. *Politeness: Some Universals in Language Use*. Cambridge: Cambridge University Press.

Burger, Harald 1991. *Das Gespräch in den Massenmedien*. Berlin, New York: De Gruyter.

Cato, Robert 1996. *Moro Swords*. Singapore: Graham Brash.

Chafe, Wallace L. 1985. Linguistic Differences Produced by Differences between Speaking and Writing. In Olson, David R. / Torrance, Nancy / Hildyard, Angela (eds) *Literacy, Language and Learning: The Nature and Consequences of Reading and Writing*. Cambridge: CUP, 105–123.

Cherny, Lynn 1999. *Conversation and Community: Chat in a Virtual World*. Stanford: CSLI Publications.

Chilton, Paul A. 1997. The Role of Language in Human Conflict: Prolegomena to the Investigation of Language as a Factor in Conflict and Resolution. *Current Issues in Languages and Society*. 4/3, 174–189.

Claridge, Claudia 2000. Pamphlets and Early Newspapers: Political Interaction vs. News Reporting. In Friedrich Ungerer (ed.) *English Media Texts Past and Present: Language and Textual Structure*. Amsterdam and Philadelphia: John Benjamins, 25–43.

Clarke, Sandra 1983. *The Elizabethan Pamphleteers: Popular Moralistic Pamphlets* 1580–1640. London: The Athlone Press.

Constant, D. / Sproull, L. / Kiesler, S. 1996. The Kindness of Strangers: Usefulness of Electronic Weak Ties for Technical Advice. *Organization Science*. 7/2, 119–135.

Conway, Maura 2004. Cyberterrorism: Media Myth or Clear and Present Danger. In Jones Irwin (ed.) *War and Virtual War: The Challenges to Communities*. Amsterdam: Rodopi, 79–95.

Crystal, David 2001. *Language and the Internet*. Cambridge: Cambridge University Press.

Culpeper, Jonathan / Bousfield, Derek / Wichmann, Anne 2003. Impoliteness Revisited: With Special Reference to Dynamic and Prosodic Aspects. *Journal of Pragmatics*. 35/10–11, 1545–1579.

Dascal, Marcelo 1997. Epistemology, Controversies, and Pragmatics. <http://www.tau.ac.il/humanities/philos/dascal/papers/dascal3.htm>; accessed 02/02/2007.

Dascal, Marcelo 1998. Types of Polemics and Types of Polemical Moves. In Cmejrrikova, S. / Hoffmannova, J. / Mullerova, O. / Svetla, J. (eds.) *Dialogue Analysis VI – Proceedings of the 6th Conference, Prague 1996*. Tübingen: Max Niemeyer, 15–33.

Dascal, Marcelo 1999. The Challenge of Human Difference and the Ethics of Communication. <http://www.tau.ac.il/humanities/philos/dascal/papers/challenge.html>; accessed 09/01/2007.

Dascal, Marcelo 2000. Types of Polemics and Types of Polemical Moves. In Cmejrkova, S. / Hoffmannova, J. / Svetla, J. (eds) *Dialogue Analysis VI* (=Proceedings of the 6th Conference, Prague 1996) vol. 1. Tubingen: Max Niemeyer, 15–33.

Dascal, Marcelo 2001. In the Uses of Argumentative Reason in Religious Polemics. In Dascal, Marcelo / Fritz, Gerd / Gloning, Thomas / Senderowicz, Yaron (eds) *Controversies in the République des Lettres: Technical Report 4, Theological Controversies*. German-Israeli Foundation (GIF): Giessen, 3–17.

Dascal, Marcelo 2003. *Interpretation and Understanding*. Amsterdam: John Benjamins.

Dascal, Marcelo 2005a. Debating with Myself and Debating with Others. In Pierluigi, Barrota / Dascal, Marcelo (eds.) *Controversies and Subjectivity*. Amsterdam: John Benjamins, 33–73.

Dascal, Marcelo 2005b. King Solomon, Ibn-Rushd, Leibniz: Three Models for Approaching the Israel/Palestine Conflict. <http://www.tau.ac.il/humanities/philos/dascal/papers/king.pdf>; accessed 06/01/2007.

Dascal, Marcelo 2006. *G.W. Leibniz: The Art of Controversies*. Dordrecht: Springer.

Dascal, Marcelo / Marras, Cristina 2002. The République des Lettres: A Republic of Quarrels. In Dascal, Marcelo / Fritz, Gerd / Gloning, Thomas / Senderowicz, Yaron (eds) *Controversies in the République des Lettres: Technical Report 3, Scientific Controversies and Theories of Controversy.* The German-Israeli Foundation for Scientific Research and Development: Giessen, 3–19.

Davis, Boyd and Jentonne Brewer 1997. *Electronic Discourse: Linguistic Individuals in Virtual Space.* Albany: State University of New York Press.

Desivilya, Helena Syna and Dana Yagil 2005. The Role of Emoticons in Conflict Management: The Case of Work Teams. *The International Journal of Conflict Management.* 16/1, 55–69.

Dewey, Martin 2007. English as a Lingua Franca and Globalization: an Interconnected Perspective. *International Journal of Applied Linguistics.* 17/3, 332–354.

Diekmann, W. 2005. *Streiten über das Streiten. Normative Grundlagen polemischer Metakommunikation.* Tübingen: Niemeyer.

Dillon, Jim T. 1988. Understanding Answers to Questions. In Michel Meyer (ed.), Questions and Questioning. Berlin: Walter de Gruyter, 98–117.

Dovring, Karin 1997. *English as Lingua Franca: Double Talk in Global Persuasion.* Westport: Praeger.

Downing, Angela 2006. The English Pragmatic Marker *Surely* and its Functional Counterparts in Spanish. In Aijmer, Karin / Simon-Vandenbergen, Anne-Marie (eds) *Pragmatic Markers in Contrast.* Amsterdam: Elsevier, 39–58.

Driver, J. L. 1988. Vain Questions. In Michel Meyer (ed.). *Questions and Questioning.* Berlin: Walter de Gruyter, 243–253.

Elder, Catherine / Davies, Alan 2006. Assessing English as a Lingua Franca. *Annual Review of Applied Linguistics.* 26, 282–301.

Enkvist, Nils Erik 1973. *Linguistic Stylistics.* The Hague: Mouton.

Esser, Jürgen 1993. *English Linguistic Stylistics.* Tübingen: Max Niemeyer Verlag.

Esser, Jürgen 2006. *Presentation in Language: Rethinking Speech and Writing.* Tübingen: Gunter Narr Verlag.

Fairclough, Norman 1992. *Discourse and Social Change.* Cambridge: Polity Press.

Fayard, Anne-Laure / DeSanctis, Gerardine 2005. Evolution of an Online Forum for Knowledge Management Professionals: A

Language Game Analysis. *Journal of Computer-Mediated Communication*. 10/4, article 2. <http://jcmc.indiana.edu/vol10/issue4/fayard.html>; accessed 12/12/2006.

Fetzer, Anita 2007. Well if that Had Been True, that Would Have Been Perfectly Reasonable: Appeals to Reasonableness in Political Interviews. *Journal of Pragmatics*. 39, 1342–1359.

Finholt, T. / Sproull, L. 1990. Electronic Groups at Work. *Organization Science*. 1/1, 41–64.

Fraser, Bruce 1998. Contrastive Discourse Markers in English. In Jucker, Andreas H. / Ziv, Yael (eds) *Discourse Markers: Descriptions and Theory*. Amsterdam: John Benjamins, 301–326.

Freeborn, Dennis / French, Peter / Longford, David 1993. *Varieties of English: An Introduction to the Study of Language*. London: MacMillan.

Fritz, Gerd 1995. Topics in the History of Dialogue Forms. In Jucker, Andreas H. (ed.) *Historical Pragmatics. Pragmatic Developments in the History of English*. Amsterdam: John Benjamins, 469–498.

Fritz, Gerd 2005a. On answering accusation in controversies. Studies in Communication Sciences. Special Issue: *Argumentation in Dialogic Interpretation*, 151–162.

Fritz, Gerd 2005b. First Person Singular in 17th Century Controversies. In Barrota, Pierluigi / Dascal, Marcelo (eds) *Controversies and Subjectivity*. Amsterdam: John Benjamins, 234–250.

Fritz, Gerd 2007. Communication Principles for Controversies: An Historical Perspective. van Eemeren, F. *et al.* (eds) Proceedings from the 6th International Conference on Argumentation. Amsterdam, 417–427.

Fritz, Gerd 2008. Review of Gottfried Wilhelm Leibniz. Journal of Historical Pragmatics. 9, 164–170.

Fritz, Gerd / Glüer, Juliane 2001a. The Pamphlet and Its Alternatives C. 1700. In Dascal, Marcelo / Fritz, Gerd / Gloning, Thomas / Senderowicz, Yaron (eds) *Controversies in the République des Lettres: Technical Report 4, Theological Controversies*. German-Israeli Foundation (GIF): Giessen, 42–79.

Fritz, Gerd / Glüer, Juliane 2001b. Rezenssionen und Repliken – Zur Kontroverse um Johann Salomo Semlers Abhandlung von freier

Untersuchung des Canon (1771–1775). In Dascal, Marcelo, Fritz, Gerd / Gloning, Thomas / Senderowicz, Yaron (eds) *Controversies in the République des Lettres: Technical Report 4, Theological Controversies.* German-Israeli Foundation (GIF): Giessen, 80–121.

Gloning, Thomas 1999. The pragmatic form of religious controversies around 1600: A Case Study in the Osiander vs. Scherer & Rosenbusch Controversy. In Jucker, Andreas H. / Fritz, Gerd / Lebsanft, Franz (eds.) *Historical Dialogue Analysis.* Amsterdam: John Benjamins, 81–110.

Gloning, Thomas 2002. Zur sprachlichen Form der Kepler/Röselin/Feselius-Kontroverse um 1600. In Dascal, Marcelo / Fritz, Gerd / Gloning, Thomas / Senderowicz, Yaron (eds) *Controversies in the République des Lettres: Technical Report 3, Scientific Controversies and Theories of Controversy.* The German-Israeli Foundation for Scientific Research and Development: Giessen, 33–85.

Gloning, Thomas 2005. Early Modern Controversies and Theories of Controversy. In Barrota, Pierluigi / Dascal, Marcelo (eds) *Controversies and Subjectivity.* Amsterdam: John Benjamins, 263–281.

Gloning, Thomas / Lüsing, Jan 2002. Die Kontroverse zwischen J.A. Gehema and M.F. Geuder (1688/1689). In Dascal, Dascal / Fritz, Gerd / Gloning, Thomas / Senderowicz, Yaron (eds) *Controversies in the République des Lettres: Technical Report 3, Scientific Controversies and Theories of Controversy.* The German-Israeli Foundation for Scientific Research and Development: Giessen, 87–142.

Glüer, Juliane 2001. Moves and Strategies in a Religious Pamphlet War: Protestants vs. Jesuits in the 1580s. In Dascal, Marcelo / Fritz, Gerd / Gloning, Thomas / Senderowicz, Yaron (eds.) *Controversies in the République des Lettres: Technical Report 4, Theological Controversies.* German-Israeli Foundation (GIF): Giessen, 18–41.

Goeze, J.M. 1778. Etwas Vorläufiges gegen des Herrn Hofraths Leßings mittelbare und unmittelbare feindselige Angriffe [. . .].

In E. Schmidt (ed.) *Goezes Streitschriften gegen Lessing*. Stuttgart: Göschen, 1–77.

Goldenbaum, U. 2004. Die öffentliche Debatte in der deutschen Aufklärung 1697–1796. In U. Goldenbaum (ed.) *Appell an das Publikum. Die öffentliche Debatte in der deutschen Aufklärung 1697–1796*. Berlin: Akademie-Verlag, 1–118.

Gordon, Thomas 1979. *Managerkonferenz: Effektives Führungstraining*. Hamburg: Hoffmann und Campe.

Graham, Sage Lambert 2007. Disagreeing to Agree. Conflict, (Im)politeness and Identity in a Computer-mediated Community. *Journal of Pragmatics*. 39, 742–759.

Grice, P. 1989. *Studies in the Way of Words*. Cambridge, Mass.: Harvard University Press.

Gross, Alan G. 2005. The Role of Subjectivity in Public Controversy. In Barrota, Pierluigi / Dascal, Marcelo (eds). *Controversies and Subjectivity*. Amsterdam: John Benjamins, 337–352.

Große, Ernst-Ulrich 1998. Massenmedien. In Ansgar Nünning (ed.), *Metzler Lexikon. Literatur- und Kulturtheorie*. Stuttgart: Metzler, 344–346.

Hamzuri, Drs. (1988). *Keris*. Indonesia: PT Karya Unipress.

Harper, Prudence Oliver 1996. The Ox-headed Mace in Pre-Islamic Iran. *Acta Iranica*. 24/2, 247–259.

Herring, S. C. 2004. Computer-mediated Discourse Analysis: An Approach to Researching Online Behavior. In Barab, S.A. / Kling, R. / Gray, J.S. (eds) *Designing for Virtual Communities in the Service of Learning*. Cambridge: Cambridge University Press, 338–376.

Hess-Lüttich, Ernest W.B. 2007. (Pseudo-)Argumentation in TV-debates. *Journal of Pragmatics*. 39, 1360–1370.

Hintikka, J. 1986. Logic of Conversation as a Logic of Dialogue. In Grandy, R.E. / Warner, R. (eds.) *Philosophical Grounds of Rationality: Intentions, Categories, Ends*. Oxford, Clarendon Press, 259–276.

Holmes, Janet / Marra, Meredith 2004. Leadership and Managing Conflict in Meetings. *Pragmatics*. 14/4, 439–462.

Janoschka, Anja 2004. *Web Advertising: New Forms of Communication on the Internet*. Amsterdam: John Benjamins.

Jeremiah, Ken 2007. Asceticism and the Pursuit of Death by Warriors and Monks. *Asian Journal of Martial Arts*, 16/2, 18–33.

Jucker, Andreas H. 1986. *News Interviews: A Pragmalinguistic Perspective*. Amsterdam: John Benjamins.

Jucker, Andreas H. 1993. The Discourse Marker Well: A Relevance-theoretical Account. *Journal of Pragmatics*. 19/5, 435–452.

Jucker, Andreas H. 2003. Mass Media Communication at the Beginning of the Twenty-first Century: Dimensions of Change. *Journal of Historical Pragmatics*. 4/1, 129–148.

Jucker, Andreas H. / Smith, Sarah W. 1998. And people just you know like 'Wow': Discourse Markers as Negotiating Strategies. In Jucker Andreas H. / Ziv, Yael (eds) *Discourse Markers: Descriptions and Theory*. Amsterdam and Philadelphia: John Benjamins, 171–201.

Jucker, Andreas H. / Smith, Sarah W. / Lüdge, Tanja 2003. Interactive Aspects of Vagueness in Conversation. *Journal of Pragmatics*. 35/12, 1737–1769.

Jucker, Andreas H. / Ziv, Yael 1998. Discourse Markers: Introduction. In Jucker, Andreas H. / Ziv, Yael (eds) *Discourse Markers: Descriptions and Theory*. Amsterdam and Philadelphia: John Benjamins, 1–12.

Kapp, Leon / Yoshihara, Hiroko and Yoshindo 1996. *Japanische Schwertschmiedekunst*. Eschershausen: Ordonnanz-Verlag.

Kasher, A. 1976. Conversational Maxims and Rationality. In J. Kasher (ed) *Language in Focus : Foundations, Methods, and Systems*. Dordrecht: D. Reidel, 197–216.

Kavanaugh, A. / Zinn, T.T. / Rosson, M.B. / Carroll, J.M. 2006. The Impact of the Internet on Local and Distant Social Ties. In Patrick Purcell (ed) *Networked Neighbourhoods: The Connected Community in Context*. London: Springer, 217–236.

Kerbrat-Orecchioni, C. 1994. *Les Interactions Verbales*. Tome III. Paris: Armand Colin.

Kim, Amy Jo 2000. *Community Building on the Web*. Berkeley: Peachpit Press.

Kresic, Marijana 2000. Kommunikationstheories und Internet. Networx 15, <http://www.mediensprache.net/networx/networx-15.pdf>; accessed 25/08/2007.

Kronick, David A. 1988. Anonymity and identity: Editorial Policy in the Early Scientific Journal. *The Library Quarterly*. 58/3, 221–237.

Lauerbach, Gerda 2007. Argumentation in Political Talk Show Interviews. *Journal of Pragmatics*. 39/8, 1388–1419.

Leech, Geoffrey 1966. *English in Advertising: Linguistic Study of Advertising of Advertising in England*. London: Longman.

Leech, Geoffrey 1999. The Distribution and Function of Vocatives in American and British English Conversation. In Hasselgård, Hilde / Oksefjell, Signe (eds.) *Out of Copora – Studies in Honour of Stig Johansson*. Amsterdam: Rodopi, 107–118.

Löffler, Heinrich 1984. Gewinner und Verlierer(-sprache) – Beobachtungen an kontrvers geführten (Fernseh-)Gesprächen. In I. Rosengren (ed.) *Sprache und Pragmatik*. Stockholm: Almqvist och Wiksell, 293–313.

Luginbühl, Martin 1999. *Gewalt im Gespräch: Verbale Gewalt in politischen Fernsehdiskussionen am Beispiel der "Arena"*. Bern: Lang.

Luginbühl, Martin 2007. Conversational Violence in Political TV Debate: Forms and Debate. *Journal of Pragmatics*. 39/8, 1371–1387.

Maletzke, Gerhard 1998. *Kommunikationswissenschaft im Überblick: Grundlagen, Probleme, Perspektiven*. Opladen: Westdeutscher Verlag.

Masia, K. 2001. The Evolution of Swords and Daggers in the Sasanian Empire. *Iranica Antiqua*, vol. XXXV, 185–289.

McMenamin, Gerald R. 1993. *Forensic Stylistics*. Amsterdam: Elsevier.

Mey, Jacob L. 1993. *Pragmatics: An Introduction*. Oxford: Blackwell Publishers.

Mills, Sara 2005. Gender and Impoliteness. *Journal of Politeness Research*. 1/2, 263–280.

Mishori, Daniel 2002. Between Physics and Metaphysics: The Monboddo-Price Correspondence (7.1780–8.1781). In Dascal, Marcelo / Fritz, Gerd / Gloning, Thomas / Senderowicz, Yaron (eds) *Controversies in the République des Lettres: Technical Report 3, Scientific Controversies and Theories of Controversy*.

The German-Israeli Foundation for Scientific Research and Development: Giessen, 143–166.
Moshtagh Khorasani, Manouchehr 2006. *Arms and Armor from Iran: The Bronze Age to the end of the Qajar Period*. Tübingen: Legat Verlag.
Mühlen, Ulrike 1985. *Talk as Show: Eine linguistische Untersuchung der Gesprächsführung in den Talkshows des deutschen Fernsehens*. Frankfurt: Peter Lang.
Mukherjee, Joybrato 2003. From corpus data to a theory of talk units. In Granger, Sylviane / Petch-Tyson, Stephanie (eds) *Extending the Scope of Corpus-based Research: New Applications, New Challenges*. Amsterdam: Rodopi, 121–134.
Mukherjee, Joybrato 2005. Stylistics. In Philipp Strazny (ed.) *Encyclopedia of Linguistics*. New York: Fitzroy Dearborn, 1043–1045.
Müller, Simone 2005. *Discourse Markers in Native and Non-native English Discourse*. Amsterdam: John Benjamins Publishing Company.
Nilsson, Stephanie 2003. *Function of Language to Facilitate and Maintain Social Networks in Research Weblogs*. Master Thesis: Umea University.
O'Sullivan, Patrick B. 1999. Personal Broadcasting. Theoretical implications of the Web. Paper presented at the annual conference of the International Communication Association's Annual Conference, San Francisco, May 1999. <http://www.ilstu.edu/~posull/PersBroad.htm>; accessed 20/08/2007.
Palander-Collin, Minna 2006. (Re)constructing Style and Language as Social Interaction through First- and Second-Person Pronouns in Early Modern English Letters. In Taavitsainen, Irma / Härmä, Juhani / Korhonen, Jarmo (eds) *Dialogic Language Use*. Helsinki: Société Néophilologigue, 339–362.
Pant, G.N. 1978. *Indian Arms and Armour: Volume I (Pre- and Protohistoric Weapons and Archery)*. New Delhi: Army Educational Stores.
Pant, G.N. 1980. *Indian Arms and Armour: Volume II (Swords and Daggers)*. New Delhi: Army Educational Stores.

Pant, G.N. 1983. *Indian Arms and Armour: Volume III (Human Armour and Shield)*. New Delhi: Army Educational Stores.

Pearce, Michael 2001. Getting behind the Image: Personality Politics in a Labour Party Election Broadcast. *Language and Literature*. 10/3, 211–228.

Prechter, Sabine 2001. *The Significance of Discourse Markers in the Development of Social Roles*. Trier: Wissenschaftlicher Verlag.

Preece, Jenny 2000. *Online Communities: Designing Usability, Supporting Sociability*. New York: John Wiley & Sons.

Pruitt, D. G. / Rubin, J. Z. 1986. *Social Conflict: Escalation, Stalemate and Settlement*. New York: Random House.

Purcell, Patrick 2006. *Networked Neighbourhoods: The Connected Community in Context*. London: Springer.

Quirk, R. / Greenbaum, S. / Leech, G. / Svartik, Jan 1985. *A Grammar of Contemporary English*. London: Longman.

Rahim, M.A. 1983. A Measure of Styles of Handling Interpersonal Conflicts. *Academy of Management Journal*. 26, 368–376.

Ratia, Maura 2005. Personal Pronouns in Argumentation: An Early Tobacco Controversy. In Skaffari, Janne / Peikola, Matti / Carroll, Ruth / Hiltunen, Risto / Warvik, Brita (eds) *Opening Windows on Texts and Discourses of the Past*. Amsterdam: John Benjamins, 123–141.

Ratia, Maura 2006. Con and Pro': Early Modern Texts in Dialogue. In Taavitsainen, Irma / Härmä, Juhani / Korhonen, Jarmo (eds) *Dialogic Language Use*. Helsinki: Société Néophilologigue, 87–106.

Reimann, Ann 2007. Man kann den Blutdurst spüren. *Spiegel Online*. <http://www.spiegel.de/netzwelt/web/0,1518,509396,00.html>; accessed 05/10/2007.

Rheingold, Howard 2000. *The Virtual Community: Homesteading on the Electronic Frontier*. New York: Harper Perennial.

Rheingold, Howard 2006. Social Networks and the Nature of Communities. In Patrick Purcell (ed.) Networked Neighbourhoods: The Connected Community in Context. London: Springer, 47–75.

Rötzer, Florian 1999. Aufmerksamkeit als Medium der Öffentlichkeit. In Maresch, Rudolf / Werber, Niels (eds) *Kommunikation, Medien, Macht*. Frankfurt: Suhrkamp, 35–58.

Schmied, Josef 1998. Discourse Markers in the Lampeter Corpus of Early Modern English Tracts. In Borgmeier, Raimund / Grabes, Herbert / Jucker, Andreas H. (eds) *Historical Pragmatics*. Reprinted from Anglistentag 1997, Gießen Proceedings. Trier: WVT Wissenschaftlicher Verlag, 57–65.

Schwitalla, Johannes 1999. The Use of Dialogue in Early German Pamphlets: On the Constitution of Public Involvement in the Reuchlin-Pfefferkorn Controversy. In Jucker, Andreas H. / Fritz, Gerd / Lebsanft, Franz (eds) *Historical Dialogue Analysis*. (Pragmatics & Beyond New Series 66). Amsterdam/Philadelphia: John Benjamins, 111–137.

Senderowicz, Yaron 2005. Debating with Myself and Debating with Others. In Barrota, Pierluigi / Dascal, Marcelo (eds) *Externalism, Internalism, and Self-Knowledge*. Amsterdam: John Benjamins, 283–299.

Settlekorn, Wolfgang 1989. Politikinszenierung im französischen Fernsehen. In Holly, W. / Kühn, P. / Püschel, U. (eds) *Redeshows – Fernsehdiskussionen in der Diskussion*. Niemeyer, Tübingen, 12–47.

Sharon-Zisser, Shirley 2005. Archaic Subjectivity and/as Controversy in Psychoanalytic Thinking. In Barrotta, Pierluigi / Dascal, Marcelo (eds) *Controversies and Subjectivity (Controversies)*. Amsterdam: John Benjamins, 371–393.

Shea, Virginia 1994. *Netiquette*. San Francisco: Albion Books.

Shepard, Leslie 1973. *The History of Street Literature: The Story of Broadside Ballads, Chapbooks, Proclamations, News-sheets, Election Bills, Tracts, Pamphlets, Cocks, Catchpennies, and other Ephemera*. Newton Abbet: David and Charles.

Smith, Dan 1997. Language and Discourse in Conflict and Conflict Resolution. *Current Issues in Languages and Society*. 4/3, 190–214.

Smith, M. A. / Kollock, P. 1999. *Communities in Cyberspace*. New York: Routledge.

Solyom, Garret / Solyom, Bronwen 1978. *The World of the Javanese Keris*. Honolulu: Asian Arts Press.

Stenström, Anna-Brita 1988. Questioning in Conversation. In Michel Meyer (ed.) *Questions and Questioning*. Berlin: Walter de Gruyter, 304–325.

Stone, Cameron Stone 1999. *Glossary of the Construction, Decoration and Use of Arms and Use of Arms and Armor in all Countries and in all Times*. Mineola: Dover Publications.

Suhr, Carla 2006. Early Modern English Witchcraft Pamphlets: The Use of Reported Speech for Interaction with Semiliterate Audiences. In Taavitsainen, Irma / Härmä, Juhani / Korhonen, Jarmo (eds) *Dialogic Language Use. Mémoires de la Société Néophilologique de Helsinki.* Helsinki: Société Néophilologique, 27–47.

Taavitsainen, Irma 1995. Interjections in Early Modern English: From Imitation of Spoken to Conventions of Written Language. In Andreas H. Jucker (ed.) *Historical Pragmatics. Pragmatic Developments in the History of English.* Amsterdam and Philadelphia: John Benjamins, 439–465.

Talhoffer, Hans 2000. *Medieval Combat: A Fifteenth-Century Illustrated Manual of Swordfighting and Close-Quarter Combat.* London: Greenhill Books.

Tannen, D. 1994. *Conversational Style, Analyzing Talk among Friends.* Ablex: Norwood.

Ungerer, Friedrich (ed.) 2000. *English Media Texts Past and Present.* (Pragmatics and Beyond New Series 80). Amsterdam: John Benjamins, 25–43.

van Dijk, Teun A. 1995. Ideological Discourse Analysis. In Ventola, E. / Solin, A. (eds) *Interdisciplinary Approaches to Discourse Analysis*. Helsinki: Helsinki University Printing House, 135–161.

van Zonneveld, Albert G. 2001. *Traditional Weapons of the Indonesian Archipelago*. Leiden: C. Zwartenkot Art Books.

Walczak, Bartlomiei / Zabinski, Grzgorz 2002. *Codex Wallerstein: A Medieval Fighting Book from the Fifteenth Century on the Longsword, Falchion, Dagger, and Wrestling*. Boulder: Paladin Press.

Wales, Katie 1996. *Personal Pronouns in Present – Day English.* Cambridge: Cambridge University Press.

Wasko, M., and S. Faraj 2005. Why Should I Share? Examining Social Capital and Knowledge Contribution in Electronic Networks of Practice. *MIS Quarterly*. 29/1, 35–58.

Weber, Elizabeth G. 1993. *Varieties of Questions in English Conversation.* Amsterdam: John Benjamins.

Weigand, Edda 2005. Conflict resolution in Court. Studies in Communication Sciences. *Special Issue: Argumentation in Dialogic Interpretation*, 193–202.

Weydt, Harald 1980. Streitsuche im Nibelungenlied: Die Kooperation der Feinde. Eine Konversationsanalytische Studie. In E.W.B. Hess-Lüttich (ed.) *Literatur und Konversation. Sprachsoziologie und Pragmatik in der Literaturwissenschaft*. Athenaion: Wiesbaden, 95–114.

Wittgenstein, L. 1969. *The Blue and Books*. Oxford: Basil Blackwell.

Wright, Sue 1997. Language as a Contributing Factor in Conflicts between States and within States. *Current Issues in Languages and Society*. 4/3, 215–237.

Yule, George 1996. *Pragmatics*. Oxford: Oxford University Press.

Index

Linguistic Insights

Studies in Language and Communication

This series aims to promote specialist language studies in the fields of linguistic theory and applied linguistics, by publishing volumes that focus on specific aspects of language use in one or several languages and provide valuable insights into language and communication research. A cross-disciplinary approach is favoured and most European languages are accepted.

The series includes two types of books:

- **Monographs** – featuring in-depth studies on special aspects of language theory, language analysis or language teaching.
- **Collected papers** – assembling papers from workshops, conferences or symposia.

Each volume of the series is subjected to a double peer-reviewing process.

Vol. 1 Maurizio Gotti & Marina Dossena (eds)
Modality in Specialized Texts. Selected Papers of the 1st CERLIS Conference.
421 pages. 2001. ISBN 3-906767-10-8. US-ISBN 0-8204-5340-4

Vol. 2 Giuseppina Cortese & Philip Riley (eds)
Domain-specific English. Textual Practices across Communities and Classrooms.
420 pages. 2002. ISBN 3-906768-98-8. US-ISBN 0-8204-5884-8

Vol. 3 Maurizio Gotti, Dorothee Heller & Marina Dossena (eds)
Conflict and Negotiation in Specialized Texts. Selected Papers of the 2nd CERLIS Conference.
470 pages. 2002. ISBN 3-906769-12-7. US-ISBN 0-8204-5887-2

Editorial address:

Prof. Maurizio Gotti Università di Bergamo, Facoltà di Lingue e Letterature Straniere, Via Salvecchio 19, 24129 Bergamo, Italy
Fax: 0039 035 2052789, E-Mail: m.gotti@unibg.it

Vol. 4 Maurizio Gotti, Marina Dossena, Richard Dury, Roberta Facchinetti & Maria Lima
Variation in Central Modals. A Repertoire of Forms and Types of Usage in Middle English and Early Modern English.
364 pages. 2002. ISBN 3-906769-84-4. US-ISBN 0-8204-5898-8

Vol. 5 Stefania Nuccorini (ed.)
Phrases and Phraseology. Data and Descriptions.
187 pages. 2002. ISBN 3-906770-08-7. US-ISBN 0-8204-5933-X

Vol. 6 Vijay Bhatia, Christopher N. Candlin & Maurizio Gotti (eds)
Legal Discourse in Multilingual and Multicultural Contexts. Arbitration Texts in Europe.
385 pages. 2003. ISBN 3-906770-85-0. US-ISBN 0-8204-6254-3

Vol. 7 Marina Dossena & Charles Jones (eds)
Insights into Late Modern English. 2nd edition.
378 pages. 2003, 2007.
ISBN 978-3-03911-257-9. US-ISBN 978-0-8204-8927-8

Vol. 8 Maurizio Gotti
Specialized Discourse. Linguistic Features and Changing Conventions.
351 pages. 2003, 2005.
ISBN 3-03910-606-6. US-ISBN 0-8204-7000-7

Vol. 9 Alan Partington, John Morley & Louann Haarman (eds)
Corpora and Discourse.
420 pages. 2004. ISBN 3-03910-026-2. US-ISBN 0-8204-6262-4

Vol. 10 Martina Möllering
The Acquisition of German Modal Particles. A Corpus-Based Approach.
290 pages. 2004. ISBN 3-03910-043-2. US-ISBN 0-8204-6273-X

Vol. 11 David Hart (ed.)
English Modality in Context. Diachronic Perspectives.
261 pages. 2003. ISBN 3-03910-046-7. US-ISBN 0-8204-6852-5

Vol. 12 Wendy Swanson
Modes of Co-reference as an Indicator of Genre.
430 pages. 2003. ISBN 3-03910-052-1. US-ISBN 0-8204-6855-X

Vol. 13 Gina Poncini
Discursive Strategies in Multicultural Business Meetings.
2nd edition. 338 pages. 2004, 2007.
ISBN 978-3-03911-296-8. US-ISBN 978-0-8204-8937-7

Vol. 14 Christopher N. Candlin & Maurizio Gotti (eds)
Intercultural Aspects of Specialized Communication.
2nd edition. 369 pages. 2004, 2007.
ISBN 978-3-03911-258-6. US-ISBN 978-0-8204-8926-1

Vol. 15 Gabriella Del Lungo Camiciotti & Elena Tognini Bonelli (eds)
Academic Discourse. New Insights into Evaluation.
234 pages. 2004. ISBN 3-03910-353-9. US-ISBN 0-8204-7016-3

Vol. 16 Marina Dossena & Roger Lass (eds)
Methods and Data in English Historical Dialectology.
405 pages. 2004. ISBN 3-03910-362-8. US-ISBN 0-8204-7018-X

Vol. 17 Judy Noguchi
The Science Review Article. An Opportune Genre in the Construction of Science.
274 pages. 2006. ISBN 3-03910-426-8. US-ISBN 0-8204-7034-1

Vol. 18 Giuseppina Cortese & Anna Duszak (eds)
Identity, Community, Discourse. English in Intercultural Settings.
495 pages. 2005. ISBN 3-03910-632-5. US-ISBN 0-8204-7163-1

Vol. 19 Anna Trosborg & Poul Erik Flyvholm Jørgensen (eds)
Business Discourse. Texts and Contexts.
250 pages. 2005. ISBN 3-03910-606-6. US-ISBN 0-8204-7000-7

Vol. 20 Christopher Williams
Tradition and Change in Legal English. Verbal Constructions in Prescriptive Texts.
2nd revised edition. 216 pages. 2005, 2007. ISBN 978-3-03911-444-3.

Vol. 21 Katarzyna Dziubalska-Kołaczyk & Joanna Przedlacka (eds)
English Pronunciation Models: A Changing Scene.
2nd edition. 476 pages. 2005, 2008. ISBN 978-3-03911-682-9.

Vol. 22 Christián Abello-Contesse, Rubén Chacón-Beltrán, M. Dolores López-Jiménez & M. Mar Torreblanca-López (eds)
Age in L2 Acquisition and Teaching.
214 pages. 2006. ISBN 3-03910-668-6. US-ISBN 0-8204-7174-7

Vol. 23 Vijay K. Bhatia, Maurizio Gotti, Jan Engberg & Dorothee Heller (eds)
Vagueness in Normative Texts.
474 pages. 2005. ISBN 3-03910-653-8. US-ISBN 0-8204-7169-0

Vol. 24 Paul Gillaerts & Maurizio Gotti (eds)
Genre Variation in Business Letters. 2nd printing.
407 pages. 2008. ISBN 978-3-03911-681-2.

Vol. 25 Ana María Hornero, María José Luzón & Silvia Murillo (eds)
Corpus Linguistics. Applications for the Study of English.
2nd printing. 526 pages. 2006, 2008. ISBN 978-3-03911-726-0

Vol. 26 J. Lachlan Mackenzie &
María de los Ángeles Gómez-González (eds)
Studies in Functional Discourse Grammar.
259 pages. 2005. ISBN 3-03910-696-1 / US-ISBN 0-8204-7558-0

Vol. 27 Debbie G.E. Ho
Classroom Talk. Exploring the Sociocultural Structure
of Formal ESL Learning. 2nd edition.
254 pages. 2006, 2007. ISBN 978-3-03911-434-4

Vol. 28 Javier Pérez-Guerra, Dolores González-Álvarez,
Jorge L. Bueno-Alonso & Esperanza Rama-Martínez (eds)
'Of Varying Language and Opposing Creed':
New Insights into Late Modern English.
455 pages. 2007. ISBN 978-3-03910-788-9

Vol. 29 Francesca Bargiela-Chiappini & Maurizio Gotti (eds)
Asian Business Discourse(s).
350 pages. 2005. ISBN 3-03910-804-2 / US-ISBN 0-8204-7574-2

Vol. 30 Nicholas Brownlees (ed.)
News Discourse in Early Modern Britain.
Selected Papers of CHINED 2004.
300 pages. 2006. ISBN 3-03910-805-0 / US-ISBN 0-8204-8025-8

Vol. 31 Roberta Facchinetti & Matti Rissanen (eds)
Corpus-based Studies of Diachronic English.
300 pages. 2006. ISBN 3-03910-851-4 / US-ISBN 0-8204-8040-1

Vol. 32 Marina Dossena & Susan M. Fitzmaurice (eds)
Business and Official Correspondence:
Historical Investigations.
209 pages. 2006. ISBN 3-03910-880-8 / US-ISBN 0-8204-8352-4

Vol. 33 Giuliana Garzone & Srikant Sarangi (eds)
Discourse, Ideology and Specialized Communication.
494 pages. 2007. ISBN 978-3-03910-888-6

Vol. 34 Giuliana Garzone & Cornelia Ilie (eds)
The Use of English in Institutional and Business Settings.
An Intercultural Perspective.
372 pages. 2007. ISBN 978-3-03910-889-3

Vol. 35 Vijay K. Bhatia & Maurizio Gotti (eds)
Explorations in Specialized Genres.
316 pages. 2006. ISBN 3-03910-995-2 / US-ISBN 0-8204-8372-9

Vol. 36 Heribert Picht (ed.)
Modern Approaches to Terminological Theories and Applications.
432 pages. 2006. ISBN 3-03911-156-6 / US-ISBN 0-8204-8380-X

Vol. 37 Anne Wagner & Sophie Cacciaguidi-Fahy (eds)
Legal Language and the Search for Clarity / Le langage juridique et la quête de clarté. Practice and Tools / Pratiques et instruments.
487 pages. 2006. ISBN 3-03911-169-8 / US-ISBN 0-8388-5

Vol. 38 Juan Carlos Palmer-Silveira, Miguel F. Ruiz-Garrido & Inmaculada Fortanet-Gómez (eds)
Intercultural and International Business Communication: Theory, Research and Teaching.
2nd edition. 343 pages. 2006, 2008. ISBN 978-3-03911-680-5

Vol. 39 Christiane Dalton-Puffer, Dieter Kastovsky, Nikolaus Ritt & Herbert Schendl (eds)
Syntax, Style and Grammatical Norms: English from 1500–2000.
250 pages. 2006. ISBN 3-03911-181-7 / US-ISBN 0-8204-8394-X

Vol. 40 Marina Dossena & Irma Taavitsainen (eds)
Diachronic Perspectives on Domain-Specific English.
280 pages. 2006. ISBN 3-03910-176-0 / US-ISBN 0-8204-8391-5

Vol. 41 John Flowerdew & Maurizio Gotti (eds)
Studies in Specialized Discourse.
293 pages. 2006. ISBN 3-03911-178-7 / US-ISBN 0-8204-8393-1

Vol. 42 Ken Hyland & Marina Bondi (eds)
Academic Discourse Across Disciplines.
320 pages. 2006. ISBN 3-03911-183-3 / US-ISBN 0-8204-8396-6

Vol. 43 Paul Gillaerts & Philip Shaw (eds)
The Map and the Landscape: Norms and Practices in Genre.
256 pages. 2006. ISBN 3-03911-182-5 / US-ISBN 0-8204-8395-4

Vol. 44 Maurizio Gotti & Davide Giannoni (eds)
New Trends in Specialized Discourse Analysis.
301 pages. 2006. ISBN 3-03911-184-1 / US-ISBN 0-8204-8381-8

Vol. 45 Maurizio Gotti & Françoise Salager-Meyer (eds)
Advances in Medical Discourse Analysis:
Oral and Written Contexts.
492 pages. 2006. ISBN 3-03911-185-X / US-ISBN 0-8204-8382-6

Vol. 46 Maurizio Gotti & Susan Šarcević (eds)
Insights into Specialized Translation.
396 pages. 2006. ISBN 3-03911-186-8 / US-ISBN 0-8204-8383-4

Vol. 47 Khurshid Ahmad & Margaret Rogers (eds)
Evidence-based LSP: Translation, Text and Terminology.
584 pages. 2007. ISBN 978-3-03911-187-9

Vol. 48 Hao Sun & Dániel Z. Kádár (eds)
It's the Dragon's Turn: Chinese Institutional Discourses.
262 pages. 2008. ISBN 978-3-03911-175-6

Vol. 49 Cristina Suárez-Gómez
Relativization in Early English (950-1250):
the Position of Relative Clauses.
149 pages. 2006. ISBN 3-03911-203-1 / US-ISBN 0-8204-8904-2

Vol. 50 Maria Vittoria Calvi & Luisa Chierichetti (eds)
Nuevas tendencias en el discurso de especialidad.
319 pages. 2006. ISBN 978-3-03911-261-6

Vol. 51 Mari Carmen Campoy & María José Luzón (eds)
Spoken Corpora in Applied Linguistics.
274 pages. 2008. ISBN 978-3-03911-275-3

Vol. 52 Konrad Ehlich & Dorothee Heller (Hrsg.)
Die Wissenschaft und ihre Sprachen.
323 pages. 2006. ISBN 978-3-03911-272-2

Vol. 53 Jingyu Zhang
The Semantic Salience Hierarchy Model:
The L2 Acquisition of Psych Predicates
273 pages. 2007. ISBN 978-3-03911-300-2

Vol. 54 Norman Fairclough, Giuseppina Cortese & Patrizia Ardizzone (eds)
Discourse and Contemporary Social Change.
555 pages. 2007. ISBN 978-3-03911-276-0

Vol. 55 Jan Engberg, Marianne Grove Ditlevsen, Peter Kastberg &
Martin Stegu (eds)
New Directions in LSP Teaching.
331 pages. 2007. ISBN 978-3-03911-433-7

Vol. 56 Dorothee Heller & Konrad Ehlich (Hrsg.)
Studien zur Rechtskommunikation.
322 pages. 2007. ISBN 978-3-03911-436-8

Vol. 57 Forthcoming.

Vol. 58 Carmen Frehner
Email – SMS – MMS
294 pages. 2008. ISBN 978-3-03911-451-1

Vol. 59 Isabel Balteiro
The Directionality of Conversion in English:
A Dia-Synchronic Study.
276 pages. 2007. ISBN 978-3-03911-241-8

Vol. 60 Maria Milagros Del Saz Rubio
English Discourse Markers of Reformulation.
237 pages. 2007. ISBN 978-3-03911-196-1

Vol. 61 Sally Burgess & Pedro Martín-Martín (eds)
English as an Additional Language in Research Publication and Communication.
259 pages. 2008. ISBN 978-3-03911-462-7

Vol. 62 Sandrine Onillon
Pratiques et représentations de l'écrit.
458 pages. 2008. ISBN 978-3-03911-464-1

Vol. 63 Hugo Bowles & Paul Seedhouse (eds)
Conversation Analysis and Language for Specific Purposes.
334 pages. 2007. ISBN 978-3-03911-469-6

Vol. 64 Vijay K. Bhatia, Christopher N. Candlin & Paola Evangelisti Allori (eds)
Language, Culture and the Law.
The Formulation of Legal Concepts across Systems and Cultures.
342 pages. 2008. ISBN 978-3-03911-470-2

Vol. 65–67 Forthcoming.

Vol. 68 Eva Alcón-Soler (ed.)
Learning How to Request in an Instructed Language Learning Context.
260 pages. 2008. ISBN 978-3-03911-601-0

Vol. 69 Domenico Pezzini
The Translation of Religious Texts in the Middle Ages.
428 pages. 2008. ISBN 978-3-03911-600-3

Vol. 70 Tomoko Tode
Effects of Frequency in Classroom Second Language Learning. Quasi-experiment and stimulated-recall analysis.
195 pages. 2008. ISBN 978-3-03911-602-7

Vol. 71 Egor Tsedryk
Fusion symétrique et alternances ditransitives.
211 pages. 2009. ISBN 978-3-03911-609-6

Vol. 72 Cynthia J. Kellett Bidoli & Elana Ochse (eds)
English in International Deaf Communication.
444 pages. 2008. ISBN 978-3-03911-610-2

Vol. 73 Joan C. Beal, Carmela Nocera & Massimo Sturiale (eds)
Perspectives on Prescriptivism.
269 pages. 2008. ISBN 978-3-03911-632-4

Vol. 74 Carol Taylor Torsello, Katherine Ackerley & Erik Castello (eds)
Corpora for University Language Teachers.
308 pages. 2008. ISBN 978-3-03911-639-3

Vol. 75 Forthcoming.

Vol. 76 Marina Dossena & Ingrid Tieken-Boon van Ostade (eds)
Studies in Late Modern English Correspondence. Methodology and Data.
291 pages. 2008. ISBN 978-3-03911-658-4

Vol. 77 Forthcoming.

Vol. 78 Marta Navarro Coy (ed.)
Practical Approaches to Foreign Language Teaching and Learning.
Forthcoming. 2009. ISBN 978-3-03911-661-4

Vol. 79 Forthcoming.

Vol. 80 Martin Solly, Michelangelo Conoscenti & Sandra Campagna (eds)
Verbal/Visual Narrative Texts in Higher Education.
384 pages. 2008. ISBN 978-3-03911-672-0

Vol. 81 Meiko Matsumoto
From Simple Verbs to Periphrastic Expressions: The Historical Development of Composite Predicates, Phrasal Verbs, and Related Constructions in English.
235 pages. 2008. ISBN 978-3-03911-675-1

Vol. 82-83 Forthcoming.

Vol. 84 Maria Grazia Guido
English as a Lingua Franca in Cross-cultural Immigration Domains.
285 pages. 2008. ISBN 978-3-03911-689-8

Vol. 85 Erik Castello
Text Complexity and Reading Comprehension Tests.
352 pages. 2008. ISBN 978-3-03911-717-8

Vol. 86-87 Forthcoming.

Vol. 88 Kiriko Sato
The Development from Case-Forms to Prepositional Constructions in Old English Prose.
226 pages. 2009. ISBN 978-3-03911-763-5

Vol. 89 Dorothee Heller (Hrsg.)
Formulierungsmuster in deutscher und italienischer Fachkommunikation. Intra- und interlinguale Perspektiven.
315 pages. 2008. ISBN 978-3-03911-778-9

Vol. 90 Forthcoming.

Vol. 91 Manouchehr Moshtagh Khorasani
The Development of Controversies: From the Early Modern Period to Online Discussion Forums.
317 pages. 2009. ISBN 978-3-3911-711-6

FSC
www.fsc.org
MIX
Papier | Fördert gute Waldnutzung
FSC® C083411

Kolibri 360 GmbH
Ferdinand-Jühlke-Straße 7
99095 Erfurt, Deutschland
produktsicherheit@kolibri360.de

Druck:
CPI Druckdienstleistungen GmbH
im Auftrag der
Kolibri 360 GmbH
Ferdinand-Jühlke-Str. 7
99095 Erfurt